LifePlan
FOR YOUR HEALTH

LifePlan
FOR YOUR HEALTH

DONALD M. VICKERY, M.D.

ADDISON-WESLEY PUBLISHING COMPANY
Reading, Massachusetts • Menlo Park, California
London • Amsterdam • Don Mills, Ontario • Sydney

Second printing, March 1979

Copyright © 1978 by Addison-Wesley Publishing Company, Inc. Philippines copyright 1978 by Addison-Wesley Publishing Company, Inc.

ISBN 0-201-03435-2
ABCDEFGHIJ-DO-79

To Shelley—for unfailing support and encouragement

Preface

How clearly do most people really understand their own health problems? Medical students learn the sad truth when they first hear stories about the legendary "Mrs. Jones," a typically confused patient. When asked about her surgical history, Mrs. Jones described her operation for "fireballs in the eucharist." Alert students quickly translate this as "fibroids of the uterus."

Unfortunately, a few misconceptions in health and medical care result in humorous anecdotes. More serious consequences include thousands of needless, costly visits to the doctor, demands that the medical care system cannot possibly meet, conflict between doctors and patients, and even unnecessary disability and death. The average American risks both health and wealth every day through lack of knowledge about: (1) the factors that affect health and how they can be controlled; (2) when and how to use medical services; and (3) the need to assume responsibility for a lifetime of health management.

While the effect on the public is the most obvious, the health care system suffers, too. Physicians and other health care professionals experience enormous personal frustration, and medical research can be held back, when patients expect care that cannot be provided. Consumers do not realize that their own medical decisions, habits, and lifestyles have far more impact on health than anything a doctor can do.

Why does this misunderstanding persist, in the face of continual improvements in health care facilities and services? There is hardly a lack of consumer health information—books, magazines, radio, and television provide it abundantly. Schools, public agencies, and volunteer organizations offer every kind of health education program. But even today, much of the information is inaccurate or misleading. More important, it has not until recently involved the individual in making key decisions. Mr. X needs to decide what to do about his chest pain, but all he can find is a description of a heart attack or sketchy news about "miraculous" surgery for heart disease. The available materials have traditionally offered little help in making difficult medical decisions.

It has become necessary, then, to face the basic question: What does the average person need to know in order to make sound decisions about his or her health? Over the last three years, an answer has been emerging in the form of an entirely new and different set of materials. In 1976 *Take Care of Yourself* was published, followed in 1977 by *Taking Care of Your Child*; both books focused on the most common medical problems and introduced charts to help readers decide when they should go to the doctor and when they can manage their medical problems at home. Largely because of the efforts of Drs. James Fries and Robert Pantell, these two books may be properly regarded as unique and pioneering efforts to make the best medical information available in usable form.

LifePlan for Your Health goes one step beyond. By focusing on an individual's control of health over a lifetime, it takes on one of our greatest and most dearly held misconceptions. For the last thirty years, we have obscured the difference between health and medicine. A true story from the early 1970s illustrates the point. In a rural area of the Midwest, where the longest life expectancy in the United States had been documented, a television reporter interviewed a typically vigorous 94-year-old woman. Eventually he asked the key question: If this is the healthiest place in the country, why don't more people live here or move here? The energetic senior citizen considered for a moment and then replied, "You know, I think it's the lack of doctors."

Have we become such dependent creatures that we would rather have a doctor's care than be healthy?

I hope that this book will help change that misconception. *You* are the key decision-maker. It is the purpose of *LifePlan* to assist you by making clear the factors that affect health, their impact on your own life, and what you can do about them. You can improve your odds on good health and long life by using the information available here. It's your decision. It's your life.

Herndon, Virginia   D.M.V.
August 1978

Acknowledgments

This brief notice is small thanks for those who contributed to *LifePlan*. Helping with another's book is never easy, and this one has been no exception.

For review of the manuscript and many useful suggestions, I am indebted to: Paul Braden, Ph.D.; Grace Chickadonz, R.N., Ph.D.; Robert Harrington, M.D.; Sarah Jane Nasser, M.P.H.; Robert Rosenberg, M.D.; and Colin Wright, MSW.

Special appreciation goes to James Fries, M.D., a master of the neglected art of constructive criticism.

Barbara Newby deserves more than thanks for succeeding at the nearly impossible task of turning my scribbling into legible manuscript.

The residents and faculty of Fairfax Family Practice Unit, Medical College of Virginia, have provided the intellectual stimulation and challenge necessary for the shaping of the concepts presented here.

Finally, recognition must be made of those leaders in the field of health whose work inspired and contributed to this book: Lester Breslow, M.D.; René Dubois, M.D.; Victor Fuchs, Ph.D.; Walsh McDermott, M.D.; Thomas McKeown, M.D.; Lewis C. Robbins, M.D.; Ann Somers; and Lewis Thomas, M.D.

Contents

**SECTION IV
YOU AND THE ENEMY—WHAT TO DO ABOUT MAJOR
DISEASES**

18
HEART DISEASE

Hardening of the arteries.   High blood pressure.   Heart
attacks.   Angina.   Heart failure.   Risk factors.   Rheumatic
fever.

19
CANCER

Cancer is many diseases.   Lung cancer and smoking.
Carcinogens—cancer-causing chemicals.   Stomach cancer—
prevented by BHT and BHA?   Thyroid cancer and X-ray
treatments in childhood.   Many cancers can be prevented;
few can be cured.   How to protect against cancers of the
lung, liver, bladder, breast, uterus, thyroid, skin.

20
STROKE

Paralysis and paresis.   Transient ischemic attacks (TIAs).
Hardening of the arteries and blood clots.   Risk factors.
Prevention.   Recovering from a stroke.

30
EPILEPSY
255

Heredity. Medication. Legal and social problems.

31
GENETIC DISORDERS
258

Heredity and genetics. Amniocentesis. Tay-Sachs disease. Down's syndrome. Phenylketonuria.

SECTION V
YOUR HEALTH RECORDS

32
PERSONAL HEALTH RECORD (PHR)
267

Including LifePlan record.

33
CHARTS
278

1. Exercise. 2. Diet. 3. Weight. 4. Smoking.

APPENDIX: FOOD VALUES
282

INDEX
297

How to Use This Book

THIS BOOK IS ABOUT YOU. YOU ARE GOING TO TELL YOUR OWN story and predict your own future. This story has a twist—you can change the ending. Indeed, the whole point is to get you to change the ending by attending to the most important factor for the future, your health.

To change the ending, you are going to have to change. If you think that your health is your doctor's responsibility, think again. If you would rather die than switch, you will. If you believe that what you don't know can't hurt you, you have not been paying attention. To live longer you must learn more and do more. Only you can give yourself a better chance at long life and good health.

Each of the five sections in this book has a specific function. Understanding each section's function will make the book easier to use and enable you to get the most out of it.

Section I provides the basis for making sound health decisions. Virtually everyone believes in one or more of the ten Myths of Medicine. You will have to dispel the myths in your own mind before you can make correct decisions concerning the health of you and your family. Understanding what affects health is clearly essential, and Chapter 2 is an absolute must. Chapters 3 and 4 deal with risks and costs of medical services or, as an economist put it, the fact that there is no free lunch. Everything we do in medicine has a cost and risk which must be weighed against potential benefits. Neglect of these chapters definitely can be hazardous to your health.

The most important writing in the entire book is that which *you* will do in Section II. With help from Section IV you will analyze your own health history and predict your future by developing your Life-Score. You will create a LifePlan (Chapter 7) for managing your health which will indicate what you must do to change that prediction to one of the best possible health. Chapter 6 explains the effects of the parents' health on the unborn child's chances for a healthy entry into life. Chapter 7 also introduces the concept of the Health Evaluation and Planning (HEP) Session, a new type of health service designed to assist you in taking care of yourself and your family. If you will be having a HEP Session, it is essential to complete Section II *before* you attend the session.

Section III deals with those facets of lifestyle which have such an overwhelming impact on health. Here you will find information on facts and fallacies as well as specific suggestions on how to change your lifestyle to your advantage. Read about smoking and alcohol even if you are a nonsmoking teetotaler—somebody you know can use your help in kicking the habit.

The major causes of death and disability are discussed in Section IV. Each disease is described in terms of its cause and effects. A discussion of whether it can be prevented, treated effectively, or detected early (screening) leads to the principal question: What, if anything, should you do to protect yourself from this disease? The answer will often surprise you.

Your LifePlan and other pertinent health information will be recorded in the Personal Health Record (PHR) in Section V. The PHR can help in your interactions with the doctor's office as well as in your management of your health. The LifePlan Record is a portion of the PHR designed to help you keep track of progress toward your health goals. Also in Section V are charts to help in attaining certain of these goals, such as controlling your weight and stopping smoking.

You may find it possible to calculate your LifeScore and develop your LifePlan without reading Sections I, III or IV. Don't do it. You will be cheating yourself. Understanding the basis for LifeScore and Life-Plan is necessary if you are to take charge of your health. Without this understanding, the chances that you will carry out your LifePlan are small.

You are invited to begin a process of knowing yourself and controlling your destiny. Such opportunities are rare and should be greeted with enthusiasm. The very first step is to realize that you control your health more than any other mortal, and to a greater degree than you thought possible. Take that step now.

I

THE PURSUIT OF HEALTH

BEFORE YOU CALCULATE YOUR LIFESCORE OR DEVELOP YOUR LifePlan—even before you begin to learn about your lifestyle and the major diseases—you need an appreciation of the "facts of life." This section will provide you with a solid basis for understanding and using the material which follows. As long as you believe in the myths of medicine, you will not understand the need for improving the management of your health. In order to formulate your priorities properly, you must understand what affects your health. To have a proper respect for medical care, you need to understand its risks as well as its benefits. To avoid the many pitfalls in the pursuit of health, you must learn the basis of decision making in health. When you finish with this section, you will be prepared to start the process of shaping your future health.

1
The Ten Myths of Medicine

UNLESS YOUR EXPERIENCE HAS BEEN UNUSUAL, THE GAP BETWEEN what you need to know about health and what you actually know is enormous. Your education in health has been a bizarre series of uncoordinated events which may have done more harm than good. It has made you a believer in some if not most of the Myths of Medicine. It is time you took a harder look at these myths.

Myth No. 1: Health depends most on good medical care

Factors which affect health are usually divided into four categories: heredity, environment, lifestyle, and medical care. The effect of heredity is difficult to measure and remains controversial. Of the remaining three, the *least* important is medical care.

If you find this hard to believe, you are not alone. Most of us were raised on Myth No. 1. But you will find it difficult to reconcile Myth No. 1 with the following facts:

- The death rate in the United States was declining for at least 150 years before medicine's greatest advances were available.

- The 1950s and 1960s saw the introduction of open heart surgery, coronary care units, heart transplants, intensive care units and other types of spectacular, high technology medical care. But the death rate stopped declining and remained steady from 1954 to 1974. For some groups (middle-aged men), it actually increased.

■ After the introduction of antibiotics, the death rate due to pneumonia for persons over the age of 65 *increased* sharply.

Beginning to wonder a little? Good. There is a great deal more you need to know. In fact, understanding what really affects health is so important that Chapter 2 is devoted entirely to it. If you read only one other chapter in this book, make sure it is "The Pursuit of Health."

Myth No. 2: Your doctor manages your health

This is a very appealing myth. How relaxing and reassuring to think that we can just put ourselves in the hands of doctors and let them worry about our health. But even the most brief consideration should make it clear that you make most of the important decisions with regard to health. Doctors cannot manage your health even if they were so inclined. *You* decide when to go to the doctor, what health facilities to use, and whether to take the doctor's advice. *You* decide on smoking, drinking, eating, exercise, and childbearing.

There are a number of indications that there is considerable room for improvement in your managerial skills, especially concerning when to go to the doctor. The National Ambulatory Care Survey of 1974 indicated that only about 17 percent of doctor visits made by the American public were serious problems while almost 50 percent were for problems which were not serious at all. (The seriousness of the visit was determined by the physician who saw the patient.) This study and others indicate that the reasons you are most likely to visit your doctor are for a routine physical examination and the common cold. The first has never been demonstrated to be of value in preserving health, and the second is a disease that cures itself and for which the doctor should recommend drugs that are also available without prescription.

Your choice of facilities seems odd, at least on occasion. For example, less than 10 percent of visits to emergency rooms are for emergencies.

Finally, you don't seem to think much of the physician's advice once you've paid for it. One well-known investigation revealed that from 25 to 50 percent of all patients never take *any* of the medicine prescribed. Another study looked at what happened to the penicillin prescribed for strep throats (streptococcal pharyngitis). It found that less than half the patients were taking the medicine at three days and that less than 20 percent of the patients completed the entire course of therapy.

The importance of your decisions as to when to use medical care can hardly be overemphasized. Surveys indicate that the average person has some sort of a symptom on one out of every three days. One hundred and twenty times a year you have the opportunity to make an unnecessary visit or miss getting help for an important problem. How well you manage these decisions will be the most important factor in deciding how much you spend for medical care, and it will have a major effect on your health.

Even more important than your use of the medical care system is your management of your lifestyle. The effects of smoking, alcohol and other drugs, weight control, and exercise far outweigh any effect that medical care may have. Don't fool yourself into thinking that your doctor can save you from your own habits. Medical care cannot undo what you've done to yourself. If you choose not to prevent it, then the next best advice is to prepare for it. Perhaps if your health insurance, life insurance, and will are in order, your family will suffer a little less.

Myth No. 3: Doctors, and only doctors, can tell whether you are healthy

This is one of our most pervasive myths. Recently a seven-year-old explained to me that she needed to see a doctor so she could find out if she was healthy this year. In a matter-of-fact fashion she discussed this "need" which she believes to be a matter of common knowledge. This should give you pause. Somehow this youngster has learned this fallacy all too well. Yet she has been taught nothing of the importance of her own habits, let alone given an understanding of what medicine can and cannot do. What chance do our children have if they do not learn the truth?

Millions of people visiting doctors to find out if they're well is a phenomenon peculiar to the last several decades. In the more distant past, most people believed that staying healthy and avoiding the doctor went together. To be sure, medical care has more to offer now, but the earlier belief is still the more accurate appraisal of the situation. It remains a fact that health is best where doctors are fewest.

What doctors can do is tell you if you have certain diseases some of the time. They are best with serious illnesses. The training of most doctors takes place almost entirely in the hospital. They are most competent in dealing with patients who are sick enough to be in the hospital and in using the hospital's facilities to deal with these patients' problems. The further you get from this setting, the less medicine has to offer. Medicine has the least to offer when there is no well-defined symptom or illness involved. The area of medicine that deals with people who do not already have a disease—preventive medicine—is one of its most neglected areas. Certainly most physicians have had only a modest exposure to preventive medicine. When you don't have symptoms, there are only a few services of the medical care system with which you need be concerned. (These are discussed in Sections II and III.) Even when there are symptoms, there are substantial limitations to what medicine has to offer since each diagnostic and therapeutic procedure has a risk of its own (see Myth No. 9).

Most disturbing in all this is the orientation both you and the doctor have toward sickness. You don't really go to the doctor to find out whether you are healthy. You go to find out whether you are sick, all the while steadfastly ignoring our very limited capability to detect disease. This leads to an absurd yet common conclusion to the routine physical: The doctor implies and the patient assumes that since nothing was found the patient has been given a clean bill of health. And this even though the patient may be 30 pounds overweight, smoking two packs of cigarettes a day, and exercising only by walking from car to home, car to office, and car to bar. You should ask yourself what it is *possible* to find before you conclude that not finding anything is a very significant event in your life. Moreover, you already know whether you are smoking, drinking too much, eating too much, or not getting enough exercise. This will count for far more than anything you can learn from your doctor. And you know that with these habits, there is no such thing as a clean bill of health.

Myth No. 4: It is vital to see the doctor as soon as a problem develops so that the disease may be treated early

No question that this would make sense *if* we could easily diagnose and cure most diseases. We cannot. For most diseases, we lack either the ability to make an early diagnosis or an effective treatment, or both.

Fortunately, most illnesses are self-limited, and your body will eventually effect the cure itself. These are the common viral problems such as colds and the flu, a multitude of minor muscle pulls, strains and sprains, as well as a whole host of skin rashes which come and go on their own. (In regard to the latter remember this piece of medical wisdom: "Only God can make a tree, but almost anything can make a rash.'') The symptoms caused by these self-limited diseases can usually be treated without a visit to the doctor.

Also in your favor is the fact that many diseases can wait to be treated without causing irreparable harm to you. The allowable time period depends on the individual problem, but generally you have longer than you think. For example, even if there is a broken bone associated with that ankle sprain, you will not cause lasting damage if you don't get treated within the first few minutes or hours if you know how to take care of yourself. On a much different scale, tuberculosis may stay hidden within the body for months or years before it causes problems. Even though we have a skin test (Tine or PPD) to alert us to the possibility of TB, the actual diagnosis is often quite difficult. Therefore, the diagnosis may be made only months or even years after the skin test turned positive. (Many people with positive skin tests never develop tuberculosis as far as we know.) Even with all these delays, we are able to treat tuberculosis effectively. It is very uncommon for this disease to have the devastating effect which was so frequent before the turn of the century.

Finally, it must be recognized that there are illnesses which can be neither cured nor effectively controlled with treatment. In truth, the doctor has little to offer you if that cough is due to lung cancer. You, on the other hand, could have lowered the chance of lung cancer to near zero by not smoking. Yet we find the notion of cure so desirable and the changing of our own behavior so difficult that we have deceived ourselves in believing that everything would be curable if we could only catch it early enough. This can cost you money, but more importantly, it may cost you a chance to save your own life.

So you, the key decision maker in health, have another decision to make. You can despair over the limits of medicine. Or you can rejoice over the enormous power of the body to make things right and *your* control of your own health. Is there really any choice?

Myth No. 5: Good doctors can almost always make the diagnosis right away

Good doctors almost never make *the* diagnosis "right away." They make a plan. A diagnosis is never absolutely certain. To pretend that it is endangers the patient. A good doctor makes a list of the reasonable possibilities (called the differential diagnosis) and then rates each possibility according to its threat to health, probability, treatability, and difficulty in diagnosis. From this a plan for dealing with the problem is formulated. This is the key. The most important thing to you is not the most likely diagnosis but how you and your doctor are going to handle the problem. For example, a diagnosis of a benign or noncancerous mole is not the last word on that skin lump. It is almost surely a benign mole—*but* it should be observed and rechecked by you, and removed if it changes shape or color.

Of course, there are times when the probability of a particular diagnosis is nearly 100 percent. But even then you should have a "what if" question in mind. What if the proposed treatment is not successful? What if we just left it alone altogether? What if it begins to change in some way? Are there things to look for? If you have been listening only for the diagnosis, you have been cheating yourself. Listen for the plan.

Myth No. 6: A regular complete checkup is important to staying healthy

Our desire to believe that we can cure anything if we could just catch it in time has led to some of our more notable follies: the executive physical and multiphasic screening. You should not confuse the desirability of early detection and cure with our capability to do the same. Medicine simply can't do this very often, despite the fact that many people have assumed that we can. Perhaps this is because they have underestimated the complexity of looking for illness in its earliest phases. At a minimum there are at least six requirements which must be met before it is worthwhile to attempt to detect a particular disease before it causes symptoms:

- The disease must have a significant effect on the quality or quantity of life.

- Acceptable methods of treatment must be available.

- Disease must have an asymptomatic (no symptoms) period during which detection and treatment significantly reduce disability and/or death.

- Treatment in the asymptomatic phase must yield a result superior to that of delaying treatment until symptoms appear.

- Tests for detecting the condition in the asymptomatic period must be available at reasonable cost.

- The incidence of the condition must be sufficient to justify the cost of screening.

To make a long story short, only a very few diseases have any possibility of meeting these requirements, and there is considerable controversy over even these few.

There is strong evidence for only three routine procedures: blood pressure, self-examination and physician examination of the breast, and Pap smears. (Even Pap smears are controversial; one large study from Canada failed to show any benefit of routine Pap smears.) Reasonable arguments may be formulated for another five to seven procedures depending on the individual's personal and family medical history. Notable for the absence of evidence supporting them are these procedures: routine physicals, multiphasic screening, diabetes testing, sickle-cell tests, electrocardiographic exercise stress tests (treadmill tests), and many others including blood tests for gout, anemia, and thyroid problems.

Who should have which tests and when is discussed for each of the major diseases in Section IV. Section II will demonstrate how these can be included in your LifePlan.

Myth No. 7: Medicine has a cure for almost every disease

This is the most incredible myth of them all and is just plain wrong. It is so far from the truth that those within medicine have a hard time understanding that many people actually do believe this. Nevertheless, according to a University of Chicago study, most adults in the United States think this myth is a statement of fact. Worse yet, the belief is more strongly held among those who are better educated and make more money.

The truth is that most illnesses cure themselves. Medicine can treat effectively some of those which do not, but cure is possible in only a few. These are the facts, and wishing it were not so will not change them.

Myth No. 8: Doctors are responsible for the rise in medical costs

Perhaps this should be called a half myth. Doctors have a major impact on medical costs, but charges for their services account for only a small part of this impact. And while it is true that costs cannot be controlled without the help of doctors, it is also true that this cannot happen unless there are some significant changes on the part of others—including you.

With certain exceptions you can rest assured that doctors' greed is not playing a substantial part in raising your medical costs. Doctors' fees account for only about 18 percent of medical care expenditures; hospital costs comprise over 40 percent. While doctors' fees have risen somewhat faster than the overall cost of living, they have risen at only about half the rate of hospital costs.

Possible exceptions are of two kinds. There are, of course, a few doctors who overcharge, submit false bills, and rip off you and your insurance company in a variety of ways. In short, there are a few crooks in the profession. The second kind is not so straightforward. There are certain specialties in which earnings have been more than substantial if not outright extravagant. Some radiologists, clinical pathologists, and surgical specialists have incomes which seem just short of outrageous to many. For example, a clinical pathologist who had the pathology "concession" at a community hospital was reported to have received 1.3 million dollars in 1973. Such a large amount is possible because he received a percentage of every laboratory test done in the hospital. From the money received, he paid two other pathologists and two chemists. If he paid the pathologists $100,000 each (probably a low guess) and the chemists $50,000 each (probably a high guess), he still made a million dollars. In the same area, a radiologist fresh out of training is said to start at a salary of approximately $95,000 per year for a 35-hour week. Interestingly enough, there do not seem to be any statistics available that allow one to compare the average incomes of these specialists to those of other persons. The physicians whose practices most closely resemble these specialists and for whom there are figures available are the obstetricians/gynecologists. As you may have guessed, obstetricians/gynecologists have the highest average income for any group of physicians for whom figures are available.

Unlike a visit to your family doctor, internist, or pediatrician, charges in these specialties are not based on the time involved for a service, but rather on the procedure involved. These procedures are usually covered by insurance. And insurance companies have a record of paying up and passing on the costs to you. Charges by these specialists are most likely to get out of hand in the hospital where they have a monopoly on services. There is no such thing as shopping from a hospital bed for the least expensive blood test or a better price on an x-ray. The bottom line is that doctors who charge by the procedure may make two or three times as much as one who does not and still work fewer hours. Primary care physicians—family physicians, internists, pediatricians—earn about as much as a master bricklayer on an hourly basis, but work more hours (58 hours per week on the average).

How much you value your physician's services should include some relevant comparisons; there are no absolute rules by which to judge fees. Here are some facts that may be helpful:

■ The average income of a physician in 1976 was approximately $60,000—a lot of money. But there was a wide variation in incomes. For example, about 30 percent of general practitioners made less than $30,000, whereas only about six percent of obstetrician/gynecologists made less than $30,000. At the opposite end of the spectrum, 42 percent of obstetrician/gynecologists made $80,000 or more, whereas only about seven percent of pediatricians had incomes in this range. Again, there are no statistics for radiologists, pathologists, and surgical subspecialists (ophthalmologists, urologists, etc.).

■ After allowing for inflation, the income of physicians increased by about 10 percent between 1966 and 1976. But the income of all persons in the nation increased by 13 percent. The greatest percentage increases were registered by corporate attorneys, plumbers, and electricians, whose incomes rose by 16 percent, 26 percent, and 30 percent, respectively.

■ Surveys done in 1975 indicated that, when benefits such as retirement plans and so on were considered, corporate lawyers' incomes were slightly higher than those of physicians.

■ If there is a race for the highest incomes, the lawyers may outdistance even the specialists who charge by procedure. You may recall that Mr. Califano had an income from his law practice of over $500,000 in the year before he became Secretary of Health, Education and Welfare.

Finally, it would be well remembered that absolute figures are only a limited help in making judgments. It seems clear that anyone—doctor, lawyer, Indian chief—should be compensated for long years of training, hard work, and superior skills. By the same token, no one should be able to make extravagant sums by exploiting a monopoly situation or a peculiarity of the insurance business.

The more important issue is not what doctors earn but what they order. Doctors decide on hospitalization, laboratory tests, x-rays, drugs, and other items which account for about 70 percent of medical care costs. But they hardly make these decisions in a vacuum. They are heavily influenced by patient demands and expectations, the threat of malpractice and, hopefully foremost, the medical needs of the patient. It is especially unfortunate that the copious use of laboratory tests and x-rays has become the standard defense against malpractice (see Myth No. 9). This is a manifestation of the influence the public's unrealistic expectations of medicine have upon the costs of medical care. Everyone seems happier with the notion that doing more is better, at least until the consequences must be faced. When costs are out of control and people are being harmed by too much medical care, then we look for villains. And who is to blame? The hospital trustees who build unnecessary additions and buy fancy equipment so they can compete with the hospital down the road? The doctor for using that unnecessary equipment once it's available? You for demanding that the full "benefit" of modern medicine be brought to bear on your minor problem? The answer, of course, is that we all deserve a share of the blame. And we all had better start doing something about it. Your job is to educate yourself so that you can manage your own health skillfully *and* be an enlightened participant in the public debate on health care costs.

Myth No. 9: Competent medical care involves little risk

All medical care involves risk, whether it is an aspirin you prescribe for yourself or heart surgery recommended by a specialist. A *necessary* operation *correctly* performed by a *skilled* surgeon may still kill or cripple. The *right* drug for the *right* diagnosis may still lead to a life-threatening reaction. Undesirable outcomes do not necessarily mean that malpractice has been committed. The risks inherent in medical care are discussed in detail in Chapter 4.

Is a bad result due to malpractice? This is often difficult to decide even for the most unbiased observers. As Medical Myth No. 9 becomes more pervasive, there is a growing tendency to equate bad results with malpractice. In addition, it seems fair to say that when there is any uncertainty about the question of malpractice, juries tend to find malpractice so that the patient will not have to bear the burden of misfortune alone. Doctors are keenly aware of the dramatic increase in the number of malpractice suits as well as the size of the award a successful suit brings. Paradoxically, the fear of malpractice has not decreased the risk of medical care. In legal battles, laboratory tests and x-rays procedures have become accepted as the best evidence that the doctor was thorough and concerned. More of these tests and procedures are ordered as doctors attempt to document the fact that they were practicing medicine appropriately. The result is that the risk of medical care has increased because of an excessive number of tests and procedures.

Myth No. 10: Medical and surgical procedures must be tested and approved before they are used on the public

In the United States, only drugs must be tested thoroughly and approved by a public agency before they can be released for general use. Any operation, x-ray, diagnostic test, or treatment not involving a drug can be used by any doctor on any patient anytime, anywhere. There is no requirement that it be demonstrated to be effective or safe. No government agency can approve it or disapprove it.

This does *not* mean that doctors routinely perform bizarre and worthless procedures on unsuspecting patients. It *does* mean that testing surgical and medical procedures is left up to whoever is interested. As a rule, the people most interested are those who develop and use the procedure, a situation which is not conducive to unbiased evaluation. (It is human nature to be biased toward your own "baby.") If you put a lot of time and effort into the development of your Super Gall-Bladder Snatcher, use it every day, and truly believe that it helps patients, you may feel that it is unethical and immoral *not* to use it. The difficulty here is the difference between *believing* and *knowing.* For you to *know* that it is worthwhile, it must be compared to something else in a scientific manner. This means some of the patients who you *believe* would benefit from it must be given some other treatment in order for there to be a comparison. The history of medicine contains many instances in which procedures believed to be effective proved to be worthless or even harmful when tested properly. You would be wise not to obscure the difference between believing and knowing.

A recent review of 29 studies on the effectiveness of tonsillectomy and adenoidectomy (T & A) illustrates these points. The reviewers found that:

- Not a single study had done an adequate job of comparing T & A to other treatments or to no treatment at all. Thus nothing could be said with certainty about the effectiveness of T & A.

- The most frequent reason given for the lack of a comparison was that it was "unethical" to withhold the operation.

- The type of doctor(s) who did the study was related to whether or not the study results were "for" or "against" T & A. For the studies conducted by physicians (pediatricians and others) who do not perform the operation but may recommend it, the results were split down the middle, 9 for and 8 against. But when the studies were conducted by the ear, nose, and throat (ENT) surgeons who do those operations, the score was 12 for, 0 against. Such a difference can hardly be due to chance.

The end result is that the many procedures and techniques are never fully evaluated. Some of the most conspicuous of these are:

- Radical mastectomy
- Coronary care units
- Intensive care units
- Tonsillectomy
- Adenoidectomy
- Coronary artery bypass graft surgery
- Hysterectomy
- Duodenal ulcer surgery
- Allergy skin testing

These procedures undoubtedly have value some of the time. But when? In many and perhaps most cases in which they are used we do not have evidence of their effectiveness. This means that your doctor must decide whether to use them without adequate information. Chapter 4 will give you more information on this subject.

If you can honestly say that you believed in none of the Myths of Medicine, you are a member of a small and select group. This group excludes not only almost all of the general public, but the majority of health professionals as well. You are off to a great start in learning to preserve your health.

If you have been a believer like most of us, be of good cheer. Confronting these myths is the first step in developing skills of unequalled importance in your life.

Whether you are a believer or not, the information which follows is meant to be interesting as well as useful. Hopefully there will be a few surprises just to keep you on your toes. Finally, the reason for the book is to allow you to take full advantage of a piece of good news: You, more than anyone else, control your health. Now is the time to learn how.

2
What Affects Health, Anyway?

YOU MAY HAVE SOME DIFFICULTY IN LETTING GO OF MEDICAL Myth No. 1. It's hard to believe that the environment and lifestyle are more important to your health than medical care. All of us have been raised on statements such as "The miracles of modern medicine have given us the longest life expectancy the world has ever known." Pure junk. Bad enough to make medicine divine, worse to ignore the facts of life expectancy. (The United States ranks twenty-second in life expectancy—behind Puerto Rico, Hong Kong, and Bulgaria, among others.) Such nonsense is believed because it is "common knowledge" that we are living longer than in the past and the medical establishment has been more than willing to take credit for it.

In reality the nation's health has been improving for at least 200 years. These two centuries may be divided into three periods with reference to health. The first and by far the longest period was dominated by the effect of environment. The second, a brief period in the late 1930s and 1940s, witnessed the most important advances in medical care. Finally, we now find ourselves in an era in which lifestyle has come to the forefront. An understanding for the relative importance of environment, lifestyle, and medical care can be gained by an analysis of these three periods.

A study of death rates over the last century is a good place to begin. The accompanying figure illustrates the death rate for the United States and the times at which major medical advances became available.

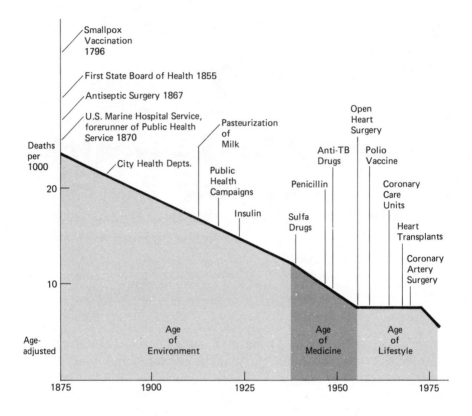

Burn these facts into your mind:

- Over 75 percent of the decline in death rate between 1875 and 1975 occurred *before* medicine's most significant discoveries became available. This decline actually began in the mid 1700s.

- The discovery of antibiotics in the 1930s ushered in a period during which the decline in death rate was accelerated. This acceleration is usually credited to a number of significant medical advances which became available during this time.

- The trend of several centuries came to an end in the early 1950s: the death rate stopped declining. For the next 20 years there was no reduction in death rate and no increase in life expectancy for the population as a whole. For middle-aged males, life expectancy actually *decreased*.

- This 20-year period of no progress coincided with the advent of high-technology medicine—coronary care units, heart surgery, and all the rest. It also coincided with a period of rapid rise in medical care costs.

■ Death rates began a modest decline in the early 1970s. This reflected a drop in the deaths due to heart attack and stroke. It coincided with reduced use of tobacco, less consumption of cholesterol and saturated fat, and increased exercise among Americans. (See Chapter 18 for more on this.)

Thus the "miracles of modern medicine" taken as a group have had little to do with the decline in the death rate. They simply do not go together historically. Now consider a few examples in more detail.

Antibiotics are widely considered to be medicine's greatest advances and are credited with a dramatic reduction in deaths due to infection. Tuberculosis and bacterial pneumonia have been leading causes of death due to infection for centuries. In 1900 the tuberculosis death rate was approximately 190 for every 100,000 persons; by 1974

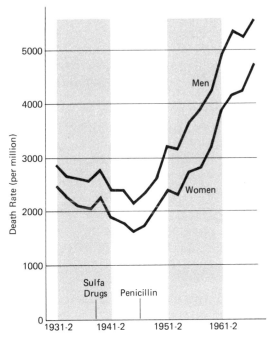

Source: Adapted from Thomas McKeown (1976), *Role of Medicine: Dream, Mirage or Nemesis?* (London: Nuffield Provincial Hospitals Trust). Used by permission.

it was less than two per 100,000. This remarkable drop is usually attributed to drugs which became available in the late 1940s. Yet the death rate due to tuberculosis was declining long before these drugs became available. In fact, 90 percent of the decline between 1838 and 1970 occurred *before* drug therapy was available.

Death rates due to pneumonia began to decrease in the late 1800s. While most of the decline in this death rate occurred before antibiotics were available, following their introduction there was a sharper decrease for persons under the age of 65. But now consider the death rate due to pneumonia for persons over the age of 65. (The data for this chart are from England and Wales but appear to apply to the United States as well.) The death rate actually began to *rise* sharply after antibiotics became available. The cause of this rise is not completely known, but most likely it is related to factors such as increased cigarette smoking and air pollution rather than problems with the antibiotics themselves. The point is that the "wonder drugs" are helpful but their effect is limited.

The table indicates the causes of infant deaths in New York City for the first 30 years of this century. Remember that antibiotics were not available until the late 1930s and early 1940s. Note that "name" infections—pertussis (whooping cough), measles, and so on—have always played a minor role in infant death. Thus the development of effective preventive or therapeutic measures for these diseases cannot be expected to have had much impact despite the attention they received.

Now consider the "pneumonia-diarrhea complex." This is not really a disease—it is not caused by a single bacterium or virus. It is an illness of living conditions—poor housing, not enough food, contaminated water, and all the rest. As real income rose and living conditions improved, this illness declined dramatically. The saddest part is that

Infant death rates, New York City, per 1000 live births

	1900	*1930*
Pneumonia-diarrhea complex	71	18
"Name" infections (including measles, tuberculosis, whooping cough, and erysipelas)	14	6
Premature birth, injury at birth	30	12
Congenital malformations	6	6
All other causes	15	2

the pneumonia-diarrhea complex still kills where conditions have not changed, most notably on certain Indian reservations and in inner-city ghettos. It has been demonstrated on at least one reservation that providing traditional medical care—drugs, doctors, hospitals—has little effect, but nontraditional care aimed at improving living conditions and educating the parents can dramatically reduce the death rate. It is a matter of national shame that funding for the latter has been dropped while funding for the former continues. Also continuing is a death rate for Indian babies which is *four times* that for white babies.

By now you should begin to have the feeling that medical care has had little to do with improvements in health and that something else has been going on. That something else is an improvement in the environment—more and better food and housing, safe water supplies, improved sanitation, and so on. All those things which you take for granted, some of which you may regard as bureaucratic nuisances, are why you are healthier than your great-great-great grandfather, not those precious pills in your medicine cabinet. The age of environment saw real income increase dramatically so that amount and quality of food, clothing and shelter increased as well. Meanwhile, the number of persons living in close contact decreased, a major factor in the decline of infectious disease. The average number of persons living in each American household has gone from 5.4 in 1790 to 2.9 today. The late 1800s and early 1900s might be called the era of sanitation. During this period, the Federal government, every state government, and most large cities formed agencies for the purpose of promoting sanitation and hygiene. Public health campaigns demonstrated that an awareness of the importance of the environment and of sanitation measures could have great effect. For example, a campaign to improve the general health of the residents of Framingham, Massachusetts was conducted between 1917 and 1923 with the support of Metropolitan Life Insurance. During that period, the infant death rate dropped by more than one-third. Even more striking was the 70 percent decrease in the death rate due to tuberculosis. This death rate declined more than twice as fast in Framingham as in communities without such a campaign. And this occurred 30 years before antituberculosis drugs were available. The fact that families no longer have to huddle together in overcrowded rooms has had more to do with controlling TB and other infections than antibiotics, clean water saves more lives than surgery, and an adequate diet has done more than all those hospitals put together.

But what happened after 1954? The major improvements in environment had already taken place; deterioration in the environment (air pollution, etc.) had begun but not yet greatly affected death rates or life expectancy. Advances in medical care were being made and through

Medicare, Medicaid, and other programs, people had access to medical care more than ever before. Yet 1954 was the beginning of 20 years of no improvement in death rates for the population as a whole and *increasing* death rates for middle-aged men. Not until the early 1970s did the death rate resume its decline.

In 1954 we entered the age of lifestyle.

Put simply, we have gotten just about all the help we can expect from the environment and medical care. We are now firmly in the grip of our own habits. Whatever substantial improvement or decline in health we experience must relate to *how* we live.

This should come as good news. You are back in the driver's seat with an opportunity to control your destiny to a very substantial degree. You know your habits are important, but do you know how important?

In a well-known study, Dr. Victor Fuchs demonstrated the relative importance of lifestyle by comparing mortality in the states of Utah and Nevada. The level of income and medical care in these two states is quite similar, though Nevada actually has a few more doctors per capita. The predominant lifestyles, however, are quite different. The influence of the nonsmoking, nondrinking, family oriented Mormons is felt throughout Utah. Nevada has high rates of cigarette and alcohol consumption as well as high divorce rates. Nevada's statistics cannot be attributed solely to the influence of Las Vegas and Reno, for the pattern persists in all parts of the state. The first table shows that Nevada's death rate is much higher than Utah's in all groups. Most

Excess of death rates in Nevada compared with Utah, average for 1959–61 and 1966–68

Age Group	Males	Females
< 1	42%	35%
1–19	16%	26%
20–29	44%	42%
30–39	37%	42%
40–49	54%	69%
50–59	38%	28%
60–69	26%	17%
70–79	20%	6%

Excess of death rates in Nevada compared with Utah for cirrhosis of the liver and lung cancer, average for 1966–68

Age	Males	Females
30–39	590%	443%
40–49	111%	296%
50–59	206%	205%
60–69	117%	227%

Source: Victor R. Fuchs, *Who Shall Live? Health, Economics, and Social Choice,* pp. 52, 54. © 1974 by Basic Books, Inc., Publishers, New York. Reprinted by permission.

have from 35 to 70 percent more deaths. These differences are enormous. No epidemic can match this; the plague was a minor illness in comparison. When we consider deaths from two diseases due to habits—lung cancer and cirrhosis of the liver—things get totally out of hand. As the second table shows, almost six times as many young men die of these diseases in Nevada as in Utah—all diseases of lifestyle, all preventable deaths.

In a famous investigation, Dr. Nedra Belloc studied the relationship between lifestyle and life expectancy in California. There was particular interest in the following habits:

- Three meals a day, avoiding snacks
- Breakfast every day
- Moderate exercise two or three times a week
- Seven or eight hours sleep a night
- No smoking
- Moderate weight
- No alcohol or only in moderation

It was found that a 45-year-old man who had up to three of these habits had a life expectancy of 21.6 years—that is, he could expect to live to about age 67. But if he had six or seven of these habits, he could expect to live 33.1 years, or to approximately age 78. In other words, an increase in life expectancy of more than 11 years was associated with the more beneficial lifestyle. The significance of this difference may be better appreciated if you realize that between 1900 and 1970 the increase in life expectancy for white men at age 40 increased by only *half a year.*

A study by Dr. Belloc and Dr. Lester Breslow indicated that a man who had six or seven of these habits was as healthy as a man *30 years younger* who had only one or two of these habits. Thirty years! How can you turn your back on being 30 years younger?

Studies on deaths due to cancer confirm the importance of lifestyle. Mormons have a cancer death rate that is only 60 percent of that for the population as a whole. Seventh-Day Adventists, who do not smoke or drink and adhere to a vegetarian diet, have a cancer death rate only 50 percent of that for the general population.

You do not have to choose between the benefits of lifestyle and medicine, but suppose for a moment that you did. What would your choice be? Consider this: Christian Scientists, who tend to have beneficial lifestyle but avoid traditional medical care, have life expectancies greater than that of the general population.

Environment, lifestyle, medical care—you now know something of their relative importance. Heredity, the fourth category of factors which affect health, must be considered least important at this point for several reasons. Foremost is the great difficulty of separating out the effects of heredity from those of environment and lifestyle. It is just plain hard to say what is due to heredity alone. Even if we knew more, we do not have the means to do much about it. For the foreseeable future, genetic manipulation will remain an enormous tangle of scientific, ethical, and legal questions without answers. Finally, we do not know the extent to which other factors can modify the contribution of heredity. For example, the risk of a family history of hypertension (high blood pressure) may be negligible if you are not overweight, have your blood pressure taken yearly, and treat hypertension should it occur.

In the past, environment was most important. As it improved, the effects of lifestyle became clear. While the achievements of medical science are significant and certainly the most dramatic, medical care must rank behind these two. Now you are in the age of lifestyle—your habits *are* your health.

Where do you go from here?

Lifestyle must be top priority. Medical science will advance, but it will not be able to undo what you have done to yourself. There are disturbing signs that the environment is staging a "comeback" as a threat to health. A recent report indicates that deaths due to lung cancer are several times as frequent in Los Angeles as in Chicago, the most likely reason being the difference in air pollution between the two cities. We are just beginning to understand environmental causes of cancer. So the bottom line is that you must take care of yourself, do your part to preserve and improve the environment, and take advantage of what medicine has to offer. Helping you to do this is the purpose of this book.

3
Making Health Decisions

WHY ARE MATTERS OF HEALTH AND MEDICINE ALWAYS SO complex and confusing? The practice of medicine has been defined as the art of making decisions based on data that are insufficient and using probabilities that are not precisely known in order to arrive at diagnoses which cannot be adequately defined for the purpose of embarking on treatment programs whose value is largely undetermined. Undoubtedly this is a bit of an exaggeration, but it is true that health decisions must often be made without the scientific information we would like. There are some good and some not so good reasons for our continuing ignorance in many areas of health.

The human body is by far the most complex system we know. Long after we have solved all the mysteries of the sun, the moon, and the stars, we will probably still be wondering exactly how we are able to chew gum and walk up stairs at the same time. Furthermore, each and every one of these complex systems is different. Nature's assembly line apparently allows for an infinite amount of variation. You are not put together exactly like anyone else. Investigating these systems is quite difficult. A body cannot be torn down and put together again like an automobile. Even if it could, most people would not permit it. They seem to have developed a real aversion to having their bodies taken apart, not to mention a definite reluctance to act as guinea pigs for medical experiments. And real guinea pigs, as well as other animals useful in laboratory experiments, always seem to be demonstrating that they are not very much like humans after all. What's good for the goose may be good for the gander, but a drug that doesn't phase a white rat may still curl your toenails. (Thalidomide is an example of a drug that did not have the disastrous effect on animals that it did on humans.) Altogether, the result is that data are insufficient, probabilities are not precisely known, definitions are often inadequate and the results of health decisions are difficult to evaluate. Nevertheless, these decisions must be made. While you need not make these decisions alone, you must understand certain concepts if you are to make them adequately.

Vickery's Laws

Each health decision must be based on an understanding of the benefits, risks, and costs involved. In this chapter you will learn of the general principles (Vickery's Laws) that must be observed in developing this understanding. These are followed by a discussion of three of the most important pitfalls in making health decisions—mistakes in the interpretation of laboratory tests, the determination of cause and effect, and recognition of the placebo effect. These principles and pitfalls are most clearly illustrated in medical decision making, but apply to many health decisions outside of medical care. One of the major goals of this book is to allow you to compare various health and medical activities. The information that follows will help you to do this accurately.

There are only two of Vickery's Laws, but they cover a lot of territory.

Law No. 1: You never get something for nothing
You must understand that every attempt to find out something about your body or to do something for your body has a definite cost and risk involved. Costs are usually a good deal more obvious than risks. You know the cost of your jogging shoes, a visit to the doctor's office, the laboratory tests, the operation. Often you will be urged to overlook these costs in your health decisions. You will be told that since your health is the most important thing, money cannot be very important. Don't believe it. Remember the rule of finite funds: What is spent on worthless procedures cannot be spent on worthwhile ones. Since there is never an unlimited amount of money, money wasted on the useless eventually prevents money being spent on the useful.

The risks of medical care are discussed in Chapter 4. Probably you are aware of many of these risks, although it is likely that you have underestimated them, especially those involved in diagnostic procedures such as x-rays, hospitalization, and screening procedures. Also, it is likely that you have overlooked the indirect risks involved in these procedures. The indirect risks are in large part a result of the limitations of medical science. For example, a laboratory test may label you with a disease that you don't really have or cause a needed treatment to be omitted. (The implications of the limits of medical science are discussed under Law No. 2.) Furthermore, the very process of looking for health problems (screening) may do harm. For example, the attempts to detect heart disease in children and diabetes in the elderly have caused many persons to act as if they were ill with these diseases when, in fact, they did not have them (see Chapters 18 and 21).

Your habits have definite risks and costs as well. Keep this in mind as you read Section III. When you can accurately compare the benefits, risks, and costs of exercise against those of medical care for heart disease, you will have arrived. You will also develop a new feeling for the truth embodied in this well-worn phrase: An ounce of prevention is worth a pound of cure.

As a general rule, those things you can do for yourself, or which your doctor can do without resorting to complex technology, have the least cost and risk and the greatest benefit. The more that complex technology is involved, the more likely it is that the cost will be high, the risk great and the benefits small.

Law No. 2: Nothing is 100 percent
No diagnosis is absolutely certain, no test is completely accurate, no treatment is always effective. Again, we have rules which seem to be topsy turvy in some way:

■   The less serious the illness, the less likely the diagnosis is certain.

■   The higher the technology used, the less likely the test is accurate.

■   The more complex the treatment, the less likely it is to be effective.

But it is hard to break the habit. It is much more comforting to believe that the diagnosis is certain, the test accurate, and the treatment effective. This belief contributes to the ease with which mistakes are made in health decisions. You should be aware of the major pitfalls in making these decisions.

The Limits of Laboratory Tests

The problem of laboratory tests deserves special consideration. Americans have come to rely more on tests than their doctors. The physician is quickly classified as being good or bad on the basis of how many tests were ordered. Those who order a large number of tests without regard to whether or not they make any sense are likely to be given the highest compliment: they are "thorough." (They are also prosperous.) Let us examine the usefulness of laboratory tests.

A laboratory test may be classified as to its sensitivity, specificity, and predictive value. Sensitivity refers to the ability of the test to detect the disease when it is present. In other words, if you have the disease, sensitivity refers to the chance that the test will indicate that you have it. A sensitivity of 95 percent is quite good, for it means that there is a 95 percent chance that the test will be positive if you have the disease. Put another way, if 100 people have the disease, the test will be positive in 95 of them.

Specificity refers to the ability of the test to distinguish between those who have the disease and those who do not. Clearly a test will not be much good if it is frequently positive in those who do not have the disease as well as in those who do. Specificity is defined as the chance that the test will be *negative* if you do *not* have the disease. Again, 95 percent would be an excellent specificity—which means that if you do not have the disease, there is a 95 percent chance that the test will be negative. Of 100 persons who do not have the disease, 95 will have negative tests. But note that five of every 100 persons without the disease will have a positive test. These are called false positives, and they are very important to keep tabs on, since they mean that the test is indicating the presence of disease when there is none.

The predictive value is the real payoff of the laboratory test. What you (and your doctor) really want to know about a laboratory test is how useful it will be in indicating the presence of a disease when it is *not* known that you have it. Remember that the definitions of sensitivity and specificity involve knowing whether or not the disease is present. Predictive value is defined as the chance that a positive test means that you actually have the disease. This bears repeating since it is often confusing: What you would really like to know is the chance that you have the disease if the test is positive.

To illustrate the importance of the predictive value, imagine for a moment this hypothetical situation: A new test has been devised to detect brain tumors. If the test is negative, then nothing further is going to be done. But if the test is positive, then you are going to have a brain operation to look for this cancer. This operation may kill or cripple you even if no cancer is found. Thus the outcome of this test is very, very important, and the last thing you want to do is to have this operation needlessly. Predictive value of the test then becomes crucial, since it indicates the chance that cancer is really present when the test is positive.

In order to determine predictive value, you must know the occurrence of a disease as well as the sensitivity and specificity of the laboratory test used to detect it. To continue our example, let us assume that the test for brain tumors has excellent sensitivity and specificity and that both of these are 95 percent. Brain tumors occur in roughly 10 out of every 100,000 persons. Now take a moment to figure out the predictive value of this test. In other words, if a test is positive, what are the chances that you actually have a brain tumor and that this dangerous operation will be worthwhile? If you're not good at figuring probabilities, then just take a guess based on your general feelings about the accuracy of laboratory tests.

If you came up with an answer of .19 percent, then you are both right and extremely unusual. That's right. Only one out of every 500 persons with a positive test will, in fact, have a brain cancer. If you find this difficult to understand, you may want to work through the calculations yourself. They go like this: For simplicity, assume that the test was done on 100,000 persons, since we said that the occurrence of brain tumors is 10 in every 100,000 persons. In this group, then, there will be 10 persons who actually have brain tumors. Because the test has a *sensitivity* of 95 percent, on the average it would detect 9.5 of these persons. Give the test the benefit of the doubt and say that it detects all 10 of the persons who actually have brain tumors. The remaining 99,990 persons do not have brain tumors. The test has a *specificity* of 95 percent, but this means that five percent are "false positives." In other words, five percent of the persons who do not have the disease will have positive tests. Five percent of 99,990 is 4,999.5. Round this off to 5,000. Thus there are a total of 5,010 positive tests, but only 10 cases of brain tumors. So only about one out of every 500 persons with positive tests (or about .19 percent) actually has a brain tumor. If an operation is done on the basis of the test, then for every operation on a person with a brain tumor there will be 500 on persons who do not have tumors. Therefore, in this hypothetical example, the odds are 500 to 1 against your operation being actually necessary if you have a positive test.

Predictive value is very sensitive to the probability that the disease exists in the first place. If you have the signs and symptoms of a particular illness, then a laboratory test may be valuable in confirming or discounting the diagnosis because the presence of these signs and symptoms has greatly increased the chance that you have the disease. For example, if there is a 50-50 chance that you have a particular disease because you have certain signs and symptoms, and the test for that disease has a sensitivity and specificity of 95 percent, then the predictive value of the test in this situation is 95 percent. In other words, in this particular setting 95 percent of those persons who have a positive test will have the disease. Laboratory tests have most value when the chances are rather good that the disease is in fact present.

They are least useful when there is only a small chance of that disease. This is likely to be the case when laboratory tests are used in an attempt to pick up diseases without symptoms in the general population. This is referred to as screening for asymptomatic disease, or simply screening. The predictive value for most laboratory tests used as a screening tool is extremely small. (See Chapter 4 for more discussion of screening.)

The problems involved in using a laboratory test for screening may be compounded by what has been called multiphasic screening. In multiphasic screening, a large number of tests, sometimes numbering 50 or more, are done in an effort to detect asymptomatic disease. Each and every laboratory test will have the type of problem mentioned above. Recall that an excellent laboratory test would only have five percent false positives; this means that out of 100 persons who did not have the disease, only five would have a positive test. Many tests are in fact defined to have just such a specificity. The normal values of many blood tests are derived by giving the test to a large number of "normal" persons (usually college students) and then setting normal values for that test so that five percent of these values fall into the "abnormal" category. *By definition then, five percent of the persons who are actually normal will have the "abnormal" result.* If you are normal, you have a five percent chance of having an abnormal result on any *one* of these tests. But what happens if you have many such tests? What are the chances that you will go through the entire multiphasic screening procedure and have completely normal results? If there are 25 tests and each has a specificity of 95 percent, your chances of having an "abnormal" result are about three out of four. That's right, if you are perfectly normal, the chance that you can have an abnormal result is about three out of four.

Keep in mind the problems of predictive value and false positives when you are tempted to request tests or your doctor indicates that he or she would like to order them. Unless they are done in a setting in which the chances are that the appropriate problem exists, then the overwhelming likelihood is that their predictive value is small. Finally, think twice the next time you are tempted to judge a physician on the basis of how many tests were ordered.

Cause and Effect

You should be aware that it is very difficult to prove the proposition of cause and effect when dealing with human disease. Only in the realm of infectious disease has it been possible to do this with regularity. In the rest of medicine we are often unable to prove whether events are simply associated or one caused the other. Medical history is full of examples in which associations were mistaken for cause and effect. For centuries it was believed that malaria was caused by bad air in marshes and swamps because people exposed to that air came down with the disease. It took a long time and some difficult medical investigation before it became clear that it was organisms carried by the mosquitos in that air which were the culprits. Nevertheless, virtually all significant medical findings have started with the detection of an association between disease and certain events. For example, it was the very strong association between cigarette smoking and lung cancer that opened the way for investigation in this area.

Such correlations may be useful even if cause and effect cannot be proven. In recent years the term "risk factors" has become popular to describe those things associated with an increased risk of a particular disease. The use of the term reminds us that the precise mechanisms by which a risk factor might cause a disease are not known. As a practical matter, a knowledge of these mechanisms may seem unimportant *if* it can be demonstrated that altering the risk factors will in fact lower the risk of disease.

On the other hand, you should be aware that obscuring the difference between associations and cause and effect sometimes results in faulty reasoning. This is painfully obvious in this country, where large portions of the population believe that penicillin, antihistamines, decongestants, or all three cure colds. The common cold is a viral illness that the body will cure by itself. No drug, including penicillin, will cure this viral illness. Yet millions of people are convinced that penicillin and other drugs are necessary when they have a cold (or the flu, another viral illness) because when they took these medicines they eventually got better. It is always difficult to answer the question "What would have happened if I had done nothing (or something else)?" but this is absolutely necessary if it is to be learned whether an association is valid. Medical scientists would express this by saying that it is always necessary to have a "control group"—that is, a group of people who did nothing or had some other treatment—so that there was something by which to compare the results of the procedure in question.

A study of the value of tonsillectomy at the Children's Hospital of Pittsburgh illustrates this point. For decades tonsillectomy has been performed to relieve frequent sore throats despite a lack of evidence that it helped in this situation. The researchers in Pittsburgh adopted the following definition of "frequent sore throats": seven sore throats in one year, five sore throats per year for two consecutive years, or three sore throats per year for three consecutive years. Children who reported to have such frequent sore throats were accepted as patients, *but no tonsillectomies were performed.* Each was followed for another year. At the end of that year, *80 percent* did not meet the definition of frequent sore throat. That is to say, 80 percent of the children had zero, one, or two sore throats during that year. Sore throats that did occur were generally mild. Now ask yourself what would have happened if tonsillectomy had been performed, but was totally without benefit? *Tonsillectomy still would have been reported as 80 percent effective in relieving frequent sore throats.* This is what can happen when there is nothing with which to compare. As it stands, the Pittsburgh group serves as a control for an evaluation of tonsillectomy. As such, it makes tonsillectomy a very bad bet in this situation. Operating will have to cure significantly more than 80 percent of children in order to be more effective than not operating. Even if it does relieve more sore throats, will it be worth the risk? About five out of every 100,000 children who have tonsillectomies *die* as a result of the operation.

Beyond the problems of simply asking the questions correctly, there is another powerful factor that is always present in human medicine: the placebo effect.

The Placebo Effect

The first law of human medicine should be that the body and mind are inseparable. You can't affect one without affecting the other. Perhaps the second law should be that what we believe is the most important factor in what we feel. The placebo effect is a demonstration of these two laws.

The term placebo is derived from a Latin word meaning "to please." Today it is used to mean a substance with little or no chemical effects that is substituted for a medicine. Pills to be used as placebos are usually composed of corn starch or a milk-sugar substance. For a placebo injection, a saline solution (salt water) is most often used. These substances in and of themselves have virtually no effect on the human body. What actually happens when they are administered depends on the expectations of the person to whom they are given, how that person interprets the giving of the medication, and what suggestions are made to him or her. This is the placebo effect. It may be seen with surgical procedures and other types of treatment as well as with pills and injections. Here are a few of the many studies which demonstrate the enormous power of the placebo effect:

Medical students were given placebos; some were told that they were taking a stimulant and others were told that they were taking a seda-

tive. They were also told that the stimulant should raise the heart rate and a sedative should decrease the heart rate. Sure enough, heart rates increased in those students who thought they were taking a stimulant and decreased in those who thought they were taking a sedative.

In order to test an operation to relieve heart pain (angina), some patients were given the operation while others were given a sham operation. The sham operation consisted of making an incision in the chest wall and then sewing it up without doing anything else. The patients did not know whether they received the real operation or the sham. Ten of 13 patients who had the real operation reported significant relief, but so did all five who had the sham operation. In a second study done in the same manner, eight patients who had the real operation had 34 percent subjective improvement while nine who had the sham operation had 42 percent subjective improvement.

In a group of patients who had just undergone surgery, placebo injections alternated with those of morphine. The placebo was found to be 77 percent as effective in relieving pain as morphine.

In a group of patients who had been taking antihistamines, a placebo was substituted without their knowledge. Yet 77.4 percent reported drowsiness, a side effect which is characteristic of antihistamines.

A group of ulcer patients were told that they would be given a new drug which had been found to give great relief. A second group was told that they would receive a new drug but that it would be impossible to predict what the results would be. Significant relief was reported in 70 percent of the first group but in only 25 percent of the second group. Both groups received the same treatment—a placebo.

Placebo injections of saline were substituted for the morphine injections of a group of addicts. The addicts did not go into withdrawal when their morphine was stopped without their knowledge, but they did go into withdrawal when the placebo injections were discontinued.

Approximately the same number of arthritis sufferers received relief from placebo as from conventional types of treatment (aspirin, cortisone). Sixty-four percent of those who did not respond to the placebo pill did experience some relief when they were given placebo injections of saline.

Responses to placebos are not limited to those things the patient can consciously expect of the placebo itself. In a famous series of experiments, Wolf showed that placebos could actually change blood-cell counts and other bodily functions despite the fact that the subjects were unaware that such biological responses were possible. Indeed they could not understand the medical terms used to describe these responses.

Researchers concerned with the placebo effect have often referred to physicians themselves as the "ultimate placebo" because the attitudes of physicians strongly affect the results of treatment. In one experiment involving both a tranquilizer and placebo, the physicians involved were asked to classify themselves as to whether they felt optimistic, pessimistic, or indifferent about the possibilities of the treatment. They also classified the patients as to whether they thought the patients were optimistic, pessimistic, or indifferent. The results of treatment correlated better with the physician's attitude about the treatment than with the attitude of the patient, regardless of whether the tranquilizer or the placebo was being used. In another study, the amount of stomach acid produced was used as a measure of patients' response to visits with different physicians, both of whom were administering placebos. The amount of stomach acid decreased by an average of 15 percent when the placebos were given by one physician, but *increased* by 12 percent when they were given by the other physician.

It has been suggested that it is the placebo effect which creates "great" physicians. They succeed where other physicians fail because they are very positive and because the patient expects them to be able to do things ordinary physicians cannot do. It must also be said that it is the placebo effect that allows charlatans to appear effective in the eyes of their patients.

Beyond this, there are many facets of the placebo effect that we do not understand. For example, it has been demonstrated that green tablets are better for treating anxiety while the same medicine with a yellow coating is better for relief of depression. Suffice it to say that experimental evidence supports the proposition that placebos are capable of affecting a broad range of mental and physical processes— including pain of angina pectoris, post-operative pain, insomnia, the common cold, coughs, headache, fever, blood-cell count, blood pressure, heart rate, adrenal gland secretion, stomach function, pupil dilation and constriction, and mood. They can even remove warts. It should be noted that placebo effects are not necessarily favorable. Just as expectations and interpretations can be negative, placebos are capable of producing problems and disease.

No one is immune to the placebo effect. It has nothing to do with being stupid or suggestible. Indeed, some investigators have found that the placebo effect is likely to be more marked in persons of higher intelligence. In one study, women were given placebos during childbirth, in postpartum pain, and later in pain produced experimentally in the laboratory. While from 30 to 50 percent of these persons received relief from the placebo in each of these situations, it was not the same 30 to 50 percent that responded. By the end of the experiment, almost everyone had responded to the placebo in one situation or another.

The placebo effect should not be regarded as a matter of deception. Rather it is a way of making clear the enormous effect which our own expectations, interpretations, and beliefs have upon mental and physical well being. That we all have a capacity for controlling these effects is cause for optimism. But keep it in mind the next time you feel certain that some pill or shot has helped you when medical science says that the particular chemical or medicine involved should not help. What medical science is really saying is that the drug has no effect over and beyond that of a placebo. It is not saying that the placebo effect may not be very powerful. As long as you expect that penicillin can cure almost any illness, it makes an excellent placebo, at least in the sense that it is likely to be effective. However, because it has the capacity to do a great deal of harm on its own through reactions, side effects, and the production of resistant bacteria, it makes a very poor placebo in reality. Finally, you may have guessed by now that the popularity of Vitamin B_{12} shots is due to their placebo effect. Physicians are willing to use them as placebos since they seldom have side effects.

This discussion has only briefly touched on certain aspects of making health decisions and you may be a bit bewildered by it. Take heart. It may have been a bit clouded by all the facts and figures, but you have taken an important step toward understanding and participating in important health decisions. Moreover, you should get the feeling that your health is a lot less dependent on sophisticated medical care and a lot more in your hands than you thought. Most of all, be assured that it is well worth the effect to understand how health decisions are made. When it comes to your own health, what you don't know *can* hurt you.

4
Medical Care: the Two-Edged Sword

IN CHAPTER 3 YOU WERE INTRODUCED TO THE SOMEWHAT COMPLEX business of making health decisions. Briefly summarized, such decisions should be based on an understanding of the benefits, risks, and costs involved. You also learned of several factors which must be taken into account in developing this understanding, especially where medical decisions are concerned—the placebo effect, interpretation of laboratory tests, and determination of cause and effect.

This chapter raises the question of benefits, risks, and costs of certain types of medical care. This discussion is far from complete. You may have assumed that, since medicine is now more science than art, most medical decisions are based on detailed information about risks and benefits even if costs have been ignored. Sadly, this is not the case. More often than not this information is incomplete or totally lacking. Worse yet, decisions to use medical care are sometimes inconsistent with the information available. As the key decision maker in matters of your own health, it is critical for you to develop an understanding of what medical care can and cannot do. The material presented here on drugs, surgery, hospitals, x-rays, and screening programs can be the basis for that understanding.

Drugs

Drugs are the most important tools of medicine. The last 50 years have seen the discovery or development of drugs which are effective in a wide variety of disorders, drugs which have revolutionized the practice of medicine. Before this time there were perhaps a half dozen drugs which could be prescribed with a legitimate expectation that they would work. It has often been noted that in the decades around 1900 the great physicians were almost all diagnosticians because treatment offered so little. This is not to say that drugs were not used. On the contrary, ineffective and often dangerous concoctions abounded. For the most part they were sold directly to the customers who used them at their own risk. The risk was great, since testing of a drug before manufacture was not required nor was there any regulation of manufacturers to ensure that it was not contaminated. A number of catastrophes, such as the death of 10 children due to contaminated tetanus toxoid vaccine, led to the demand that drugs be tested and their manufacture regulated to ensure purity.

In 1927, the Food and Drug Administration became a separate regulatory agency empowered to oversee the testing of drugs. For the most part this testing concerned only new drugs, so that drugs in use before 1927 were exempted from many of the provisions of the regulations established at that time. More importantly, the testing established at this time was concerned with the *safety* of a drug, not whether it was an effective drug. It was not until 1962, 35 years later, that questions concerning the effectiveness of drugs became a part of the FDA's program.

Efforts have continued to be concentrated on new drugs and prescription drugs. It is only recently that attention has been turned to the drugs which may be purchased without a prescription. These nonprescription drugs account for a majority of all the drugs used in the country. Moreover, nonprescription drugs contain the same chemicals which are often prescribed for minor illnesses such as colds and the flu. As it stands now there is little evidence of effectiveness for many of the decongestants, antihistamines and cough medicines that Americans consume in such huge amounts. However, it seems unlikely that these drugs will be withdrawn from the market since they are big business, and a large part of the population has come to rely upon them. It has been suggested more than once that this industry and the public's dependence upon these drugs give testimony to the power of the placebo effect. Space does not permit a discussion of the effectiveness of individual drugs. But a general rule for the use of drugs is clear: Before you take any drug, be assured that you have authoritative information that the drug is, in fact, effective. Remember that a drug does not have to be proven effective to appear on the drugstore shelf or to be prescribed by a doctor.

The risks of drugs are of three basic types. The first type consists of those effects directly due to the chemical itself and are related to the amount taken. Every drug is a potential poison, and at some point the harmful effects of the chemical involved begin to outweigh the beneficial effects. For example, aspirin irritates the lining of the stomach enough to cause some blood loss in virtually everyone who takes it, but for most people this is not a significant problem unless the amounts of aspirin taken are quite large.

The second type of risk is that of an allergic reaction. These are especially important because they are somewhat unpredictable, and the reactions may be severe even though only a small amount of drug has been taken. (See Chapter 29 for a discussion of allergic reactions.)

Finally, there are indirect effects such as those seen with antibiotics. Bacteria, the "germs" against which antibiotics work, may develop resistance to an antibiotic after repeated exposures. This means that the antibiotic will no longer be effective against this type of bacteria. Thus we have something of a paradox in which the more antibiotic used, the more likely it is that the bacteria will develop resistance to it. This has already happened with the bacteria causing gonorrhea and with the bacteria associated with many infections acquired in the hospital, and it is beginning to occur in the bacteria identified as the leading cause of pneumonia.

Drugs carry substantial risks. Consider the following:

- Dr. Leighton Cluff and his associates at Johns Hopkins Hospital followed 714 patients admitted to general medical beds. They found that 122 patients suffered 184 adverse drug reactions. Drug reactions were responsible for five percent of these admissions. Also, 13.6 percent of the patients suffered a drug-related problem after admission and six of these patients died as a result.

- In a second study, the same group found that certain drugs were more likely to be associated with an adverse reaction. Barbiturates, codeine, penicillins, and thiazide diuretics produced 70 percent of the drug problems despite the fact that they accounted for only 17 percent of all medication.

- A British survey found that 193 out of 731 patients (18 percent) admitted to a general medical hospital suffered undesirable consequences of drug therapy. Seventeen of the 67 deaths (25 percent) that occurred among these patients were due to adverse drug reactions.

■ Most drug reactions are related directly to the chemical effect of the drug and only a small percentage (less than 10 percent) are due to allergic reactions to the drug.

■ It has been estimated that each drug prescribed has a 50 to 75 percent chance of being taken at the wrong time, in the wrong dosage, or is the wrong drug in the first place. It would seem that drugs obtained without a prescription must have a similar chance of being used incorrectly.

Drugs are mixed blessings. Those used most often (tranquilizers, decongestants, antihistamines, and the like) are of uncertain value for many patients who take them. Those with the capacity for great benefit often have the capacity for great harm as well. All of them present some risk to your health. Give them the respect they deserve.

While drugs account for only about 10 percent of the total amount spent on health care in the United States, they are far from inexpensive—as anyone knows who has had a prescription filled recently. Moreover, there is a justifiable concern that they are far more expensive than they need to be. The drug industry has long had the highest profit margin of any major industry in the nation. Drug manufacturers have contended that this is necessary in order to have funds to invest in drug research. However, the best indications are that only from five to 15 percent of their income is spent on drug research, while 40 percent goes for manufacturing costs and 25 percent is spent on advertising. The proportion of income that is profit and that spent on advertising are both higher than for any other major industry. There is good evidence that high profits are possible because of lack of price competition among drug firms and pharmacies, the extensive promotion of drugs, and less than optimal prescribing practices by physicians.

However, you should be aware that a major factor in determining the price of a drug is the pricing policy of the pharmacy that sells it. Prescribing by the chemical (generic) name rather than the brand name is important in many cases, but this does not ensure that the pharmacy will pass along the lower cost of the drug to you. Further, it should be noted that in a few instances (digitalis, tricyclic antidepressants) the brand name drugs may be in fact superior to the generic formulation.

As a rule, for over-the-counter drugs, the cheapest is the best. For prescription drugs, you should find out if your doctor is prescribing by generic or brand name and why. Finally, you will need to shop around in order to take advantage of the wide variation in pricing policies by pharmacies. In a Seattle program which attempts to address all these factors, the cost per prescription is about one-half the national average.

Surgery

In the discussion of Medical Myth No. 10, it was made clear that surgical procedures are not required to be tested and/or approved before being adopted as "standard." In Chapter 3 you learned of the importance of avoiding problems due to placebo effect or mistaking association with cause and effect. These problems are particularly difficult to avoid in evaluating surgical procedures because the development of "control groups" is much more difficult. It is one thing to give placebo drugs, it is quite another to do placebo operations. But avoiding "control studies" leads to a clearly unacceptable situation—the acceptance of operations of unknown benefit but of significant risk and cost.

The history of surgical procedures to relieve heart pain (angina) illustrates this point. Before coronary artery bypass graft (CABG) surgery became the rage, at least a half-dozen operations were promoted for the relief of angina. All claim to be effective in relieving the pain in 60 to 80 percent of patients. One of the most popular of these was called internal mammary artery ligation. In this operation, two arteries in the chest wall were tied off in an effort to cause more blood to flow into the blood vessels of the heart. This was a simple, safe procedure which did not require putting the patient to sleep. Originated in Italy, this operation spread like wildfire around the globe because it seemed safe, simple and effective. Certain physicians in this country had persistent doubts as to its effectiveness, and finally two controlled studies were performed. In each of these studies, one group of patients received the entire operation while a second group received a sham operation in which the same procedure was performed except that the arteries were not tied off. In one study, 34 percent of the patients who had the entire operation reported improvement and 42 percent of those who had the sham operation reported improvement. In the second study, 10 of 13 patients who had the real internal mammary artery ligation procedure reported significant improvement in their angina, but so did all five who had the sham operation. Thus the internal mammary artery ligation operation turned out to be nothing more than an impressive demonstration of the placebo effect.

Unfortunately, most operations are not as simple and safe as the internal mammary artery ligation. In the minds of many physicians this makes it harder to do a sham operation. But it also means that the harm done if the surgery is ineffective is much greater. For the vast majority of surgical procedures there have not been adequate studies, and the result is that they have not been shown to be definitely good or definitely bad. But all have risks and costs.

Here are a few points to ponder with respect to surgery:

■ Introduced in 1894, radical mastectomy remains the standard operation for breast cancer in the United States (but not in Europe). The disability and disfigurement of this operation is considerably greater than that with simple mastectomy. Yet a review sponsored by the Harvard School of Public Health found that studies comparing the two indicate that radical mastectomy is no better and may be worse than simple mastectomy in terms of improving survival with breast cancer. Furthermore, there are no data that clearly demonstrate that doing any surgical procedure for breast cancer is better than doing nothing. In the words of Dr. B. A. Stoll: "A highly responsible body of scientific opinion has suggested that neither surgical treatment nor radiation therapy is likely to affect the outcome of [breast cancer] in the vast majority of patients presenting." It is known that the incidence of and death rate from breast cancer are essentially unchanged over the last 75 years. In 1930, 40 percent of those who had breast cancer died of the disease. Today it is the same.

■ One analysis of hernia operations indicated that they may increase the quality of life by avoiding the need for a truss—but may *decrease* life expectancy.

■ Coronary artery bypass grafting is up to 90 percent effective in relieving angina. While there is considerably better evidence to support the proposition that this operation improves circulation to the heart than there was for the internal mammary ligation operation, it has never been subjected to the acid test of comparison with a sham operation. Thus how much of this benefit is due to placebo effect is unknown. Approximately 50,000 of these procedures will be performed in the United States this year.

■ Tonsillectomy and adenoidectomy are the most frequently performed operations in the United States. It is estimated that nearly a million such operations will be performed this year alone. Yet a recent review of the evidence for and against these operations concluded that there were no studies that conclusively demonstrated the value of these operations for any problem. Further, they were definitely ineffective for many of the problems for which they had been commonly used in the past, such as recurrent sore throats or difficulty in swallowing. Most thoughtful physicians would agree, however, that these operations do make sense in certain situations, such as an abscess in the area of the tonsil or substantial interference with breathing due to blockage of the throat. Even if one accepts the notion that there are good reasons for these operations, it is still clear that they are overused. For example, a Seattle study revealed that less than one-third of these operations were performed for reasons usually regarded as valid.

■   The reasons gynecologists give for doing hysterectomies range all the way from low back pain to cancer of the uterus. As in the case of tonsillectomy and adenoidectomy, there are no studies that absolutely demonstrate the effectiveness of hysterectomy, but there are conditions for which the best physicians would accept hysterectomy as appropriate therapy. Again, even accepting these conditions as indications for the operation, it is likely that many hysterectomies are done unnecessarily. For example, the College of Physicians and Surgeons of Saskatchewan (Canada) found that in some hospitals up to 59 percent of hysterectomies were unjustified according to the criteria it had developed. For all hospitals approximately one-fourth of hysterectomies were unjustified. Such studies may give some indication as to why the rates for hysterectomy in the United States and Canada are twice that for Great Britain, where the financial incentive to perform operations is much less.

Most people appreciate that surgery is a risky business. Death rates of various operations are one indicator of risk involved, but they do not give information on the risk of disability or pain and suffering. For example, some operations may have little risk of death but a significant risk of loss of a limb or eye, or the production of considerable pain. Nevertheless, the best information we have on the risks of surgery relates to death rates. The accompanying table gives these rates for several common operations.

The total cost of surgery is not known exactly. In 1977, total expenditures for health care in the United States were approximately 160 billion dollars. A reasonable estimate is that 64 billion dollars of these expenditures (40 percent), were directly related to surgery. This estimate does not include the costs of disability or days lost from work. As anyone who has had an operation knows, the costs of surgery on an individual basis are astounding. The average cost of a coronary artery bypass grafting operation is approximately $14,000. The cost for a hernia operation is approximately $1,400. When costs of disability and days of work loss are included, the total cost of a hysterectomy in 1976

Death rates for several common surgical procedures

Procedure	Deaths Per 100,000 Procedures
Coronary Artery Bypass Grafting	5,000
Cholecystectomy (Gallbladder)	400
Radical Mastectomy	400
Appendectomy	352
Tonsillectomy	5
Abortion—All	3.9
With first three months of pregnancy	1.7

For comparison:
   Death rate for pregnancy and childbirth: 14.8 per 100,000 live births
   Death rate for general anesthesia (gas) *without* surgery: 2 per 100,000 procedures

Source: Estimates based on information from various U.S. Government sources.

was estimated to be $5,432. The causes of the high cost of surgery are many, and include the way in which most hospitals are organized and the manner in which insurance companies pay for surgical services. Byproducts of these are: (1) The bulk of most hospitals' income is dependent upon the amount of surgery that is performed and (2) surgeons earn substantially more than most nonsurgeon physicians such as family practitioners, pediatricians, and internists. The financial incentive for both hospitals and surgeons is to do more surgery rather than less.

Hospitals

The nonsurgical activities of hospitals involve patients with problems that vary widely in terms of their severity and the need for diagnostic and treatment procedures. This makes evaluation of the benefits of hospitalization very difficult. Indeed there are no studies that allow a specific value to be placed on the role of the hospital. Nevertheless, it seems clear that the hospital is necessary for the best care of many patients. It also seems clear that the benefits of the hospital—and especially some of the newer and more specialized units within the hospital—have been overrated. Consider the following:

■ The Coronary Care Unit (CCU) is regarded by most Americans as a necessity for the treatment of persons with heart attacks (myocardial infarction). Yet several studies from Great Britain indicate that most patients do as well with home care as with CCU care and that many patients with heart attacks (elderly patients without complications) actually do better at home than in the CCU.

■ Dr. Paul Griner of the University of Rochester found that patients with congestive heart failure did as well on the general medical ward as in the CCU.

■ When the CCU first appeared in the 1960s, some enthusiasts predicted it would prevent up to 50 percent of deaths due to heart attacks. It now appears that the major effect of the CCU is to postpone a small percentage of deaths until after discharge from the hospital. Thus, the CCU's effect on surviving for six months, one year, or five years after a heart attack is small and may be negligible. In retrospect, this is hardly surprising. Persons who have heart attacks have severe disease, and the CCU does nothing to affect the basic disease.

■ The Intensive Care Unit (ICU), like the CCU, is an area of high technology and intensive use of highly trained personnel. A study of 226 critically ill patients admitted to the ICU at the Massachusetts General Hospital yielded these startling results: At the end of one month, 123 patients (54 percent) were dead, 70 were still hospitalized, and 31 were at home. Only one of the 103 survivors had fully recovered. At the end of 12 months, 164 patients (73 percent) were dead, 10 were still hospitalized and 51 were home. Only 27 (12 percent) of the original 226 patients had fully recovered.

Much of the risk of hospitalization relates to the use of drugs, and this is discussed above. But there are many other risks involved. The hospital environment is infamous for the stress it places on the patient. It is noisy, the food often leaves a good deal to be desired, and it comes equipped with roommates whose habits are totally different from yours. Its routine seems peculiar, as if devised by persons whose only previous experience is in making schedules for boot camps. It is staffed by persons who are forever barging in when you are trying to sleep but can't be found when you need them. Here *many* things go bump in the night.

A study from Yale investigated the risks associated with hospitalization by observing what happened to 1,014 patients admitted to the University medical service over a period of eight months. All mishaps and untoward events were recorded as "episodes." An episode was classified as minor if it was short and subsided without specific treatment, moderate if it required significant treatment or prolonged hospitalization, and major if it was life threatening or contributed to death. All episodes that were due to error were *excluded*, so this study gives information on hospitalization risks that are not due to error. The results were as follows: There were 240 episodes and 198 patients. Twenty percent of the patients had a prolonged or unresolved episode. There were 110 minor, 82 moderate, and 48 major episodes. Sixteen of the episodes ended in death. Of the deaths, four were reactions to diagnostic procedures (two occurred during barium enemas), six were due to infections acquired in the hospital, four were involved reactions to drugs, and two occurred as a result of treatment procedures. The death rate associated with hospitalization was 1.6 percent. This means that admission to a hospital for medical diagnosis and therapy may be as risky as many serious surgical procedures.

Between 1965 and 1976, the cost of a semiprivate hospital room in the United States rose by 254 percent and operating room charges rose by 232 percent. These items rose at more than two and one-half times the rate of the rise in the Consumer Price Index (a measure of inflation). Of the approximately 160 billion dollars spent on health in 1977, approximately 63 billion went for hospital services. Note also that the cost per day of specialized units such as ICU's and CCU's is usually twice that of the regular hospital room, and ICU charges may exceed $500 per day. In the Massachusetts General Hospital study mentioned above, the average cost per patient was $14,304. The total cost for the 226 patients was $3,132,704.00. By far the greater part of this money was spent on patients who did not survive. It has been estimated that if each patient who died received the "benefit" of such a stay in an ICU, the total hospital charge for final hospitalization (excluding physicians' fees) in the United States would be 28 billion dollars a year.

X-Rays

There is no question that x-rays can be an extraordinarily useful tool and constitute one of the greatest advances in medical technology. There is increasing evidence, however, that many x-rays which are ordered are in fact not useful in the care of the patient. The University of Washington School of Medicine investigation revealed that the x-rays of the skull which are routinely ordered following head trauma do not aid in diagnosis and treatment. In 120 patients with cough, Stanford University physicians reported that a chest x-ray affected treatment decisions in only two out of 120 cases. Another investigation followed 495 patients who had x-rays of the upper gastrointestinal track, often called the "upper GI series." It was found that about 70 percent of the x-rays were normal and that x-rays changed therapy in only seven percent.

Despite the fact that x-rays are routinely ordered upon hospital admission and as a part of routine medical and dental examinations, the use of x-rays in this fashion has not been demonstrated to be of value. And no x-ray has ever been demonstrated to be useful as a screening procedure with the possible exception of x-rays of the breast (xeromammography) in women with a personal or family history of breast cancer (see below). In general, x-rays are most likely to be of benefit in serious illnesses when the physician has a specific question in mind. They tend to be of least value when the illness is minor or when they are used as a screening tool.

X-rays have long been known to be capable of producing cancer (oncogenic) and mutations in offspring (mutagenic). These effects are related to the amount of radiation involved in the x-ray and how much of the radiation reaches the ovaries and testes (gonads). It is not known what level of radiation is safe, or even whether there is a safe level. Radiation levels assumed to be safe in the past have proven not to be. For example, at one time many children with large tonsils or adenoids, acne, or ringworm of the scalp, were treated with x-ray therapy to these areas. Now, 20 to 30 years later, we are seeing the effects: cancer of the thyroid and the oral cavity.

The best information available seems to indicate that there is no absolutely safe level and that the effects of radiation tend to be cumulative. Thus the best personal policy is to avoid x-rays unless they are truly necessary. Note also that the amount of radiation in various x-rays varies tremendously. There is a good deal less radiation involved in an x-ray of a limb for a possible fracture, or even in a single chest x-ray, than there is in a series of x-rays of the upper or lower gastrointestinal track (Upper GI, barium enema).

X-ray equipment is expensive and radiologists are well paid. The result is that x-rays themselves are costly and that there is a powerful financial incentive to utilize x-ray facilities in order to recover their cost. X-ray units are usually quite profitable for hospitals as well as for radiologists practicing outside hospitals. The cost of x-rays is a significant portion of the cost of hospital care and physicians' services.

A very important factor leading to increased cost of x-rays is the fact that many patients (66 percent in one survey) believe that the ordering of many x-rays indicates an excellent physician. This attitude is reflected in the decisions of courts and juries who have often required the performance of an x-ray as evidence that the physician was conscientious and thorough. This is the major reason why skull x-rays continue to be ordered for patients who have suffered head trauma despite the fact that the physician knows that it will not help in diagnosis or treatment. Thus the overuse of x-rays is a classic example of overestimating benefits and underestimating risks both by patients and physicians.

Screening

Nobody likes to deal with diseases that are untreatable. Given the emphasis on helping in their profession, doctors especially are disturbed when they find themselves unable to change the course of a disease. Without new treatments, there is an overwhelming tendency to believe that the old treatment would be better if it could be started earlier in the course of the illness. Yet there is evidence for this in only a very small number of cases. Nevertheless, the vast majority of Americans have come to accept as fact the notion that any attempt to detect disease at an "early" stage is always a good thing. This is a particularly cruel and wasteful misconception.

In the discussion of Medical Myth No. 6 in Chapter 1, you are introduced to the requirements for screening as adopted by the World Health Organization. Briefly stated, to be worthwhile a screening program must demonstrate that it is able to detect disease reliably before it causes symptoms, that treatment is more effective when begun before symptoms arise, and that this detection and treatment can be accomplished at an acceptable risk and cost. These criteria are accepted throughout the world as the rational basis for screening programs. Yet they are regularly ignored by various groups in the United States. You cannot rely on others to determine whether a screening program is worthwhile. For your own protection you must gain some familiarity with the problems of screening programs if you are to benefit from those that are worthwhile while avoiding those that are not.

In the preceding chapter, we discussed how the usefulness of laboratory tests is destroyed when there is only a relatively small chance that the disease is present. This is nearly always the case in screening programs. The table on the next page illustrates this by relating the occurrence of a number of major health problems to the predictive value of an excellent test for those problems. The test is a hypothetical one and is given a sensitivity and specificity of 95 percent. (Unfortunately, few screening tests have such excellent sensitivity and specificity.) Note that three of the most common health problems (smoking, obesity, and alcoholism) require no laboratory test to make the diag-

Effect of occurrence on predictive value

Health Problem	Occurrence Per 100,000	Predictive Value %
Smoking	35,000	91
Obesity	25,000	86
Hypertension (high blood pressure)	15,000	77
Alcoholism	4,200	45
Coronary artery disease (ischemic heart disease)	2,800	35
Diabetes (all types)	1,270	20
Glaucoma	360	6.4
Gonorrhea	285	5.2
Tuberculosis	80	1.5
Cancer of the breast (per 100,000 women)	73	1.4
Cancer of colon and rectum	45	.85
Lung cancer (all types) For males age 65: 150	26	.49
Syphilis	11	.20
Bladder cancer	7	.14

nosis. Recall also from Chapter 3 that the use of many screening tests (multiphasic screening) compounds the problems of these tests. The end result may be that there is a very great probability that a normal person will have an "abnormal" result on at least one part of the multiphasic screening program.

Although these problems with the tests used for detection are very significant, they may not be as great as those involved in demonstrating that treatment is more effective when begun before symptoms appear. As noted above, the reasoning behind most screening programs is something of a paradox. It is the very lack of an effective treatment that leads to the notion that screening is necessary in the first place. Given the widespread prejudice in favor of screening, evaluation of the effectiveness of treatment is often inadequate or omitted altogether.

Such evaluation is not easy. One of the inherent fallacies of screening is that all screening programs make it appear that survival is improved. To illustrate, let us assume there is a cancer that is uniformly fatal six months after symptoms appear and the diagnosis is made.

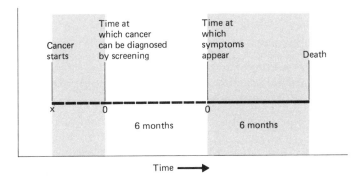

With screening, survival 12 months. *But* treatment was totally ineffective.
"Increase" in survival is artifact of early detection.
Without screening, survival 6 months;

Treatment is totally ineffective. Now suppose we devised a screening program that detects this cancer six months before it causes symptoms. For those who are detected by screening, this is the time at which diagnosis is made. This is shown in the figure above. When the results of this screening program are reported, it will be said that patients detected by screening lived one year after diagnosis, whereas those diagnosed on the basis of symptoms will have survived only six months after diagnosis. It will seem logical to conclude that the combination of screening and treatment improved survival by six months. *But treatment was totally ineffective.* We didn't add six months to the life expectancy of the patient. We simply added six months to the time in which the cancer was known to exist. Some would say that we robbed the patient of the last six months of normal life by telling him or her about the cancer six months earlier than he or she would have known otherwise. Is it a good thing to inform someone that they have a disease if there is nothing that can be done about it? You will have to formulate your own answer to this, but it is far from obvious that it is of benefit to tell someone who is feeling well and who is without symptoms that they have an untreatable and incurable disease. The only certain beneficiaries of such screening programs are those who are promoting those programs. If nothing is lost by waiting for the disease to cause symptoms before starting treatment, there seems to be little point in undergoing the cost and risk of the screening procedure.

A large portion of Section IV of this book is devoted to discussions of the most frequently advocated screening procedures. The conclusions reached in those discussions may be summarized as follows:

■ *Procedures for which there is good evidence of effectiveness:* Blood-pressure checks, self examination and physician examination of breasts, Pap smear.

■ *Procedures that are probably effective:* Tuberculosis skin testing, tonometry (glaucoma testing), VDRL (blood test for syphilis), tests for hidden blood in stool, proctosigmoidoscopy.

■ *Procedures for which there is little or no evidence of effectiveness:* Annual physical examinations, multiphasic screening, blood tests for diabetes, x-rays for lung cancer, electrocardiographic exercise stress tests ("treadmill tests"), and many others—including blood tests for anemia, gout, arthritis, and thyroid disease.

■ *Procedures that may be of benefit to those with certain items in their personal or family medical history:* Thyroid examination, xeromammography (x-rays) of breasts.

Information as to who should have these procedures and at what ages is given in Section II as well as in Section IV.

The risks of screening procedures are often dismissed as of no consequence. Do not let anyone sell you a screening procedure on the basis that even if it does no good, it does no harm. Screening procedures can harm you in at least four ways:

■ It should be clear by now that the risk of false positive laboratory tests is high. Accepting such a test as proof of a disease obviously has great potential for harm by exposing you to the hazards of unnecessary treatment or by labeling you as "diseased" when you are not. Moreover, the attempt to prove that an abnormal laboratory test is just a false positive may be costly, inconvenient, and a danger to your health. In at least one instance, an investigation to prove that a laboratory test was simply a false positive eventually culminated in the death of a patient due to a complication of an x-ray procedure.

■ Diagnostic tests do have inherent dangers. There really is radiation in those x-rays and, once in a great while, people really do have heart attacks during uncomfortable, stressful tests.

■ Screening programs may have side effects not directly related to the test used. For example, Dr. Abraham Bergman studied the effects of screening programs for heart murmurs and sickle-cell anemia in children. In both instances, it was found that a significant number of these children and their families acted as if the child had a disease when, in fact, there was none. The overall result was that more disease and disability was created by these programs than was detected. Similarly, it has been demonstrated that from 77 to 100 percent of persons over the age of 60 will be labeled as diabetic on the basis of the "best" laboratory test for this disease. It hardly makes sense to label every person over the age of 60 as diabetic, especially when this may lead to treatment with dangerous drugs of unknown benefit.

■ They cost money. And even if they did cost only money, they still would be unacceptable. Money spent on the useless cannot be spent on the useful.

The total costs of screening programs are always difficult to ascertain. Analysis of the budgets of various governmental organizations and voluntary disease-oriented groups seldom reveals the monies actually being spent for screening procedures. Figures for cost within private physicians' offices are even more difficult to obtain. It is known that the cost of individual screening procedures varies enormously, from $300 or more for the "executive physical" to about 13 cents for a single test of the stool for hidden blood. As a rule of thumb, the more expensive the screening procedure, the less likely it is to be worthwhile. Beware of those who attempt to get around this by arguing that if many such tests are done, then the cost per test will be decreased. Clearly, if the test is ineffective, then doing one is bad and doing many is worse. And you already know that doing many screening tests increases the likelihood of problems with false positive results.

The bottom line is that only a few screening tests are worthwhile. They do not need to be done with great frequency and their cost is quite reasonable. Obtain the benefit of these tests by incorporating them into your LifePlan. Equally important, avoid the trap of believing that any attempt to detect disease early is better than nothing at all.

A Final Word

In medical care, it is often difficult or impossible to decide whether the benefits outweigh the risks and costs. Many times information on these factors is simply not available. Even when it is, a whole new set of problems may present themselves. For example, a group of experts recently concluded that where appendectomies were concerned it was necessary to spend 43 million dollars in order to save one life. Balancing the benefits and risks of appendectomy is difficult enough, but adding the question of cost makes things infinitely more difficult. Raised to believe that a human life is priceless, we are not equipped with guidelines or simple formulas for using this kind of information. Yet it is vitally important for each of us to confront these facts and to be involved, for these are the realities we face.

Below is the prayer of Sir Robert Hutchinson that hangs on the wall of the Children's Ward at The London Hospital. It is clearly the prayer of a physician, but it has a message from which we may all profit:

From inability to let well alone,
From too much zeal for the new
And contempt for what is old,
From putting knowledge before wisdom,
Science before art, and cleverness before
Common sense,
From treating patients as cases, and from
Making the cure of the disease more
Grievous than the endurance of the same,
Good Lord, deliver us.

II

TAKING STOCK
OF YOUR HEALTH

IN LIFESCORE YOU WILL ENCOUNTER THE FACTS THAT HAVE THE most to do with your health. How you score on each item will illustrate the importance of that factor in your life. Your LifeScore will give you an excellent idea of where you have been and where you are headed with respect to health.

If childbearing is planned or you are already pregnant, find out what your baby's chances are. It is not enough to "eat for two"—thinking for two is much more important.

In the final analysis, the point of this book is to help you manage the facts of LifeScore for the best possible results. To do this you must have a plan for your life—a LifePlan. The reasoning behind each item in LifePlan is given in detail in Sections III and IV. You may find it easiest to simply read these sections first, or you may refer to them as you go along. (Each item in the LifePlan contains a reference to the appropriate chapter.) Either way, remember that the goal is a LifePlan you understand and accept. Without this you are adrift without chart and compass.

Most of us will need some help in putting our LifePlan together. Getting this help is what a Health Evaluation and Planning (HEP) Session is all about. It's the kind of visit to the doctor's office that you have needed for a long time.

5

LifeScore

YOUR LIFESCORE IS THE FIRST OF THE THREE STEPS IN DEVELoping your own health management plan. By completing your LifeScore, you will determine the facts which control your chances for a healthy future. This is worth repeating: These are the facts which dictate the odds for or against your being healthy tomorrow. You may be a bit reluctant to accept this. We have all heard these stories before: "My grandfather smoked two packs of cigarettes and drank a six-pack of beer every day of his life and lived to the age of 90." At least some of these stories are true, which proves that the LifeScore cannot be that important, right? Wrong. It is precisely because the information in LifeScore *is* important that such tales assume a life of their own. It is very nearly the same as if you put a loaded gun to your head and pull the trigger. If the gun goes off and blows your mind in a literal sense, this unhappy event is hardly surprising. But if the gun should fail to fire, now that is an unexpected turn of events and a tale worth retelling. Now, if you put the gun to your head every day and it fails to fire until you reach 90, your story will never be forgotten. After all, we all want to think we can beat the odds.

But what *are* the odds? What are the chances you can get away with smoking or eating too much or exercising too little? LifeScore is one way of illustrating how your habits and health history affect the probability of good health. It can be used to estimate your life expectancy, a very basic measure of your prospects for the future. Are you planning to travel when you retire? Want to see your child graduate from school? Expect to be chief executive officer before fishing becomes your occupation and preoccupation? Are you counting on being around then?

Life expectancy is not all there is to it. LifeScore also gives a good indication of how healthy you will be while you are around. Will life be worth living if you get short of breath with the slightest effort or fatigue makes every day a struggle? Many who have lost their health think it is not.

Determining your LifeScore will enable you to understand what is affecting your health. This understanding forms the basis for the second step: plotting a strategy for the best health—your LifePlan. In the third step you will calculate your Potential LifeScore using your LifePlan. This will demonstrate how your LifePlan has improved the chances for a long and healthy life.

You may have filled out other medical questionnaires. The Life-Score is different. It is shorter because it deals only with facts known to have an impact on health, and not every piece of information that might be of interest to a doctor at some point in the future. It contains references to other chapters so that you can understand each question before you answer it. It will be more fun than questionnaires that have many questions but don't tell you what the answers mean.

Instructions are given with each question. If you do not understand the question, and especially if you do not understand *why* the question was asked, consult the chapter listed as a reference.

LifeScore Worksheet

I. HABITS

1. **Exercise** Chapter 8

To qualify as a minute of conditioning, it must be a minute with the heart rate at 120 beats per minute or more. Beware of overestimating activities in which there may be a lot of standing around—for example, tennis. As a rule, golf, bowling, baseball and volleyball do *not* result in conditioning.

Your Score

If your minutes of conditioning per week come to:

Less than 15	score	0	_____
15–29		+2	_____
30–44		+6	_____
45–74		+12	_____
75–119		+16	_____
120–179		+20	_____
180 or more		+24	_____

2. **Weight** Chapter 9

Read in Chapter 9 about using the weight table you will find on page 126 to determine how many pounds overweight you are.

If you are overweight by:

0–5 pounds	score	0	_____
6–15		−2	_____
16–25		−6	_____
26–35		−10	_____
36–45		−12	_____
46 or more		−15	_____

3. **Diet** Chapter 9

If you eat a well-balanced diet, score +4 _____

If you avoid saturated fats and cholesterol, score +2 _____

Your Score

4. **Smoking** Chapter 10

One cigar is considered to be the equivalent of one cigarette. If you smoke only a pipe, enter −4   _____

If the number of cigarettes you smoke per day comes to:

1–9	score −13	_____
10–19	−15	_____
20–29	−17	_____
30–39	−20	_____
40–49	−24	_____
50 or more	−28	_____

5. **Alcohol** Chapter 11

Cocktails are assumed to contain 1½ ounces of hard liquor. If you are pouring doubles, multiply accordingly. One pint equals 16 ounces, or about 10 cocktails. One eight-ounce beer is the equivalent of one cocktail. Six ounces of wine also is the equivalent of one cocktail.

If your daily cocktail consumption comes to:

0	score 0	_____
1–2	+1	_____
3–4	−4	_____
5–6	−12	_____
7–9	−20	_____
10 or more	−30	_____

6. **Accidents** Chapter 12

The actual time you wear seat belts while driving is probably one-half your first guess (unless that guess was zero). Take a minute to come up with a more accurate estimate.

If the driving time during which you wear a seat belt is:

Less than 25%	score 0	_____
About 25%	+2	_____
About 50%	+4	_____

		Your Score
About 75%	+6	_____
About 100%	+8	_____

7. For women only (Contraception) Chapter 14

If you have had a hysterectomy or tubal ligation or have reached the menopause, skip this section.

If you use:

Nothing and would *not* have an abortion	score −10	_____
Mechanical method and would *not* have an abortion	0	_____
Birth-control pills and would *not* have an abortion	+4	_____
Nothing but *would* have an abortion	+4	_____
Birth-control pills and *would* have an abortion	+5	_____
Mechanical method and *would* have an abortion	+10	_____
Bad bonus: If you smoke and use birth control pills	−10	_____

Habits Total _____

II. MENTAL HEALTH Chapter 16

The Holmes Scale and a discussion of it are found in Chapter 16. Record your score in the appropriate space.

If your Holmes score is:

Less than 150	score 0	_____
150–250	−4	_____
250–300	−7	_____
More than 300	−10	_____

Your Score

III. IMMUNIZATIONS Chapter 15

Determine whether your immunizations are up to date for each of the diseases listed. (Those listed are for adults. See Chapter 15 for information on immunizations for children.)

If you are not current on:

Tetanus   score   −2   _____

Diphtheria*   −1   _____

IV. PERSONAL HISTORY

Tuberculosis Chapter 22

If you have been in close contact for a year or more with someone with tuberculosis, score −4   _____

Radiation Chapter 19

If you have had radiation (x-ray) treatment of tonsils, adenoids, acne or ringworm of the scalp, score −6   _____

Asbestos Chapter 19

If you work with asbestos regularly and do *not* smoke, score −2   _____

If you work with asbestos regularly and *do* smoke, score −10   _____

Vinyl chloride Chapter 19

If you work regularly with vinyl chloride, score −4.   _____

Environment Chapter 17

If you live in a city or suburb, score −6.   _____

Venereal Disease Chapter 25

If sexual activity has been frequent *and* with many different partners, score −1.   _____

_____
* High risk of exposure only.

Your Score

For Women Only (Risk of uterine cancer) Chapter 19

If you began regular sexual activity before age 18, score −1. _____

If sexual activity has been frequent *and* with many different partners, score −1. _____

If you are Jewish, score −1.* _____

Personal History Total _____

V. FAMILY HISTORY

Heart Attacks (Myocardial Infarction) Chapter 18

For each parent, brother, or sister who had a heart attack before age 40, score −4. _____

For each grandparent, uncle, or aunt who had a heart attack before age 40, score −1. _____

High Blood Pressure (Hypertension) Chapter 18

For each parent, brother, or sister with high blood pressure requiring treatment, score −2. _____

For each grandparent, uncle, or aunt with high blood pressure requiring treatment, score −1. _____

Diabetes Chapter 21

For each parent, brother, or sister with juvenile-onset diabetes, score −6. _____

For each grandparent, uncle, or aunt with juvenile-onset diabetes, score −2. _____

For each parent, brother, or sister with adult-onset diabetes requiring treatment with insulin, score −2. _____

For each grandparent, uncle, or aunt with adult-onset diabetes requiring treatment with insulin, score −1. _____

For Women Only (Cancer of the·breast) Chapter 19

If your mother or a sister has had cancer of the breast, score −4. _____

_____
* See Chapter 19.

Your Score

Glaucoma Chapter 26

If you have a parent, grandparent, brother, sister, uncle, or aunt with glaucoma, score −2.   _____

Gout Chapter 24

If you have a parent, grandparent, brother, sister, uncle, or aunt with gout, score −1.   _____

Family History Total   _____

VI. MEDICAL CARE

If you have had the following procedures regularly, score the points indicated:

Blood pressure check every year: +4 points   _____

Self-examination of breasts monthly plus examination by physician every year or two: +2 points   _____

Pap smear every year or two: +2 points   _____

Tuberculosis skin test (PPD or Tine) every five to 10 years: +1 point   _____

Tonometry every four years after age 40: +1 point   _____

VDRL (blood test for syphilis) every four to six years while sexually active: +1 point   _____

Test for hidden blood in stool every two years after age 40, every year after 50: +1 point   _____

Proctosigmoidoscopy once after age 50: +1 point   _____

Medical Care Total   _____

I.	Habits	_____	Be sure to get the signs of the numbers right so that you add or subtract correctly.
II.	Mental Health	_____	
III.	Immunizations	_____	
IV.	Personal History	_____	
V.	Family History	_____	

VI. Medical Care   _____

     TOTAL   _____

     Now Add   __200__

     To Obtain Your LifeScore   _____

A LifeScore of 200 is about "average." A LifeScore above 215 indicates a positive lifestyle which gives you an excellent chance at enjoying better than average health. If you scored 230 or more, the odds are overwhelmingly in your favor. A LifeScore below 185 means that your chance at a healthy future is clearly decreased. If your LifeScore is below 170, consider your life to be in danger. Below 150, make out a will and get your affairs in order.

Or you can get your act together. You can do something about almost all of the things that decrease your LifeScore. This is what LifePlan is all about.

How long do you have? Another way of illustrating the impact of your decisions on your health is to calculate your personal life expectancy. For men, the formula is:

$$\underset{\text{LifeScore}}{\underline{\qquad\qquad}} \div 200 \times 70 \text{ years} = \underset{\text{Life Expectancy}}{\underline{\qquad\qquad\qquad}}$$

For women:

$$\underset{\text{LifeScore}}{\underline{\qquad\qquad}} \div 200 \times 75 \text{ years} = \underset{\text{Life Expectancy}}{\underline{\qquad\qquad\qquad}}$$

These estimates assume that you do not have a chronic disease such as diabetes. The effect of such a disease on health and life expectancy depends on the disease and its severity. Your doctor can give you an indication of what the effect may be.

The values given to the various factors comprising the LifeScore are based on a large number of studies. Unfortunately, there has been no study that defines the exact relationship among these factors or determines their absolute value. But it would be a great mistake to dismiss these risks simply because we cannot be as precise as you would like. LifeScore is an approximation, but it accurately reflects the best information on what affects your health.

Well, what does the future look like? Is *your* management of *your* health saving or losing life? Perhaps you had not realized that you were in charge of your health, but by now you should feel the need for a plan—a LifePlan for saving your life.

6

What Will Your Baby's Chances Be?

APPROXIMATELY 80 PERCENT OF ALL PREGNANCIES END IN THE BIRTH of a healthy child. The remaining 20 percent end with a spontaneous abortion (miscarriage), a stillbirth, or a child with significant congenital abnormalities. (Induced abortions have been excluded.) In one-third to one-half of the spontaneous abortions and stillbirths, no abnormality is identified. Even when an abnormality is found, it is often impossible to say exactly what caused the abnormality or if the abnormality was responsible for loss of the fetus. Nevertheless, we now know a good deal about the effect of the parents' habits on the health of an unborn child. You can take steps to substantially decrease the threat of death or deformity to your own child.

Smoking
Several studies have indicated that spontaneous abortions are more frequent in mothers who smoke. A recent report from Columbia University indicates that light smokers (less than one pack per day) are 1.6 times more likely than nonsmokers to spontaneously abort, while heavy smokers (one pack or more per day) are 2.3 times more likely than nonsmokers to abort.

The association between smoking and congenital abnormalities is less strong. However, the British Perinatal Mortality Study indicated 55 percent more congenital abnormalities in infants born to smoking mothers than to those born to nonsmoking mothers.

Children born to smoking mothers have also been reported to weigh less at birth, be shorter as young children, and have more lead in their blood than those born to nonsmokers.

Alcohol

As in adults, the effect of alcohol on the unborn child is directly proportional to the amount to which it is exposed. However, recent medical studies indicate that the fetus is more sensitive to alcohol than you are. As few as two cocktails a day substantially increase the risks of mental and physical retardation as well as birth defects.

The child of an alcoholic bears the burden of the mother's addiction. The constant, excessive use of alcohol makes it very likely that the child will have permanent mental and physical problems. Moreover, the *child* is an alcoholic and thus may experience seizures and delirium tremens (the D.T.'s) after birth due to withdrawal from alcohol—just as the mother may do on withdrawal. "Horror show" is an indelicate piece of medical slang, but it accurately describes the scene of an alcoholic in the D.T.'s giving birth to a seizing baby.

Drugs

Perhaps the only good thing that has come out of the thalidomide tragedy is an increased awareness of the danger drugs pose to the fetus. Still there are disturbing indications that the message is taken lightly. A study of the pregnancies of 300 women who were considered to be normal and healthy in every way revealed that:

■ All had taken at least one drug during the pregnancy.

■ The average number of drugs taken was seven.

■ One woman took 23 different drugs during her pregnancy.

You should understand that it is impossible to say with certainty that *any* drug is absolutely safe during pregnancy. The best rule is that all drugs should be avoided if possible and some must be avoided absolutely. No drug, including those available without a prescription, should be used without discussing it with your physician. The accompanying table lists some common drugs and the problems they are known to cause.

Children of mothers addicted to narcotics or barbiturates are in much the same predicament of those whose mothers are addicted to alcohol. Again, there is the possibility of a "horror show" as addict gives birth to addict.

Medication	Potential Problem in Infants
Aspirin (during last three months of pregnancy)	Yellow jaundice Bleeding Premature labor
Aspirin-phenacetin combination	Oxygen-carrying ability of blood decreases
Acetaminophen (Tylenol, Tempra, Valadol)	Kidney problems
Alcohol—chronic abuse or high doses	Seizures Growth retardation Birth defects

Antidepressants (tricyclic)
  Imipromine (Tofranil)
  Amitryptyline (Elavil, Etafron, Triavil)
	Birth defects

Antihistamines Diphenhidramine (Benadryl)	Seizures

Antinausea drugs
  Meclizine (Bonine)
  Cyclizine (Marezine, Migral)
  Chlorocyclizine
	Birth defects
	Birth defects
	Birth defects

Antibiotics
  Sulfa drugs
  Tetracycline
	Yellow jaundice
	Malformed teeth
	Suppressed bone growth
	Cataracts

Kanamycin Streptomycin	Hearing loss Hearing loss
Bronchial medications Potassium iodide	Goiter

Hormones
  Estrogens
  (diethylstilbestrol)
  Androgens
  Progestins
	Vaginal cancer
	Masculinization of daughter
	Birth defects
	Growth retardation

LSD	Limb defects

Medication	Potential Problem in Infants
Tranquilizers	
Diazepam (Valium)	Decreased body temperature, cleft palate
Chlordiazepopide (Librium)	Seizures
Barbiturates	Seizures
Chlorpromazine (Thorazine)	Temperature regulation
Promethazine (Phenergan)	Bleeding
Vitamin excess	
C	Skin and intestinal problems
Pyridoxine	Birth defects
Vaginal preparations	
Flagyl	Cancer (in rats) Mutations (in bacteria)

Marijuana use has been reported to be associated with damage to chromosomes, but there is insufficient information to be certain of its effects. For now it should be regarded as being about the same as alcohol—more than light use is trouble.

Radiation

X-rays and other types of radiation may cause deformities or death in an unborn child. There is some evidence that the chance of the child developing a malignancy (leukemia) later on is also increased. Radiation is most dangerous when exposure occurs at the beginning of the pregnancy. In the last three months of pregnancy, the risk is reduced. The use of an abdominal lead shield (gonadal shield) will reduce it further. The rule, then, is to avoid x-rays altogether if possible. In the event that they are absolutely necessary, they should be delayed as long as possible and an abdominal shield used if feasible.

Age

Very young mothers and older mothers have an increased risk of unsuccessful pregnancies. As age increases, so does the chance of chromosomal abnormalities (see Chapter 31). This accounts for a good deal of the risk in older mothers. A combination of factors probably accounts for the remainder of this risk as well as the increased risk in very young mothers. A discussion of *what* these factors may be is beyond the scope of this book. Suffice it to say that medical care cannot significantly alter them.

Nutrition

It is clear that nutrition is important in pregnancy and that inadequate nutrition is one of the reasons unsuccessful pregnancies are more common among the poor. Yet it is very difficult to measure this effect precisely and to separate it from other factors that affect the health of the poor mothers. Inadequate nutrition rarely contributes to unsuccessful pregnancies in the nonpoor. This leads to a somewhat unsatisfactory conclusion: Nutrition is important, but exactly how and to what extent it affects pregnancies is not known.

Acute Illness

Any severe acute illness may cause a spontaneous abortion or stillbirth. Such illnesses are seldom associated with congenital malformations. However, rubella (German measles) is a mild acute infection which carries a high risk of congenital problems (deafness, cataracts, heart disease, retardation) if contracted during early pregnancy. Of course, if you have had the illness in the past, or if you have been immunized, you needn't be concerned about the possibility of getting rubella while pregnant. But if neither of these events has occurred, you should be immunized *before* you get pregnant to eliminate a significant risk to your baby (see Chapter 15).

Chronic Illness

Many chronic illnesses impose some increased risk for both mother and unborn child. Diabetes is the most important example. The degree of risk depends on the disease and its severity, so each situation must be assessed separately. If you have a chronic disease, discussing its effects on pregnancy is a must *before* you get pregnant.

Medical Care

Not so long ago it was unusual for the doctor to see a pregnant woman before the time of delivery regardless of her wealth or social position. Now regular visits during pregnancy are routine among those able to pay for them. Government support of these services for the poor has been cited as a major reason why death and disability associated with pregnancy and childbirth have decreased in the last 15 years, although it should be remembered that many other programs have been aimed at improving the health of the poor during this same period.

Medical care during pregnancy should be regarded as a necessity. A major purpose of these visits should be the opportunity to educate parents and answer their questions. Often this is accomplished best when a nurse practitioner or nurse midwife participates in prenatal care. Regular visits may detect certain problems such as toxemia of pregnancy before they become severe. Testing for blood type (especially RH factor) incompatability will allow appropriate preparations for delivery to be made. Other factors that affect the method of delivery (position of baby, size of mother's pelvis) can be determined also. Close medical supervision is essential with any chronic disease such as diabetes.

What Are Your Baby's Chances?
The following will give you some idea of how you are affecting your baby's chances:

Your Baby's Score

Smoking

Write in one-half your smoking score from your LifeScore (Chapter 5).   _____

Drinking

Your drinking score from your LifeScore (Chapter 5).   _____

Drugs

For each of the drugs in the table on page 66 that you have used during pregnancy (except aspirin), score −2. For aspirin, score −2 only if you used substantial amounts in the last three months of pregnancy.   _____

If you have used more than two drugs during pregnancy, score −2.   _____

Radiation

If you had x-rays of abdomen, chest, or upper leg in first six months of pregnancy, score −3.   _____

Age

If you are over 20, subtract your age from 30:

30 − _____ (your age) = _____ .   _____

If this number is negative, record it as your score. Otherwise your score is 0.

If you are 20 or younger, subtract 20 from your age and record this as your score:

_____ (your age) − 20 = _____ .   _____

Your Baby's Score

Rubella

If you had the disease or were immunized before you
became pregnant, score +4.   _____

Medical Care

If you have received regular medical care during your
pregnancy, score +9.   _____

Now add 100 to the total to get your Baby's Score.

Total = _____

_+100_

Baby's score _____

To estimate the chance of successful pregnancy, divide your Baby's
Score by 115.

_____ ÷ 115 = _____ %
Baby's Score   Chance of successful
                          pregnancy.

This estimate assumes that you do not have any serious illness. As
with LifeScore, there has been no large scale study which has directly
tested its accuracy; it is an estimate based on many studies of various
aspects of pregnancy. But it does illustrate what is known about your
effect on your unborn child. Don't deceive yourself by dismissing a risk
because we cannot determine its magnitude precisely. Give your baby
the best chance you can.

Contrast in Expectations

To illustrate a calculation of the Baby's Score, consider those for
two women with very different backgrounds. The first is 28 years old,
never smoked, averages less than one cocktail per day, uses only an
occasional aspirin, had rubella as a child, and has received medical
care throughout her pregnancy. X-rays of her pelvis will probably be
necessary just before delivery in order to determine whether a cesarean
section will be necessary.

The second woman is one of the many unwed teenage mothers. She
is 15, smokes half a pack of cigarettes a day, has three or four beers
every evening, has used many drugs routinely, including Valium and
Librium. Her first contact with a physician was in her eighth month of

pregnancy. She has never been immunized against rubella and does not believe she has ever had the disease. A blood test confirms that she is not immune to rubella.

The scores for their babies are compared below:

	Your Baby's Score	
	First Woman	Second Woman
Smoking		
Write in one-half your smoking score from your LifeScore (Chapter 5).	0	−8
Drinking		
Your drinking score from your LifeScore (Chapter 5).	0	−4
Drugs		
For each of the drugs in the table on page 66 that you have used during pregnancy (except aspirin), score −2. For aspirin, score −2 only if you used substantial amounts in the last three months of pregnancy.	0	−4
If you have used more than two drugs during pregnancy, score −2.	0	−2
Radiation		
If you had x-rays of abdomen, chest or upper leg in first six months of pregnancy, score −3.	0	0
Age		
If you are over 20, subtract your age from 30: 30 − 28 (your age) = 2 .	0	
If this number is *negative*, record it as your score. Otherwise your score is 0.		
If you are 20 or younger, subtract 20 from your age and record this as your score: 15 (your age) − 20 = −5 .		−5
Rubella		
If you had the disease or were immunized before you became pregnant, score +4.	4	0

Your Baby's Score

Medical Care

If you have received regular medical care during your pregnancy, score +9.

	9	0
Total	13	−23

	First Woman	Second Woman
Total =	13	−23
	+100	+100
Baby's score	113	77

	Baby's Score		Chance of successful pregnancy
First Woman	113	÷ 115 =	98%
Second Woman	77	÷ 115 =	67%

7
LifePlan

HOW DID YOU DO ON YOUR LIFESCORE? WAS IT WHAT YOU EXPECTED? Is it a cause for celebration or consternation? What would you like it to be? Let's assume that the answer to the last question is "as high as possible." It seems likely that no matter whether you scored high or low, you would be interested in improving your chances for a long, healthy life. To do this, you need a LifePlan which ensures that the odds are in your favor.

There are three steps to developing your LifePlan and putting it into action. The first is to understand the problems involved and what can be done about them. This is what Sections III and IV are about. The second step is to set the goals for your LifePlan. The importance of these goals will be illustrated by calculating your Potential LifeScore and Potential Life Expectancy. Finally, you will begin the process of putting your LifePlan into action by recording it in the Personal Health Record in Section V, and, where appropriate, using the other materials in that section to help you achieve your goals.

Step 1: Understanding the Problem

Each chapter in Sections III and IV addresses itself to a subject that is important to your LifePlan. The material in these chapters is designed to help you decide what you should do about that particular subject.

Section III concerns itself with lifestyle. This is required reading for all of us. Section IV concerns itself with major medical problems. Heart disease, cancer, and strokes are the three leading causes of death in the United States. Diabetes is the sixth leading cause of death, and the chapter on that subject is important because it will help you to understand what diabetes is *not* as well as what it *is*. Anemia and thyroid disease are also problems about which it is as important to know what they are *not* as to know what they *are*. Tuberculosis, arthritis, gout, and venereal disease are potentially serious problems but you can decrease the threats that they present to you. Glaucoma is a preventable cause of blindness. The chapter on allergy and asthma can keep you from labeling yourselves with medical problems you do not have. The chapters on epilepsy and genetic disorders are important not only because your life may be touched by these problems, but also because our attitude as a society has a significant impact on the illnesses they cause.

This is quite a bit of reading. It is not easy, but it is important. To help you in the completion of the remainder of this chapter, these chapters are referenced at appropriate points.

Step 2: Setting Your Goals

Here's where you get down to business. You now know all about how to give yourself the best chances for health and long life. Now you must say just what you are willing to do. You must set the goals of your LifePlan. To help you do this, each of the goals you should consider for your LifePlan have been listed below. The appropriate chapter or chapters in Sections IV and V are referenced. For your convenience, the ideal goal is presented in an abbreviated form. Simply record your goal in the space provided.

Setting Your LifePlan Goals

I. HABITS

Exercise Chapter 8   Your Goal

Ideal: Within reason, the more the better, but
        at least 15 minutes of conditioning
        three times a week   _____

Weight Chapter 9

Ideal: Within five pounds of your ideal weight
        according to the table on page 126   _____

Diet Chapter 9

Ideal: Balanced diet, avoid saturated fats and
        cholesterol   _____

Smoking Chapter 10

Ideal: No smoking: Second best is to reduce
        amount or switch to pipe or cigar   _____

Drinking Chapter 11

Ideal: Zero to one cocktail per day on the
        average   _____

Seat Belts Chapter 12

Ideal: Worn 100 % of time while driving or
        riding in a car   _____

Contraception Chapter 14

Ideal: The safest method acceptable to you   _____

II. MENTAL HEALTH

Holmes Score Chapter 16

Ideal: Score of less than 150 in a year   _____

III. IMMUNIZATIONS Chapter 15

Ideal: All immunizations up to date   _____

Your Goal

IV. MAJOR DISEASES

Heart Disease and Stroke Chapters 18 and 21

Ideal: Regular exercise   See Habits

Weight within five pounds of ideal   See Habits

No smoking   See Habits

Blood pressure check once a year   _____

Cancer of the Lung Chapters 10, 17 and 19

Ideal: No smoking   See Habits

Avoid air pollution   _____

Avoid exposure to asbestos   _____

Cancer of the Breast Chapter 19

Ideal: Monthly Self-Examination   _____

Yearly Doctor Examination   _____

Xeromammography after age 40 if
mother or sister had breast cancer   _____

Cancer of the Uterus Chapter 19

Ideal: Pap Smear every year or two   _____

Cancer of the Colon Chapter 19

Ideal: Proctosigmoidoscopy once after age 50   _____

Test stool for hidden blood every two
years after age 40, yearly after age 50   _____

Cancer of the Thyroid Chapter 19

If you have had radiation treatment of tonsils,
adenoids, acne or ringworm of the scalp:
yearly examination by physician   _____

Cancer of the Liver Chapter 19

Ideal: Less than three cocktails a day   See Habits

Avoid exposure to vinyl chloride   _____

	Your Goal
Cancer of the Skin Chapter 19	
* Consider: Monthly self-examination	_____
Avoid prolonged, excessive exposure to sun	_____
Cancer of the Testes Chapter 19	
* Consider: Monthly self-examination of testes	_____
Diabetes Chapter 21	
Ideal: Weight within five pounds of ideal	See Habits
Tuberculosis Chapter 22	
Ideal: Skin test (PPD or Tine) every five to 10 years if no history of exposure	_____
Glaucoma Chapter 26	
Ideal: Tonometry every four to five years after age 40 (after age 30 if family history of glaucoma)	_____
Gout Chapter 24	
Ideal: Weight within five pounds of ideal	See Habits
Venereal Disease Chapter 25	
Ideal: Avoid frequent sexual activity with many different partners	_____
Blood test (VDRL) every five to six years while sexually active	_____

Let us now consider the new you. It seems natural to wonder how much your LifePlan is going to do for you. To find out about this, calculate your Potential LifeScore and your Potential Life Expectancy. These are what your LifeScore and life expectancy will be if you are successful in following your LifePlan. To do this we will recalculate the LifeScore based on your LifePlan goals rather than what you have actually been doing. We will call this the New You Score.

In Sections 1, 2, and 3 of the New You Score, points are awarded or lost in the same fashion as in the LifeScore (Chapter 5). Again, you

---

* These measures are reasonable but unproven. They deserve consideration for your LifePlan, but are not given points in either your LifeScore or New You Score.

simply use your LifePlan goals instead of what you are actually doing. For example, if you are currently smoking about a pack (20 cigarettes) a day but have set a goal of no smoking, you lost 17 points on your LifeScore but you lose *no* points on the New You Score. If you set a goal of 1 to 9 cigarettes per day, your New You Score is -13.

In Sections 4, 5, and 6 each item has special instructions for scoring.

The New You Score

	Points
I. HABITS	
Exercise	_____
Weight	_____
Diet: Balanced diet, avoid saturated fats and cholesterol	_____
Smoking	_____
Drinking	_____
Seat belts	_____
Contraception	_____
Habits Total	_____
II. MENTAL HEALTH	
Holmes Score	_____
III. IMMUNIZATIONS	
Immunizations	_____

IV. PERSONAL HISTORY

Tuberculosis

A skin test every year for five years after discovery of the exposure, then every five years after that, allows you to add back three of the points lost because of an exposure to tuberculosis.   _____

Radiation

Yearly thyroid examinations by your physician will add back five of the points you lost because of this exposure.   _____

Asbestos

Ending this exposure allows you to add back half of the points lost because of it.   _____

Points

Vinyl Chloride

Ending this exposure allows you to add back half of the points lost because of it.   _____

Urban Environment

Changing your environment allows you to add back five of the points lost here.   _____

For men and women (Risk of venereal disease)

A VDRL every year or two will allow you to add back one of the points lost here.   _____

For Women Only (Risk of uterine cancer)

Yearly pap smears allow you to add back the points lost because of these items in your history.   _____

Personal History Total   _____

V. FAMILY HISTORY

Heart Attacks (Myocardial Infarction)

If you set your goal at the ideal for preventing heart disease, you may add back one-half the points lost because of a family history of heart attacks.   _____

High Blood Pressure (Hypertension)

If you will have a yearly blood pressure check, you may add back the points lost because of a family history of hypertension.   _____

Diabetes

If you will keep your weight to within five pounds of ideal, you may:

Add back one-third of the points that you lost because of juvenile diabetes in parents, brothers or sisters.   _____

Add back one-third of the points lost because of juvenile diabetes in a grandparent, aunt or uncle.   _____

Add back two-thirds of the points lost because of adult diabetes in parents, brothers or sisters.   _____

Add back two-thirds of the points lost because of adult diabetes in grandparents, aunts or uncles.   _____

Points

Cancer of the Breast

If you will practice monthly self-examination, have a physician examination yearly, and have xeromammography after age 40, you may add back three of the points lost because of this cancer in your mother or sister.

_____

Glaucoma

If you will have tonometry yearly after age 30, you may add back the points lost because of a family history of glaucoma.

_____

Gout

If you will keep your weight to within five pounds of ideal, you may add back the point lost because of a family history of gout.

_____

Family History Total   _____

VI. MEDICAL CARE

These are the screening procedures which are worthwhile. Add the points indicated if you made the procedures part of your LifePlan.

Blood pressure check every year: +6 points   _____

Self-examination of breasts monthly plus physician examination every year or two: +3 points   _____

Pap smear every year or two: +2 points   _____

Tuberculosis skin test (PPD or Tine) every five to ten years: +1 point   _____

Tonometry every four years after age 40: +1 point   _____

VDRL (bloood test for syphilis) every four to six years while sexually active: +1 point   _____

Test for hidden blood in stool every two years after age 40, then yearly after age 50: +1 point   _____

Proctosigmoidoscopy once after age 50: +1 point   _____

Medical Care Total   _____

There is little data concerning the following items, so it is not possible to determine their value at present. However, they make sense and are well worth considering for your LifePlan. They are discussed in Chapter 19.

Monthly self-examination of the skin	No Points
Monthly self-examination of testes	No Points

Now add up the New You Points:

I.	Habits	_____
II.	Mental Health	_____
III.	Immunizations	_____
IV.	Personal History	_____
V.	Family History	_____
VI.	Medical Care	_____
	Total	_____
	Now Add	200
	To Obtain The New You Score	_____

The New You Score should be a significant improvement over your LifeScore unless:

- You already had an excellent LifePlan. Keep up the good work.

- You set no goals which will improve your health. Go to the back of the class and start all over again.

The New You Score has one very important drawback. It does not take into account *when* you begin your LifePlan. Obviously it is better to begin at age 20 than age 50. Whatever benefit your LifePlan brings will depend on the age at which it is implemented. A measure of this benefit is the *Potential LifeScore.*

To calculate your Potential LifeScore, determine the difference between your LifeScore and the New You Score.

_____ – _____ = _____

New You Score   LifeScore   The Difference

Next, determine your Delay Factor from the Delay Factor table.

Delay factor

Age	Delay Factor
20 or less	1.0
21–30	.9
31–40	.7
41–50	.5
51–60	.3
61–70	.2
71 and over	.1

Multiply this by the difference found above to find the points your new LifePlan can add to your LifeScore.

$$\underline{\hspace{3cm}} \times \underline{\hspace{3cm}} = \underline{\hspace{3cm}}$$
Delay Factor   The Difference   Added Points

Add these points to your original LifeScore to get your potential LifeScore.

$$\underline{\hspace{3cm}} + \underline{\hspace{2cm}} = \underline{\hspace{3cm}}$$
Original LifeScore   Added Points   Potential LifeScore

You can calculate your Potential Life Expectancy.

For men:

$$\underline{\hspace{4cm}} \div 200 \times 70 \text{ years} = \underline{\hspace{3cm}}$$
Potential LifeScore   Potential Life
Expectancy (years)

For women:

$$\underline{\hspace{4cm}} \div 200 \times 75 \text{ years} = \underline{\hspace{3cm}}$$
Potential LifeScore   Potential Life
Expectancy (years)

If you have not reached senior-citizen status, you may be a bit scornful of some extra time at the end of your life. You will feel differently about it when that time arrives. More than this, remember that your LifeScore relates not only to the number of years you will have, but also to how well you will feel during those years. The only ones of us who will be glad to see the end are those who have been dying for years anyway.

Step 3: Putting Your LifePlan Into Action

The key to implementing your LifePlan seems simple enough: Write it down in such a way that you understand what you want to do and you can easily keep tabs on yourself. The LifePlan portion of your Personal Health Record (Section 5) was designed to help you accomplish this. So now, before you become involved in something else, transfer your LifePlan goals to this section. When you have completed this, take a moment to fill out the rest of your Personal Health Record according to the instructions accompanying it. (This is essential if you are scheduled for a Health Education and Planning (HEP) session.)

Also included in Section 5 are some materials that will help you take the first step in meeting specific goals you have set for yourself. Despite their simplicity, checklists and charts have been proven over and over to be among the most valuable tools for helping us to achieve our aims, especially where our own habits are concerned. You will find materials for exercise, diet, weight control, and smoking in this section.

The Health Evaluation and Planning Session

It is a rare individual who can completely develop a LifePlan without raising some important, unanswered questions. Getting the help you need to make your LifePlan workable could be the most important investment you ever make. It would seem logical that there should be a session with a health professional for the sole purpose of assisting the individual to develop a plan for staying healthy—a LifePlan if you will. Given the importance of this plan, you might expect that a substantial portion of the health care system's resources would be devoted to these visits and they would be a regular part of everyone's life.

There are, of course, no such visits.

And so it has been necessary to invent them—Health Evaluation and Planning (HEP) sessions. The concept is simple: By using this book and completing your LifeScore, LifePlan, and PHR, you get as far as you can on your own. Then you attend a HEP session to get the help of a physician or nurse in resolving any remaining problems. While you are there, whatever procedures you need—blood pressure, pap smear, etc.—can be done. But remember the title—this visit is dedicated to assisting you in evaluating and planning for your own health. Do your homework before you arrive. If you are not willing to participate actively, the HEP session will be little better than an "annual physical" even if it costs much less. And an annual physical you don't need.

HEP sessions are becoming available as a part of several special projects. If such a session is not available to you through such a project, take up the matter of your LifePlan with your doctor or nurse practitioner. This may be a bit unexpected. Many health professionals believe that the public is not really interested in learning how to be healthy. But most are willing to teach. You may be surprised at their willingness to help and answer questions once you take the initiative. Allow enough time—at least 30 minutes—to get your questions answered. (The routine office visit is usually 15 minutes or less.)

You shouldn't need a HEP session very often, perhaps every three or four years, once a year at most. (Procedures such as a Pap smear can be obtained by themselves at less cost.) You may only need one in a lifetime if you keep up with new medical information. The key is whether or not you have the information you need. If your LifePlan is on track and your questions have been answered, the HEP session is unnecessary.

Finally, the question of the "complete physical" comes up continually. Isn't this a good idea every so often? If you have never had such a physical in your adult life, by all means have *one*. After the first one, whatever value they have drops off very quickly. Be sure that you get your questions answered while you are there. In other words, turn it into a HEP session. Having paid all that money, you should make it as worthwhile as possible.

One Man's LifePlan

To illustrate how a LifeScore, New You Score, and LifePlan are completed, consider how it was done by George, good friend and fairly average person. George is 38 years old and likes to think of himself as a hard-nosed, hard-driving businessman. Since he has a habit of talking to himself, it was easy to follow his reasoning as he went through Section 2.

For LifeScore, George's thinking out loud went something like this:

Exercise—hate the thought. Play golf every weekend because I like it and it's good for business. Bet my heart rate only goes above 120 when I'm closing a deal.

Weight—I am 5 foot 10 inches tall and weigh 175 pounds. Let's say I have a large frame—I'm only one pound overweight according to the table on page 126. Scratch that. The truth is, I am stretching it to say I have a medium frame, so I'm 15 pounds overweight.

Diet—Well-balanced, no doubt. Avoiding saturated fats and cholesterol, no way.

Smoking—I try to keep it under a pack a day. My wife claims it's closer to two packs a day. I'm losing so many points that I'm going to stick with my estimate—about 10 to 19 cigarettes a day.

Drinking—I think I'm drinking more and enjoying it less, but I doubt if I'm averaging more than three cocktails a day.

Seat Belts—Don't believe in them.

For Women Only—It'll be interesting to see what my wife thinks of this.

Mental Health—Let's see now, on my Holmes Schedule, since I got divorced, remarried, have a mortgage over $10,000, changed my occupation and place of residence last year, I managed to score 210.

Immunizations—Tetanus is up to date and I have no risk of exposure to diphtheria as far as I know.

Personal History—Of the things listed here, the only ones that apply are the x-ray treatment to the tonsils I had as a boy and the fact that I live in the city.

Family History—Let's see, I did have an uncle who died of a heart attack at age 39. Both my mother's parents were supposed to have been diabetic, but that was when they were really up in their years and they just took pills, no insulin.

Medical Care—I never have time for these.

After George finished mumbling to himself, his LifeScore questionnaire looked like this:

I. HABITS

1. Exercise Chapter 8

To qualify as a minute of conditioning, it must be a minute with the heart rate at 120 beats per minute or more. Beware of overestimating activities in which there may be a lot of standing around—for example, tennis. As a rule, golf, bowling, baseball and volleyball do *not* result in conditioning.

Your Score

If your minutes of conditioning per week come to:

			Your Score
Less than 15	score	0	*0*
15–29		+2	
30–44		+6	
45–74		+12	
75–119		+16	
120–179		+20	
180 or more		+24	

2. Weight Chapter 9

Read in Chapter 9 about using the weight table you will find on page 126 to determine how many pounds overweight you are.

If you are overweight by:

0–5 pounds	score	0	
6–15		−2	*−2*
16–25		−6	
26–35		−10	
36–45		−12	
46 or more		−15	

3. Diet Chapter 9

If you eat a well-balanced diet, score +4   *4*

If you avoid saturated fats and cholesterol, score +2

4. Smoking Chapter 10

One cigar is considered to be the equivalent of one cigarette. If you smoke only a pipe, enter −4

If the number of cigarettes you smoke per day comes to:

1–9	score	−13	
10–19		−15	*−15*
20–29		−17	
30–39		−20	

Your Score

40–49	−24	_____
50 or more	−28	_____

5. **Alcohol** Chapter 11

Cocktails are assumed to contain 1½ ounces of hard liquor. If you are pouring doubles, multiply accordingly. One pint equals 16 ounces, or about 10 cocktails. One eight-ounce beer is the equivalent of one cocktail. Six ounces of wine also is the equivalent of one cocktail.

If your daily cocktail consumption comes to:

0	score 0	_____
1–2	+1	_____
3–4	−4	*−4*
5–6	−12	_____
7–9	−20	_____
10 or more	−30	_____

6. **Accidents** Chapter 12

The actual time you wear seat belts while driving is probably one-half your first guess (unless that guess was zero). Take a minute to come up with a more accurate estimate.

If the driving time during which you wear a seat belt is:

Less than 25%	score 0	*0*
About 25%	+2	_____
About 50%	+4	_____
About 75%	+6	_____
About 100%	+8	_____

7. **For women only (Contraception)** Chapter 14

If you have had a hysterectomy or tubal ligation or have reached the menopause, skip this section.

If you use:

Nothing and would *not* have an abortion	score −10	_____

		Your Score
Mechanical method and would *not* have an abortion	0	_____
Birth-control pills and would *not* have an abortion	+4	_____
Nothing but *would* have an abortion	+4	_____
Birth-control pills and *would* have an abortion	+5	_____
Mechanical method and *would* have an abortion	+10	_____
Bad bonus: If you smoke and use birth control pills	−10	_____

Habits Total ___−17___

II. MENTAL HEALTH Chapter 16

The Holmes Scale and a discussion of it are found in Chapter 16. Record your score in the appropriate space.

If your Holmes score is:

Less than 150	score	0	_____
150–250		−4	___−4___
250–300		−7	_____
More than 300		−10	_____

III. IMMUNIZATIONS Chapter 15

Determine whether your immunizations are up to date for each of the diseases listed. (Those listed are for adults. See Chapter 15 for information on immunizations for children.)

If you are not current on:

Tetanus	score	−2	___0___
Diphtheria*		−1	_____

---

* High risk of exposure only.

Your Score

IV. PERSONAL HISTORY

Tuberculosis Chapter 22

If you have been in close contact for a year or more
with someone with tuberculosis, score −4   *0*

Radiation Chapter 19

If you have had radiation (x-ray) treatment of tonsils,
adenoids, acne or ringworm of the scalp, score −6   *−6*

Asbestos Chapter 19

If you work with asbestos regularly and do *not* smoke,
score −2   *0*

If you work with asbestos regularly and *do* smoke,
score −10   *0*

Vinyl chloride Chapter 19

If you work regularly with vinyl chloride, score −4.   *0*

Environment Chapter 17

If you live in a city or suburb, score −6.   *−6*

Venereal Disease Chapter 25

If sexual activity has been frequent *and* with many
different partners, score −1.   *0*

For Women Only (Risk of uterine cancer) Chapter 19

If you began regular sexual activity before age 18, score
−1.   _____

If sexual activity has been frequent *and* with many
different partners, score −1.   _____

If you are Jewish, score −1.*   _____

Personal History Total   *−/2*

V. FAMILY HISTORY

Heart Attacks (Myocardial Infarction) Chapter 18

For each parent, brother, or sister who had a heart
attack before age 40, score −4.   *0*

_____

* See Chapter 19.

Your Score

For each grandparent, uncle, or aunt who had a heart attack before age 40, score −1.   *−1*

High Blood Pressure (Hypertension) Chapter 18

For each parent, brother, or sister with high blood pressure requiring treatment, score −2.   *0*

For each grandparent, uncle, or aunt with high blood pressure requiring treatment, score −1.   *0*

Diabetes Chapter 21

For each parent, brother, or sister with juvenile-onset diabetes, score −6.   *0*

For each grandparent, uncle, or aunt with juvenile-onset diabetes, score −2.   *0*

For each parent, brother, or sister with adult-onset diabetes requiring treatment with insulin, score −2.   *0*

For each grandparent, uncle, or aunt with adult-onset diabetes requiring treatment with insulin, score −1.   *0*

For Women Only (Cancer of the breast) Chapter 19

If your mother or a sister has had cancer of the breast, score −4.

Glaucoma Chapter 26

If you have a parent, grandparent, brother, sister, uncle, or aunt with glaucoma, score −2.   *0*

Gout Chapter 24

If you have a parent, grandparent, brother, sister, uncle, or aunt with gout, score −1.   *0*

Family History Total   *−1*

VI. MEDICAL CARE

If you have had the following procedures regularly, score the points indicated:

Blood pressure check every year: +4 points   *0*

Self-examination of breasts monthly plus examination by physician every year or two: +2 points   *0*

		Your Score
Pap smear every year or two: +2 points		*0*
Tuberculosis skin test (PPD or Tine) every five to 10 years: +1 point		*0*
Tonometry every four years after age 40: +1 point		*0*
VDRL (blood test for syphilis) every four to six years while sexually active: +1 point		*0*
Test for hidden blood in stool every two years after age 40, every year after 50: +1 point		*0*
Proctosigmoidoscopy once after age 50: +1 point		*0*
	Medical Care Total	*0*

I.	Habits	*−17*	Be sure to get the
II.	Mental Health	*−4*	signs of the numbers right
III.	Immunizations	*0*	so that you add or
IV.	Personal History	*−12*	subtract correctly.
V.	Family History	*−1*	
VI.	Medical Care	*0*	
	TOTAL	*−34*	
	Now Add	200	
	To Obtain Your LifeScore	*164*	

George was pretty surprised at his LifeScore of 164 and thought it should be higher. He was distinctly unhappy when he figured (with the aid of his pocket calculator) that his life expectancy was 164/200 × 70 years, or 57.4 years. This amounted to a prediction that he would die before he got to retirement. This was hardly comforting.

So George looked through Sections III and IV and came to the following conclusions which he muttered while filling out his LifePlan goals.

Exercise—This is where I really lost out in the LifeScore. With all those options from Chapter 8, I really believe I can get in 15 minutes of conditioning three times a week.

Weight—If I will stick to the exercise and begin to get a handle on when and why I'm eating, the weight will take care of itself. I can get down to within five pounds of my ideal weight.

Diet—I'm really not sure about the saturated fats and cholesterol. I'm going to hold off on this.

Smoking—I really don't think I can hack stopping completely while getting this other stuff started. I'll save that until next year. In the meantime, I'm going to switch to a pipe.

Drinking—I'm not going to promise on this either.

Seat Belts—The ones in my new car are much more comfortable. I think I'll shoot for wearing them at least half of the time.

Mental Health—Nothing I can do about what's happened, but my mortgage will be under $10,000 by the end of the year and I think I can slow the pace of change quite a bit.

Immunizations—I'll continue up to date.

Major Diseases—I've already covered most of this with my habits. Having a blood pressure check once a year is no problem. I don't work with asbestos, but avoiding air pollution is impossible in the city. It's easy enough to agree to have a proctosigmoidoscopy and to test the stool for hidden blood since I'm not at the age I need to do it yet. The truth is I probably will have these done. Since I had the radiation, I definitely have to have the yearly examination of the thyroid by my physician. I think I'll get into the self examination of the skin and testes business. Excessive exposure to the sun is no problem, I hardly see the light of day now. I'll get a skin test for tuberculosis at the same time I have the blood pressure check. The venereal disease stuff sounds a little old fashioned, but with the new wife it sounds like a heck of a good idea and it will even protect me from a couple of diseases.

George's LifePlan goals look like this:

I. HABITS

Exercise Chapter 8   Your Goal

Ideal: Within reason, the more the better, but
         at least 15 minutes of conditioning
         three times a week   *15 min. x 3/wk.*

Your Goal

Weight Chapter 9

Ideal: Within five pounds of your ideal weight
according to the table on page 000

within 5

Diet Chapter 9

Ideal: Balanced diet, avoid saturated fats and
cholesterol

balanced

Smoking Chapter 10

Ideal: No smoking: Second best is to reduce
amount or switch to pipe or cigar

pipe

Drinking Chapter 11

Ideal: Zero to one cocktail per day on the
average

3 or less

Seat Belts Chapter 12

Ideal: Worn 100 % of time while driving or
riding in a car

50 %

Contraception Chapter 14

Ideal: The safest method acceptable to you

—

II. MENTAL HEALTH

Holmes Score Chapter 16

Ideal: Score of less than 150 in a year

123

III. IMMUNIZATIONS Chapter 15

Ideal: All immunizations up to date

✓

IV. MAJOR DISEASES

Heart Disease and Stroke Chapters 18 and 21

Ideal: Regular exercise   See Habits

Weight within five pounds of ideal   See Habits

No smoking   See Habits

Blood pressure check once a year   *✓*

Your Goal

Cancer of the Lung Chapters 10, 17 and 19

Ideal: No smoking   See Habits

       Avoid air pollution   _____

       Avoid exposure to asbestos   ___✓_____

Cancer of the Breast Chapter 19

Ideal: Monthly Self-Examination   _____

       Yearly Doctor Examination   _____

       Xeromammography after age 40 if
       mother or sister had breast cancer   _____

Cancer of the Uterus Chapter 19

Ideal: Pap Smear every year or two   _____

Cancer of the Colon Chapter 19

Ideal: Proctosigmoidoscopy once after age 50   ___✓_____

       Test stool for hidden blood every two
       years after age 40, yearly after age 50   ___✓_____

Cancer of the Thyroid Chapter 19

If you have had radiation treatment of tonsils,
adenoids, acne or ringworm of the scalp:
yearly examination by physician   ___✓_____

Cancer of the Liver Chapter 19

Ideal: Less than three cocktails a day   See Habits

Avoid exposure to vinyl chloride   _____

Cancer of the Skin Chapter 19

* Consider: Monthly self-examination   ___✓_____

Avoid prolonged, excessive exposure to sun   ___✓_____

Cancer of the Testes Chapter 19

* Consider: Monthly self-examination of testes   ___✓_____

---

* These measures are reasonable but unproven. They deserve consideration for your LifePlan, but are not given points in either your LifeScore or New You Score.

	Your Goal
Diabetes Chapter 21	
Ideal: Weight within five pounds of ideal	See Habits
Tuberculosis Chapter 22	
Ideal: Skin test (PPD or Tine) every five to 10 years if no history of exposure	✓
Glaucoma Chapter 26	
Ideal: Tonometry every four to five years after age 40 (after age 30 if family history of glaucoma)	✓
Gout Chapter 24	
Ideal: Weight within five pounds of ideal	See Habits
Venereal Disease Chapter 25	
Ideal: Avoid frequent sexual activity with many different partners	✓
Blood test (VDRL) every five to six years while sexually active	✓

Using this LifePlan, George calculated his New You Score thus:

	Points
I. HABITS	
Exercise	+12
Weight	0
Diet: Balanced diet, avoid saturated fats and cholesterol	+4
Smoking	-4
Drinking	-4
Seat belts	+4
Contraception	
Habits Total	+12

II. MENTAL HEALTH	
Holmes Score	0

Points

III. IMMUNIZATIONS

Immunizations   *0*

IV. PERSONAL HISTORY

Tuberculosis

A skin test every year for five years after discovery of
the exposure, then every five years after that, allows you
to add back three of the points lost because of an exposure
to tuberculosis.   *0*

Radiation

Yearly thyroid examinations by your physician will
add back five of the points you lost because of this
exposure.   *−1*

Asbestos

Ending this exposure allows you to add back half of   *0*
the points lost because of it.

Vinyl Chloride

Ending this exposure allows you to add back half of   *0*
the points lost because of it.

Urban Environment

Changing your environment allows you to add back
five of the points lost here.   *−6*

For men and women (Risk of venereal disease)

A VDRL every year or two will allow you to add back   *0*
one of the points lost here.

For Women Only (Risk of uterine cancer)

Yearly pap smears allow you to add back the points
lost because of these items in your history.

Personal History Total   *−7*

V. FAMILY HISTORY

Heart Attacks (Myocardial Infarction)

If you set your goal at the ideal for preventing heart
disease, you may add back one-half the points lost because   *−1*
of a family history of heart attacks.

Points

High Blood Pressure (Hypertension)

If you will have a yearly blood pressure check, you may add back the points lost because of a family history of hypertension.

0

Diabetes

If you will keep your weight to within five pounds of ideal, you may:

Add back one-third of the points that you lost because of juvenile diabetes in parents, brothers or sisters.

0

Add back one-third of the points lost because of juvenile diabetes in a grandparent, aunt or uncle.

0

Add back two-thirds of the points lost because of adult diabetes in parents, brothers or sisters.

0

Add back two-thirds of the points lost because of adult diabetes in grandparents, aunts or uncles.

0

Cancer of the Breast

If you will practice monthly self-examination, have a physician examination yearly, and have xeromammography after age 40, you may add back three of the points lost because of this cancer in your mother or sister.

Glaucoma

If you will have tonometry yearly after age 30, you may add back the points lost because of a family history of glaucoma.

0

Gout

If you will keep your weight to within five pounds of ideal, you may add back the point lost because of a family history of gout.

0

Family History Total   *-1*

VI. MEDICAL CARE

These are the screening procedures which are worthwhile. Add the points indicated if you made the procedures part of your LifePlan.

Blood pressure check every year: +6 points

+6

Points

Self-examination of breasts monthly plus physician examination every year or two: +3 points

Pap smear every year or two: +2 points

Tuberculosis skin test (PPD or Tine) every five to ten years: +1 point .... +1

Tonometry every four years after age 40: +1 point .... +1

VDRL (bloood test for syphilis) every four to six years while sexually active: +1 point .... +1

Test for hidden blood in stool every two years after age 40, then yearly after age 50: +1 point .... +1

Proctosigmoidoscopy once after age 50: +1 point .... +1

Medical Care Total .... +11

There is little data concerning the following items, so it is not possible to determine their value at present. However, they make sense and are well worth considering for your LifePlan. They are discussed in Chapter 19.

Monthly self-examination of the skin .... No Points

Monthly self-examination of testes .... No Points

Now add up the New You Points:

I.   Habits .... +12

II. Mental Health 0

III. Immunizations 0

IV. Personal History .... −7

V.   Family History .... −1

VI. Medical Care .... +11

Total .... +15

Now Add 200

To Obtain The New You Score 215

George liked the looks of the New You Score a lot better. Next he calculated his Potential LifeScore and Potential Life Expectancy as follows:

To calculate your Potential LifeScore, determine the difference between your LifeScore and the New You Score.

$$\underline{\hspace{1em}215\hspace{1em}} - \underline{\hspace{1em}164\hspace{1em}} = \underline{\hspace{1em}51\hspace{1em}}$$

New You Score   LifeScore   The Difference

Next, determine your Delay Factor from the Delay Factor table. Multiply this by the difference found above to find the points your new LifePlan can add to your LifeScore.

$$\underline{\hspace{1em}.7\hspace{1em}} \times \underline{\hspace{1em}51\hspace{1em}} = \underline{\hspace{1em}36\hspace{1em}}$$

Delay Factor   The Difference   Added Points

Add these points to your original LifeScore to get your potential LifeScore.

$$\underline{\hspace{1em}164\hspace{1em}} + \underline{\hspace{1em}36\hspace{1em}} = \underline{\hspace{1em}200\hspace{1em}}$$

Original LifeScore   Added Points   Potential LifeScore

You can calculate your Potential Life Expectancy.

For men:

$$\underline{\hspace{1em}200\hspace{1em}} \div 200 \times 70 \text{ years} = \underline{\hspace{1em}70\hspace{1em}}$$

Potential LifeScore   Potential Life
                                                       Expectancy (years)

For women:

$$\underline{\hspace{4em}} \div 200 \times 75 \text{ years} = \underline{\hspace{4em}}$$

Potential LifeScore   Potential Life
                                                       Expectancy (years)

Frankly, George was a bit disappointed that despite what he thought was a very good LifePlan, he had only worked himself back up to just about a normal life expectancy. This bothered him a bit. So did a few things that he began to think about when he read the chapter on mental health. He also had some questions about the family history of diabetes. Since he did not have any access to a formal HEP session, he took these questions up with his personal physician. While his physician was not too interested in the details of working out a LifeScore or a Potential Life Expectancy, he was impressed that George was asking some good questions. After answering the specific questions, he suggested to George that there was still room for improvement and that a group approach might help. He put George in touch with an exercise group that met during the lunch hour. In addition to increasing the amount of exercise, he predicted that George would find it easier to lose weight and to reduce his alcohol consumption.

When last heard from, George had really gotten a thing about running. Not just jogging, real running. He found that running at the cocktail hour was best. After a good 20-minute run, he rewarded himself with a single cocktail. The switch to the pipe never really worked, but with the running he found he didn't want to smoke cigarettes either. He hasn't recalculated his LifeScore yet, but he figures that when he does he will have a clearly increased life expectancy.

An Example For Women Only

Harriet, George's new wife, had a number of questions about this part of the LifeScore. Her responses are given below:
(From **I. Habits**)

7. For Women Only Chapter 14

Contraception—If you have had a hysterectomy, tubal ligation or have reached the menopause, skip this section.

If you use:

Nothing and would *not* have an abortion	score −10	_____
Mechanical method and would *not* have an abortion	+0	_____
Birth control pills and would not have an abortion	+4	_____
Nothing, but *would* have an abortion	+4	_____
Birth control pills and *would* have an abortion	+5	_+5_
Mechanical method and *would* have an abortion	+10	_____

<table>
<tr><td></td><td></td><td>Your Score</td></tr>
</table>

Bad Bonus:
If you smoke and use birth
control pills   −15   *−15*

(From **IV. Personal History**)

For Women Only (**Risk of Uterine Cancer**) Chapter 19

If you began regular sexual activity before age 18, score
−1   *−1*

If you are Jewish, score −1   *−1*

(From **V. Family History**)

For Women Only (**Cancer of the breast**) Chapter 19

If your mother or a sister has had cancer of the breast,
score −4   *−4*

Her questions: (1) Are too many points being lost? (2) Are birth control pills really that good without smoking and that bad with smoking? (3) Is the business about sexual activity before age 18 a little old-fashioned? Responses were respectively: (1) It is impossible to be 100 percent certain of how many points should be awarded, but see what happens when the Potential LifeScore is calculated. (2) Birth control pills do have some problems, but not as many as an uninterrupted string of pregnancies *except* if combined with smoking. (3) No moral judgments are intended—this is just a measure of the risk of cancer of the uterus.

Harriet's LifePlan goals included (1) stopping smoking, (2) a Pap Smear every two years, (3) monthly self examination of the breast with a physician examination every year or two, and (4) xeromammography after age 40. By setting these goals she converted her LifeScore of −16 for the above items to a New You Score of +4.

Harriet concluded (and we agree) that while she was at greater risk than the average woman, she also had more than the average woman to gain from these procedures.

III

YOUR LIFESTYLE AND YOUR HEALTH

THIS IS WHERE THE ACTION IS. YOUR LIFESTYLE TODAY HAS MORE to do with your tomorrow than any other factor. You cannot give yourself a decent chance if you ignore this information. Don't wait until the game is over to learn how you should have played.

8
Exercise

HOW IMPORTANT IS EXERCISE? IT MAY WELL BE THE SINGLE MOST important thing you can do if you want to live a long and healthy life. Studies of persons who lived to great age—into their 90s and beyond—indicate that these persons have at least one thing in common: regular, vigorous exercise. There is a great deal more variation in other habits such as diet and the use of alcohol. While exercise has a wide variety of beneficial effects, the most remarkable are in the prevention of heart disease and the strengthening of bones.

The relationship between exercise and heart disease has been investigated extensively. J. N. Morris has conducted a number of studies in Great Britain that demonstrate the effect of exercise on heart disease. A comparison was made between postal workers who carried mailbags and those who sat at desk jobs. The mail carriers had fewer heart attacks and were less likely to die or be seriously disabled if they did have one. Similar results were found in conductors and drivers of double-decker buses. Conductors must move through the bus and up and down the stairs, while the drivers remain seated. In every age group, the conductors had fewer heart attacks and fewer deaths from heart attacks than the drivers. Since the stress of driving in London traffic could not be denied, Morris then took both groups (drivers and conductors) and classified them according to total physical activity (off the job as well as on). The results were the same: less heart disease among the physically active.

Morris also investigated the relationship between heavy physical work and heart disease. Middle-aged men involved in heavy work had less heart disease and developed it later in life than those who had jobs that required little or no physical activity. At autopsy the hearts of physically inactive workers showed as much evidence of heart disease as the hearts of physically active workers 10 to 15 years older.

In another study from Great Britain, the relationship between walking to work and evidence of heart disease on electrocardiograms was studied. It showed that even men who had only a very short walk to work (one to nine minutes) had less evidence of heart disease than those who did not walk to work at all. It could be that the automobile is killing more of us by making it easy to avoid exercise than by dismembering us on the highway.

Recently the results of a 10-year study of 17,000 men between the ages of 35 and 74 were reported. For each of these men, an estimate of the amount of energy (calories) used in exercise each week was made. It was found that those who spent less than 2,000 calories a week in exercise were 64 percent more likely to suffer a heart attack than those who spent more. There was a total of 572 heart attacks in the group. It was estimated that 166 of these could have been prevented if the entire group had exercised at the higher level. (The amount of exercise involved in expending 2,000 calories a week is discussed a little later in this chapter.)

The remarkable impact of exercise on heart disease is in part due to its beneficial effects on the other risk factors of heart disease. (The risk factors are discussed in more detail in Chapter 18.) People who exercise regularly are much less likely to be overweight. Not only does the exercise burn up calories, but also there is evidence that it actually suppresses appetite. Blood pressure is reduced by exercise. In fact, the combination of exercise and weight reduction often allows persons with hypertension (high blood pressure) to control their blood pressure without the use of medication. This control may be better than was possible with drugs. It is common for smokers to discontinue this habit as they begin exercise programs. Finally, P. D. Wood and his associates have demonstrated that a group of active joggers had lower total cholesterol than a group of men the same age who did not run. More importantly, they showed that the joggers had a higher level of HDL cholesterol, which protects against heart disease, and a lower level of LDL cholesterol, which is associated with a greater risk of heart disease. (See Chapter 18 for more on the "good" and "bad" types of cholesterol.)

A study from Harvard University and the Trinity School of Medicine in Dublin indicates that the effects of exercise may outweigh the effects of diet. Six-hundred Irishmen between 30 and 60 years of age who had lived in Boston for 10 or more years were compared with brothers who had never left Ireland. The Irish brothers ate 500 calories more a day and almost twice as many eggs as their American brothers (averaging a pound of butter and 14 to 18 eggs per week). Yet, the Irish brothers weighed 15 percent less, had lower cholesterol and only one-half the incidence of high blood pressure of their Boston brothers. The most likely cause for this was the Irish brothers' greater level of physical activity, primarily in the form of bicycling and walking. Not only does exercise push you in the right direction with respect to weight and smoking, but it may also outweigh the effect of diet on weight, blood pressure, and cholesterol.

Exercise also offers protection against heart disease beyond its effect on other risk factors. As mentioned above, studies of persons who lived to great age show that exercise is the most constant feature and that risk factors may vary a good deal. In a well-known study by J. C. Cassel, heart disease in Evans County, Georgia, was studied over a seven-year period. Two groups, white sharecroppers and black men, had less than half the incidence of heart disease of a third group, who were all white men. Further analysis revealed that it was the level of physical activity which was largely responsible for the difference in heart disease. Blood pressure, cholesterol, smoking, weight, and diet could not account for it.

The message is clear: When it comes to protecting your heart, there is no substitute for exercise.

Without sufficient exercise, bones become "demineralized"—lose their calcium and become brittle. If a person is put at complete bed rest, this process starts almost immediately—and progresses rapidly. This is one reason why doctors recommend that activity be resumed as soon as possible even after major operations or heart attacks. Demineralization of bones also has been documented in astronauts returning from space, where lack of gravity robs activity of its exercise value. Weak and brittle bones due to lack of exercise are common in the aged. In this setting, the implications go beyond the risk of a broken bone alone. Almost all of us have had an elderly friend or relative who was doing well until a hip was broken, and then went rapidly downhill. Fractures in the elderly can mean the beginning of the end. Strong bones may prevent a premature end to an active and useful life.

Exercise is important for living better as well as longer. People who exercise regularly feel and look younger than those who don't. Improvement in muscles and the circulation undoubtedly contribute to the freedom from fatigue and feeling of well-being that the physically fit enjoy. Moreover, it is likely that they are more productive at their jobs, although there is no conclusive proof of this yet. Even if the connection between being in good shape and being productive is an illusion, it is a powerful one. The boss will always find it difficult to promote you if you are flabby and seem to be out of breath with every minor exertion. It just doesn't agree with the image of the dynamic, effective worker.

What Kind of Exercise Is Best?

For the purposes of health, physical fitness means endurance, not strength or speed. Sustained exercises that mildly stress the heart and lungs are preferable to the stop-and-go variety. Jogging, swimming, rowing, walking, and bicycling lend themselves to this type of conditioning. Weight lifting or short sprints are unlikely to provide this conditioning. Note that the value of many activities—tennis, for example—depends on how you play the game. If you are moving all the time by running after balls, avoiding breaks between points, and so on, then you are getting valuable exercise. On the other hand, it has been shown that a pretty decent game of tennis can be played while nearly standing still. In the long run, you will lose if you learn to win without moving. As a rule golf, bowling, volleyball, and baseball are not very good exercise. A Stanford study of men aged 35 to 74 concluded that these sports gave no protection against heart disease, whereas running, swimming, basketball, handball, and squash did.

Experiments at the University of Texas support the belief that exercise requiring a good deal of muscle tension but little motion— such as weight lifting—is to be avoided. This is termed static isometric exercise. It results in a marked increase in blood pressure, but does not produce a substantial rise in the amount of blood pumped by the heart. This is in contrast to exercise in which there is a great deal of motion of muscle and joints, such as running or swimming, called dynamic isotonic exercise. In this type of exercise, the blood pressure does not rise a great deal, but the amount of blood pumped by the heart is greatly increased. Thus static isotonic exercise produces considerable strain but without the conditioning benefit of dynamic isotonic exercise. The Texas physicians concluded that static isometric exercise is of no concern to persons with normal hearts, but may pose a hazard for those with heart problems. This is consistent with the observation that some heart attacks seem to be associated with static isometric activities such as changing a tire or shoveling snow, but relatively few are associated with dynamic isotonic activities such as jogging or cross-country skiing. Keep in mind that the evidence for this is still tentative and that these conclusions cannot be regarded as an absolute certainty. But they do make sense.

Daily exercise is best but three or four sessions a week is quite adequate. It is better to do 30 minutes of conditioning three times a week than 90 minutes once per week—although one session per week is better than none. J. N. Morris recently reported that persons who exercised vigorously only on weekends had fewer heart attacks than those who never exercised.

If you have knee problems or other reasons for avoiding continuous weight-bearing on your legs, then bicycling, swimming, or an exercycle may be best.

None of these considerations are absolute. You must satisfy only yourself. Choose something that allows you to get the amount of exercise you need, but make it something you will *do*. And look for opportunities to exercise within your daily routine—walk instead of ride, use the stairs instead of the elevator, and so on. If you like the structure of more formal programs, the Royal Canadian Air Force Exercises, *Complete Conditioning*, and the *Canadian Fit Kit* (a homefitness program) can be recommended. You'll find information about them at the end of this chapter.

Getting Started

What about starting an exercise program? Isn't there some risk? After all, endurance is created when the body becomes strong in response to physical *stress*. Some physicians claim that everyone over the age of 40 needs an "exercise prescription" so that the stress of exercise will not cause a heart problem. This "prescription" is obtained from your friendly local cardiologist after you submit to an electrocardiographic exercise stress test, sometimes called a treadmill test. Some health authorities have been so unkind as to suggest that an economic motive underlies the creation of this "need," just as in the case of the "need" for more coronary artery bypass graft surgery (see Chapter 18). They point out that:

- There are more cardiologists than are needed.

- While it was previously limited to persons with known or strongly suspected heart disease, the cardiologists' market has expanded to include everyone over the age of 40.

- Stress testing is quite profitable, costing from $50 to $150.

Whatever the motive, there are several reasons why it is quite unlikely that you need a stress test before beginning an exercise program. First, put the stress of exercise in proper perspective. If you are prone to a heart attack, perhaps you should consider other stresses and their risks. One authority noted the risks of several activities and expressed them as multiples of the risk of heart attack at rest:

Activity	Risk
Rest	1
Cross-country skiing	3–4
Sexual intercourse	5
Unaccustomed, severe exercise	6–12
Electrocardiographic exercise stress test	30–60

If you want to avoid all stress, then you should avoid the sustained, moderate stress of the skiing. But you will also have to give up sex, never attempt to run a block to catch a bus, and, above all, never submit to a stress test in a cardiologist's office. You must also avoid arguments with family members, conflicts at work, watching your favorite team, and anything else that might get you excited. The point is, of course, that none of us can live stress-free lives. At least exercise in the long run may *decrease* the odds of a heart attack. Which of your other stresses will do that?

Next you must consider how good the stress test is at identifying persons at high risk for a heart attack and what alternatives are available. The stress test is far from perfect as an indicator of heart disease, especially in persons with no other evidence of heart disease. In one study of persons without symptoms of heart disease, 47 percent of those with "abnormal" stress tests did *not* have any heart disease (47 percent false positive). A study of persons who *did* have heart disease found that as many as 62 percent had "normal" tests (62 percent false negatives). With so many false positives and false negatives, the usefulness of this test is severely limited.

Finally, assume that you *do* have heart disease and are prone to a heart attack. What now? You can sit back and wait for it to happen or you can begin an exercise program and do something to change the odds. The only real question is whether your exercise should be medically supervised. To determine whether you should have a discussion with your doctor before you begin your exercise program, ask yourself the following questions:

- Do you ever have chest pain when you exert yourself?

- Do you get short of breath with mild exertion?

■   Do you have pain in your legs when you walk which disappears with rest?

■   Do you regularly have swelling of the ankles (not associated with the menstrual cycle in women)?

■   Has a doctor ever told you that you have heart disease?

If you answered "yes" to any of these questions and are over 35, see your doctor. If you gave any "yes" answers and are 35 or younger, give your doctor a call first before starting your program. The odds are overwhelmingly against heart disease and you may be able to clear up the problem over the phone. In any event, your doctor can help you determine whether the electrocardiographic stress test will help with the decision on medical supervision. Most often it will not.

Common sense says to *start slowly and increase the amount of exercise gradually.* You don't need a doctor to tell you this. If you haven't exercised in years and run a two-mile race, you are asking for trouble. You have weeks, months if you like, to reach the goals discussed below. You have time. Start each session slowly, too. A little warm-up will go a long way to prevent muscle strain and soreness. If you can't decide where to start and how fast to increase activity, refer to the RCAF Exercise, *Complete Conditioning,* or Canadian home fitness programs to get going. But get going.

How Much Is Enough?

While almost everyone agrees that exercise is a good idea, opinion on how much varies. It has been claimed that as little as 30 minutes a week can result in "total fitness." Most authorities doubt that this is the case for most people. Certainly it cannot take any less than this. What follows is what I believe to be the best advice based on what we know at present.

The best way to know you are exercising properly is to take your pulse before, during, and after your exercise session. Most adults have heart rates of 60 to 75 beats per minute while at rest. Raising this to 120 beats per minute or more indicates adequate exercise for most people. Sustaining activity at this level for 15 minutes three times per week is known to benefit the heart. This should represent the absolute minimum routine exercise program. An optimal program would be approximately 45 minutes *per day,* but 45 minutes three times *per week* is probably adequate. Getting 45 minutes per day is probably easier than you think. It is a matter of believing exercise is important, and then taking advantage of stairs, walking, and so on to get in the needed minutes within your routine.

As you get into shape, you will note that (1) your resting heart rate is lower, (2) it takes more exercise to raise the heart rate to 120 beats per minute, and (3) your heart rate returns to the resting rate more quickly following exercise. This indicates that muscles, heart, and lungs are becoming more efficient and effective. Well-trained athletes often have resting heart rates under 50 beats per minute. John Havlicek of the Boston Celtics, who seemed to never stop running on the basketball court, is said to have a resting rate of 36. (Hopefully this is not true, because (1) it is so low that it's a little frightening and (2) it makes the rest of us seem so out of shape.) Forty-five minutes of exercise three times per week won't put you into the superstar category, but it *will* make you live longer and feel better.

If for some reason you are averse to taking your pulse, an alternative approach is suggested by the study of Harvard alumni cited above. The accompanying table gives the amount of time necessary to burn 2,000 calories in several different types of exercise. The physicians who did this study felt that the *intensity* of the exercise was important in providing protection against heart attacks. This is probably so but it does not mean that less intense exercises are not beneficial (especially to older individuals) or that lesser amounts of time spent in exercise have no benefit. But the table will give you some idea of the value of different kinds of exercise without taking your pulse, as well as indication of the amount of exercise necessary for quite good protection against heart attacks.

Exercising comes naturally. You don't need fancy equipment or someone to tell you how and when. You need some common sense and a little perseverance. If you will honestly admit the importance of exercise, it will be easy to find the time and the place, It's simply a matter of priorities. Do you really believe your life doesn't deserve 45 minutes per week?

Recommended Reading

The Canadian Fit Kit. Available from Supply and Services, Canada, Printing and Publishing, Ottawa, Canada K1A 0SP. $5.94. A unique package of materials including an excellent booklet and a phonograph record. Especially good for those just starting out since it contains a gradual exercise program based on the results of the Canadian Home Fitness Test (that's where the record comes in).

Activity	Calories/hour	Time needed to burn 2,000 calories
Good		
skating (moderate)	345	5 hrs. 48 min.
walking (4½ mph)	401	5 hrs.
tennis (moderate)	419	4 hrs. 45 min.
canoeing (4 mph)	426	4 hrs. 41 min.
Better		
swimming (crawl, 45 yards/min)	529	3 hrs. 47 min.
skating (vigorous)	531	3 hrs. 45 min.
downhill skiing	585	3 hrs. 25 min.
handball	591	3 hrs. 23 min.
tennis (vigorous)	591	3 hrs. 23 min.
squash	630	3 hrs. 10 min.
running (5.5 mph)	651	3 hrs. 4 min.
bicycling (13 mph)	651	3 hrs. 4 min.
Best		
cross-country skiing (5 mph)	709	2 hrs. 50 min.
karate	778	2 hrs. 34 min.
running (7 mph)	847	2 hrs. 22 min.

(These figures are for a 152-lb. person. If you weigh more, you'll burn up more calories in the same time; if you weigh less, you'll burn fewer.)

Source: The *Executive Fitness Newsletter*, published bi-weekly by the Rodale Press, Inc., 33 East Minor St., Emmaus, Pa. Reprinted by permission.

Complete Conditioning: The No-Nonsense Guide to Fitness and Good Health. David Shepro and Howard G. Knuttgen. Addison-Wesley Publishing Company, Reading, Mass., 1977. $3.95. Practical and sensible information presented in some detail. Can help you if you want an individualized program but need some structure.

5BX and XBX. The Canadian Air Force Exercise Programs for Men and Women. Available from several publishers including Dell, N.Y. 1975. $1.95. A completely structured program with little variation but little guessing too.

9
Diet

ARE YOU WHAT YOU EAT? DEPENDING ON YOUR INTERPRETATION of the question, the correct answers are yes, somewhat, and so what. Yes, your body can only work with what you put into it. But your body can get what it needs from a wide variety of foods, so it is only somewhat dependent on your picking the "right" foods. And we know for certain so little about the effect of any particular food on health that a "so what" is very tempting.

This situation allows you some choice in your approach to diet. If you prefer to stick with the things for which there is good evidence, then the approach will be straightforward, even to the point of being disappointingly simple. If you prefer the theoretical, then there is really no limit to the things you can expect from—or blame on—your diet. Almost everything you have ever eaten someone once thought was the kiss of death, and those things that have never passed your lips are considered to be an absolute necessity by someone else. This is the You-Are-What-You-Eat game, and any number can play. The first step is to assume that disease is related to diet. Next you need a medical fact without explanation. For example, you note that the Japanese have a lot of cancer of the stomach or that the Bantu don't seem to have much cancer of the large bowel. Then select some part of the diet as the cause—the Japanese like smoked fish and the Bantu have a great deal of fiber in their foods. There, now you can say that smoked oysters and charbroiled hamburgers must be avoided and a little cardboard is good for everybody. These two examples are logical guesses—there are many that are simply wild shots in the dark. But logical guesses still are just guesses. If you accept as fact every plausible suggestion for linking variations in diet with variations in disease, you will find yourself with a complex and contradictory set of dietary rules.

Entrepreneurs and charlatans whose income depends on the promotion of "health" foods play the You-Are-What-You-Eat game with a vengeance. The more guesses, the more "health" foods you need, the more money they make. They play the Frontiers-of-Science game for the same reason—profit. In this game some experimental finding is used to justify a food or food supplement. A classical example is the vitamin E-and-aging myth. In the laboratory, cell cultures are said to be "old" when they exhaust the media in which they grow and stop dividing. Vitamin E added to the cell culture can lengthen the time before cell division ceases. (This is not unexpected since vitamin E is an antioxidant. Added in sufficient quantity it should be similar to other antioxidants that have this same effect.) Presto chango—we are told that modern medical science has discovered that vitamin E prevents aging. Interestingly enough, there is an alternative interpretation that has not been promoted. Uncontrolled division of cells is the hallmark of cancer. Perhaps vitamin E causes cancer by allowing cells to divide. Which interpretation do you choose? You already know which one was chosen by those who sell vitamin E.

The hottest Frontiers-of-Science game involves choline. Indeed, choline may turn out to be of some help in the manic phase of a manic-depressive psychosis. Only a very few of us are psychotic in this manner. If you think that science has shown that it is good for everything from hypertension to hyperactivity, you played the Frontiers-of-Science game even if you didn't know it. The results of playing this game are identical to those with the You-Are-What-You-Eat game: a complex and contradictory set of dietary rules based on guesswork and inspired by the profit motive.

Almost nobody can get enthusiastic about the alternative. It is too simple to create much interest or dramatic impact. Worse yet, it leaves little hope for a wonder diet that painlessly cures all ills and guarantees long life. Almost everything the average American needs to know relates to only two factors: (1) weight and (2) a balanced menu.

If your weight is what it should be, then you have gone a long way toward achieving an optimum diet even if you never touch bran flakes and have eggs for breakfast every day. If you are overweight, then you are in trouble even if you take 10 different vitamins religiously while avoiding butter and eggs like the plague. The association between obesity and health problems is so strong that it overwhelms any single dietary factor. And, as noted in Chapters 10 and 18, weight may go along with nondietary factors that affect health. That is, overweight people may be more likely to be smokers and nonexercisers. There just aren't very many people who exercise regularly and remain 30 pounds overweight. Overnourishment is America's diet dilemma. When undernourishment does occur, it is almost always a socioeconomic problem, not a dietary one.

Determining your weight is easy enough, but what is a "balanced" diet? In high school we learned that eating something from each of the four basic food groups each day would give us everything we needed. This definition of balance remains as good as any because medical science has not contributed a great deal to defining an ideal diet. We do know that, given adequate financial resources, diseases due to a deficiency in vitamins or minerals are rare. Furthermore, they are rare regardless of whether a person's dinner comes from the best supermarket, McDonald's, or an organic farm. All of this tends to make one think that there is a good deal of flexibility in achieving balance and that the need for supplements to diet is rare. There are only three common exceptions to the "need for supplements" rule and these occur under special circumstances. Breast-fed infants should receive a vitamin D supplement, while bottle-fed infants need extra iron. Pregnant women may benefit from additional folic acid. For the rest of us, the problem is not too little of anything but too much of everything.

Do not underestimate the difficulty of creating a medical problem by excluding something from your diet. Consider the following:

- To produce signs of vitamin C deficiency in one presumably normal adult (a doctor), it was necessary for that adult to eat *nothing* but milk and boiled potatoes for more than four months. One glass of orange juice would have botched the whole experiment.

- Human disease due to a diet deficient in vitamin E has never been reported. Never. Not even experimentally. Problems that *resemble* vitamin E deficiency in animals have been reported in children with serious intestinal diseases, but only very rarely.

- Pyridoxine (vitamin B_6) deficiency has only rarely been reported. Experimentally it cannot be produced by excluding it from the diet.

- Vitamin K is produced by bacteria in the large bowel and therefore adequate levels do not depend upon diet.

- To produce disease due to a thiamine (vitamin B_1) deficiency, thiamine must be excluded from the diet for 50 to 200 days. To produce disease due to pantothenic acid (vitamin B₅) deficiency requires 12 weeks.

■ Disease due to deficiency of "vitamins" such as biotin, choline, and PABA has never been reported. Period.

■ American diets are especially unlikely to produce deficiencies since vitamins and minerals are added to so many foods—flour, cereals, juices, milk, margarine, and so on.

You will really have to eat a pretty weird diet for a long time to do yourself in by way of a nutritional deficiency.

Beyond weight control and a balanced diet, it is worthwhile for everyone to consider the questions of cholesterol and sugar. Whether or not diet affects cholesterol in such a way as to reduce heart disease and stroke is currently a subject of heated controversy within the medical profession. Here are some facts to ponder:

■ About 80 percent of cholesterol is manufactured by the body, so eliminating cholesterol alone from the diet would not be expected to have a marked effect. However, the body makes cholesterol from saturated fats, so reducing both saturated fats and cholesterol may be more effective.

■ How diet affects the balance between HDL and LDL cholesterol is not clear. (See Chapter 18 for a discussion of the types of cholesterol and their importance.)

■ In the most comprehensive study to date, a diet low in cholesterol and saturated fats *did* lower cholesterol levels, and deaths due to heart attacks *did* decrease. *But* deaths due to other causes, especially cancer, increased, so there was no difference in the overall death rates between persons on the special diet and those who ate a routine diet.

■ Other studies generally support the proposition that a low-cholesterol, low-fat diet has some effect but that it may not be as great as that of exercise, smoking, obesity and other risk factors.

At this time a reasonable approach would be to avoid foods rich in cholesterol and saturated fats, but not make a fetish of it.

Sugar is a basic food. It is not guilty of the imaginary horrors (cellulite, depression, etc.) for which it is blamed. You can reduce without an artificial sweetener; a teaspoon of sugar has about 16 calories. However, highly refined sugar does contribute to tooth decay.

Children especially should be wary of prolonged contact of this type of sugar with their teeth. Again, avoiding excessive use (candies, etc.) without being obsessed seems reasonable.

Some have advocated no-salt diets in an effort to prevent high blood pressure and the heart disease and stroke that high blood pressure causes. It is true that in societies whose members eat almost no salt, there is no high blood pressure. When these societies become "westernized" and begin to use salt, high blood pressure rears its ugly head. The problem is that it appears that the diet must contain virtually no salt in order to have a protective effect. This does not mean just not adding salt from the shaker. Salt must be eliminated entirely from food preparation as well. You would have to prepare all foods from the basic ingredients, never use canned or frozen food, never eat out. All in all, not a very practical suggestion. Less severe salt restriction is useful in the treatment of both high blood pressure and heart failure once they are present.

Your major concerns, then, should be weight control and a reasonably balanced diet. A discussion of these subjects is followed by information on food additives, fiber, cholesterol and fats, and organic foods.

Weight Control

This is not about "going on a diet." This term has come to mean a brief period of unpleasant eating habits before getting back to your regular diet. Implicit is the thought that after this period of suffering you can get back to enjoying food. It is hardly surprising that this approach seldom results in meeting the goal of maintaining an acceptable weight for the rest of your life. The whole emphasis is on the extremes of eating. First you starve, then you celebrate not starving by eating. Even if your reducing diet "works," the best that can be hoped for is that your weight will go up and down like a yo-yo. The stronger the reducing diet, the more likely you are to bounce around. Do you really think you can face an all-liquid diet for the rest of your life? Not only will you fail to control your weight, there is evidence that rapid fluctuations in weight are more hazardous than being steadily over-weight.

Your goal should be to adopt eating habits that allow you to control your weight for the *rest of your life*. This may not be as tough as you think. Consider this: If you are overweight, chances are that you got that way over a period of years or even decades, not days or weeks. The number of excess calories you consumed per day may have been very small—they just added up over a long period. So your diet may not need as much change as you think. And you don't have to achieve your desired weight in a matter of days. If it takes a year—or even two—there's no problem so long as the desired weight is maintained. Finally, if you are not gaining weight, then you are balanced with respect to calories—you are using up all the calories you eat. *Any* reduction in calories eaten or increase in the calories burned up will result in weight loss.

This leads to a consideration of the one great, simple truth which governs all of weight control: Weight is determined by the relationship between the number of calories eaten and the number burned up. If these numbers are equal, weight is maintained at a steady level. If you eat less than you burn, weight goes down. If you eat more than you burn, weight must go up. This has nothing to do with medicine, good foods or bad, cellulite or baby fat. It is a law of physics and can't be changed by you, your doctor or anyone else.

What happens if you establish a deficit of 500 calories per day— that is, you eat 500 calories less than you burn? (This is a small change and could be accomplished by omitting two soft drinks, for example.) Since there are about 3,500 calories in each pound of your body fat, it will take 7 days to lose a pound. In a year the loss will be 50 pounds. So long as you burn more calories than you eat, weight loss will continue.

This does not mean, of course, that giving up one of your soft drinks will cause you to waste away to nothing. As you lose weight, it takes fewer calories to accomplish any particular activity. Just as it takes more energy to lift 200 pounds than 150 pounds, you will have to use less energy to get your 150-pound body up the stairs than your 200-pound version. Undoubtedly this is one reason why persons who control their weight are more active and feel better than those who are over-weight. It also means that you burn fewer calories and, if your activities remain exactly the same, the deficit caused by skipping the soft drink will get smaller and smaller until finally you come into balance again and weight becomes steady. But steady at a lower weight. The table you see here indicates the number of calories required to maintain a given weight for a person of average activity.

A calorie deficit can be produced only by eating less or burning more by being more active—or both. The combination of a little more exercise and a little less calorie intake seems to be a natural. Exercise is a positive step that helps to balance out all those negatives concerning eating. We all get tired of being told what not to do. Some physicians think that exercise actually helps suppress appetite and make it easier to eat less. As we have seen, as weight goes down, you feel like doing more. Not to mention that it is encouraging to have the weight come off more quickly than doing just one or the other. Chapter 8 explains the many other advantages of exercise.

Present Weight	Present Daily Intake *(PDI: Calories it takes to maintain present body weight)**	Daily Calorie Intake to lose 1 lb/wk *(500 calories/day less than PDI)*	Daily Calorie Intake to lose 2 lbs/wk *(1000 calories/day less than PDI)*
295	5015	4515	4015
290	4930	4430	3930
285	4845	4345	3845
280	4760	4260	3760
275	4675	4175	3675
270	4590	4090	3590
265	4505	4005	3505
260	4420	3920	3420
255	4335	3835	3335
250	4250	3750	3250
245	4165	3665	3165
240	4080	3580	3080
235	3995	3495	2995
230	3910	3410	2910
225	3825	3325	2825
220	3740	3240	2740
215	3655	3155	2655
210	3570	3070	2570
205	3485	2985	2485
200	3400	2900	2400
195	3315	2815	2315
190	3230	2730	2230
185	3145	2645	2145
180	3060	2560	2060

* Your weight $\times$ 17 = Approximate number of calories which maintains present weight of active person

Present Weight	Present Daily Intake *(PDI: Calories it takes to maintain present body weight)**	Daily Calorie Intake to lose 1 lb/wk *(500 calories/day less than PDI)*	Daily Calorie Intake to lose 2 lbs/wk *(1000 calories/day less than PDI)*
175	2975	2475	1975
170	2890	2390	1890
165	2805	2305	1805
160	2720	2220	(1720)
155	2635	2135	1635
150	2550	2050	1550
145	2465	1965	1465
140	2380	1880	1380
135	2295	1795	1295
130	2210	1710	1210
125	2125	1625	1125

There is no need to spend a lot of time counting calories in the food you eat or calculating the calories burned in different activities. The laws of physics work both ways, so all you need to know is your weight. If weight is steady, you are in caloric balance. If it is going down, you have a caloric deficit. If it is going up, you have a caloric excess. Don't attempt to control your weight without a scale. It's like going to sea without a compass. Remember that you must weigh yourself at the same time of day, dressed (or undressed, preferably) exactly the same. Also be aware that fluid changes can complicate day-to-day comparisons. A comparison of weekly averages or trends can be made to allow for the effect of fluid changes.

So there you are, armed with the truth about calories, the proud owner of a bathroom scale, overweight but determined to do something about it. How, exactly, are you going to go about it? No one method works for all, most work for just about no one. The fad diets, be they no carbohydrates, no fat, high protein, or whatever, by their very nature are unlikely to help you reach your goal of an acceptable weight for the rest of your life. Some, like the liquid-protein diet, can kill you.

Weight Watchers has had more success than most doctors and its program will fit the needs of some. What follows is a program based on the principles set forth above, the belief that poor eating habits are learned, and that these can be replaced by learning better habits.

A Method of Weight Control

■   *Find out what, when, where, and why you eat.* Most of us are not consciously aware of our eating habits and cannot remember accurately what our diet has been. A diary such as that shown here kept for two weeks can overcome this problem. (A diary form can be found in Section V.) There are usually a few surprises. One person who kept such a diary was asked if she still believed that she was "eating like a bird." She replied that she did, but now knew that the bird weighed 200 pounds and had an appetite to match.

Keep a chart of daily weights (see Section V) during this time. Weigh yourself without clothes at the same time each day—best time is just after awakening. *Do not attempt to lose weight.* The whole point of the chart is to find out how you *usually* eat. If you make changes and begin to lose weight, you will not find out how your usual eating habits have gotten you into your present predicament.

■   *Analyze why you eat.* Eating results when cues to eat are received. Cues can be of many types and no two persons respond exactly the same to all possible cues. There are some things, however, that are true

DIET CHART

Date _____   Weight _____

Time	Food	Amount	Location	Reason	Place setting used
12:10	Tunafish Sand.	2	Kitchen	Lunch	
	Chowder	Large Bowl	Table		
	Crackers	8			
	Ice Cream	3 Scoops			
2:15	Candy Bar	1 reg.	Living Rm.	Bored	

for just about everyone, including you. First, hunger is not nearly as important a cue as you think—you seldom seek out food because of hunger pangs in the pit of your stomach. Second, how you feel has a great deal to do with eating. Many, if not most, overweight persons have learned to eat in response to being anxious or bored. Third, external cues such as the sight of food, mealtimes and coffee breaks, and being where you usually eat (kitchen, restaurant, and so on) are important.

It is important to realize that eating as a reaction to these cues involves substantial rewards. These can be represented as follows:

Cue		*Reaction*		*Reward*
Hunger	→	Eating	→	Satisfaction
Nervous	→	Eating	→	Calmer
Angry	→	Eating	→	Calmer
Bored	→	Eating	→	Occupied
Excited	→	Eating	→	Even Better!

By studying your eating diary you can determine which cues cause you to eat.

■ *Make a plan.* This plan is not a diet in the usual sense. No foods are prohibited. You will not have to restrict yourself to low calorie foods. You don't even have to count calories. But you do have to make a plan and carry it out.

The object of this plan is to change eating habits by changing cues. Try the following:

□ Get a new place setting (placemat, plate, bowls, utensils—everything) as different as possible from that which you have now. From now on everything you eat will be from this setting. Bedtime snacks, leftovers from your children's plates, even a candy bar or a stick of gum—*everything* is eaten from this setting. The only exceptions are beverages without calories, such as tea without sugar and black coffee. If meals are regularly eaten away from home, then pack your lunch with the setting or at least take part of the setting, such as the utensils, with you as a reminder of the entire setting. At home get out the whole setting—placemat, plate, and the rest—each and every time.

□ Eat in one and only one place in the home. You may have been eating significant amounts of food without realizing it because "snacking" was going on all over the place. Avoid going out to dinner during the first month of your plan.

□ Avoid doing anything else while eating. You won't believe how many "munchies" are consumed unconsciously in front of the TV or while reading a book. If you are going to eat, sit down with your new place setting and enjoy it.

□ Keep food out of sight. Nobody can resist taking a bite if food is always out where it can be seen and obtained easily. Keep serving dishes off the table during meals. Nothing is more tempting than an almost empty dish. We all have the urge to "help" clean up and not "waste" the food.

■ *Make some small changes.* After you have followed your plan for several weeks, you will have a new awareness of your eating habits. This awareness will give you greater control over those habits. Now is the time to exercise a little of this control to eliminate some unnecessary calories. Great changes are not necessary. Remember that you have months, even years to lower weight. Frequently weight loss has already begun because the plan reduced the amount of food being eaten without thinking. No further change may be necessary. If weight loss has not started, here are some suggestions to get it started:

□ Reduce the size of servings by about one-quarter.

□ Serve with a teaspoon instead of a tablespoon.

□ Brush your teeth immediately after meals. Helps to keep you from going back for more.

□ Substitute a low calorie food for a high calorie food. As you know, calorie counting and food restrictions are not an important part of the plan. But if you can make a substitution you like, then you help your own cause. Table A at the end of this chapter lists some high and low calorie foods. See if there isn't a trade which would make you happy.

■ *Reward yourself.* Every time you lose half a pound, give yourself a reward. The reward should be:

□ something you can give yourself promptly,

□ something that will really please you, and

□ something you can't eat (sorry).

Money often works well—half-dollars and dollars are the most popular amounts. Small amounts can be accumulated for larger purchases later. But the reward can be anything from magazines to marbles. The important things are that it is available soon after the weight loss and that it is something you want just for yourself.

Daily weights can vary up and down due to temporary changes in body fluids and other factors. Still, give yourself a reward every time you lose half a pound even if you gain it back the next day.

In addition to your daily weights, keep track of your weight on a weekly basis. Pick one daily weight (Saturday morning's, for example) as the "week's weight," or calculate your average weight for the week, or both. This will help to make trends more vivid. For weight losses on a weekly basis, give yourself a larger reward.

■   *Choose reasonable goals.* Please don't try to lose more than a pound a week. Attempting more creates too much strain. Remember, you are trying to create habits you can live with for the rest of your life.

You will have to choose the weight you would like to achieve ultimately. The table on the next page gives standard desirable weights, but some words of caution are necessary. The range of weights called desirable is quite wide. Don't deceive yourself by believing you have a large frame when you don't. Your mirror may be of more help than the table; an honest look will tell you whether you are fat or not. Don't overemphasize the final goal. You have time. Once you have controlled your eating, losing 30 pounds should take a year. Losing 100 pounds should take three years. Pay attention to the half pounds and the hundreds will take care of themselves.

A Balanced Diet

It is surprising how lopsided a diet can be and still not cause a deficiency of vitamins and minerals, at least not one that causes a medical problem. Perhaps one reason is that some balance is necessary simply to provide some variety. Certainly it helps that American menus have traditionally emphasized variety. Even "vegetarians" eat a wide range of foods and have eliminated only a small portion of a regular diet from their menus.

Still, it hardly makes sense to take a chance when a well-balanced diet is easy to maintain. Foods are traditionally divided into four major groups, but dividing them into six groups has some advantages. Table B at the end of this chapter lists common foods in each group. A well-balanced diet would include portions from each group as follows:

Group	Portions Per Day
Milk	2 to 2½
Vegetable	2 to 3
Fruit	4 to 6
Bread	4 to 7
Meat	5 to 8
Fat	2 to 4

Desirable Weights
Weight in Pounds According to Frame (In Indoor Clothing)

Men of Ages 25 and Over *(with shoes on: 1-inch heels)*

HEIGHT FEET	HEIGHT INCHES	SMALL FRAME	MEDIUM FRAME	LARGE FRAME
5	2	112–120	118–129	126–141
5	3	115–123	121–133	129–144
5	4	118–126	124–136	132–148
5	5	121–129	127–139	135–152
5	6	124–133	130–143	138–156
5	7	128–137	134–147	142–161
5	8	132–141	138–152	147–166
5	9	136–145	142–156	151–170
5	10	140–150	146–160	155–174
5	11	144–154	150–165	159–179
6	0	148–158	154–170	164–184
6	1	152–162	158–175	168–189
6	2	156–167	162–180	173–194
6	3	160–171	167–185	178–199
6	4	164–175	172–190	182–204

Women of Ages 25 and Over *(with shoes on: 2-inch heels)*

4	10	92–98	96–107	104–119
4	11	94–101	98–110	106–122
5	0	96–104	101–113	109–125
5	1	99–107	104–116	112–128
5	2	102–110	107–119	115–131
5	3	105–113	110–122	118–134
5	4	108–116	113–126	121–138
5	5	111–119	116–130	125–142
5	6	114–123	120–135	129–146
5	7	118–127	124–139	133–150
5	8	122–131	128–143	137–154
5	9	126–135	132–147	141–158
5	10	130–140	136–151	145–163
5	11	134–144	140–155	149–168
6	0	138–148	144–159	153–173

For girls between 18 and 25, subtract 1 pound for each year under 25.

Source: Prepared by the Metropolitan Life Insurance Company, derived primarily from data of the Build and Blood Pressure Study, 1959, Society of Actuaries.

These proportions are not absolutely rigid requirements. For example, eating less from the Fat group would be quite healthy for almost everyone. For most of us the problem is too much fat and carbohydrate, so protein is the only need that is of real concern. Table C at the end of this chapter indicates the protein requirements for various age groups. Take care of your protein needs, make sure you get plenty of fruits and vegetables, and everything else will take care of itself.

A word about vegetarian diets. If you eat a wide variety of vegetables, then most dietary requirements are satisfied. One exception: If the diet is strictly vegetables and includes no milk or eggs, then you're not getting enough vitamin B_{12}. If you insist on such a diet, then a vitamin B_{12} supplement would be wise.

The Appendix to this book gives detailed information on many foods. Use it to get some ideas on how to arrange a balanced diet you can enjoy. And don't neglect reading about Group 7, which is innocently entitled "Miscellaneous." Many of us are getting lots of calories and nothing else from the beverages listed. These have been omitted from the basic food groups for good reason—have they become basic for you?

Best Guesses About Diet and Disease

Fiber helps hold water in the stool, making it softer and bulkier. This helps prevent constipation, especially in older people. Including fiber in your diet is worthwhile, but don't count on it to prevent cancer or diverticulosis of the large bowel. Even if fiber is related to these problems, it may well be that a lifetime of high-fiber diet is required to make a difference. Certainly there is no evidence that fiber will cure the problem once it has developed.

Food additives present difficult choices. Some, such as the food dyes, we could do without in my opinion. Their contribution is not essential and at least some of them do produce cancer in animals. It is very unlikely that they have anything to do with hyperactivity in children. Preservatives such as nitrites do make a contribution. Without them certain foods such as sausages, luncheon meats, and so on would not be available as a practical matter. But they do cause bladder cancer in mice. Avoiding them when possible seems a reasonable approach.

Just to keep things unsettled, we have the case of BHA and BHT. These antioxidants are added to cereals and other products to keep them fresh. There is evidence that these additives have contributed to the *decline* in stomach cancer (see Chapter 19). So it seems there must be at least two exceptions to the rule of avoiding additives if you can.

It is depressing to be told that we must choose between the cancer risk of artificial sweeteners and the risk of death and disease associated with being overweight. Are Tab and Diet Pepsi really the keys to weight control? Are we so helplessly dependent on this stuff that the only alternative is a lifetime of flab? Obviously not, and their importance has been overemphasized by a coalition of fat but influential people and the soft drink industry. On the other hand, their risk clearly seems to be related to dosage, so that occasionally using them would seem to present little danger. Again, avoiding them when possible seems reasonable.

Why Are We Guessing?

You may be a bit disturbed that we are guessing when we should be knowing. In this country the emphasis for decades has been on research for cures rather than prevention. Little wonder we know a lot about treating these problems but not much about preventing them. Our treatments have proven expensive, dangerous, painful—and often ineffective. Perhaps now is the time to begin really believing that an ounce of prevention is worth a pound of cure. Surely it is time we began seriously attempting to find answers to how diet relates to health and disease.

TABLE A
Food substitutions

For This		Substitute This		
Beverages	*Calories*		*Calories*	*Calories saved*
Milk (whole), 8 oz.	165	Milk (buttermilk, skim), 8 oz.	80	85
Prune juice, 8 oz.	170	Tomato juice, 8 oz.	50	120
Soft drinks, 8 oz.	105	Diet soft drinks, 8 oz.	1*	104
Coffee (with cream and 2 tsp. sugar)	110	Coffee (black with artificial sweetener)	0	110

* See individual bottle label for possible variations.
Source: Pharmaceutical Division, Pennwalt Corporation. Used by permission.

For This		Substitute This		
Beverages (Cont'd)	*Calories*		*Calories*	*Calories saved*
Cocoa (all milk), 8 oz.	235	Cocoa (milk and water), 8 oz.	140	95
Chocolate malted milk shake, 8 oz.	500	Lemonade (sweetened), 8 oz.	100	400
Beer (1 bottle), 12 oz.	175	Liquor (1½ oz.), with soda or water, 8 oz.	120	55
Breakfast foods				
Rice flakes, 1 cup	110	Puffed rice, 1 cup	50	60
Eggs (scrambled), 2	220	Eggs (boiled, poached), 2	160	60
Butter and Cheese				
Butter on toast	170	Apple butter on toast	90	80
Cheese (Blue, Cheddar, Cream, Swiss), 1 oz.	105	Cheese (cottage, uncreamed), 1 oz.	25	80
Desserts				
Angel food cake, 2" piece	110	Cantaloupe melon, ½	40	70
Cheese cake, 2" piece	200	Watermelon, ½" slice (10" diam.)	60	140
Chocolate cake with icing, 2" piece	425	Sponge cake, 2" piece	120	305
Fruit cake, 2" piece	115	Grapes, 1 cup	65	50
Pound cake, 1 oz. piece	140	Plums, 2	50	90
Cupcake, white icing, 1	230	Plain cupcake, 1	115	115
Cookies, assorted (3" diam.), 1	120	Vanilla wafer (dietetic), 1	25	95

Table A *(Cont'd)*

For This		Substitute This		
Desserts (Cont'd)	*Calories*		*Calories*	*Calories saved*
Ice cream, 4 oz.	150	Yoghurt (flavored), 4 oz.	60	90

Fish and Fowl

Tuna (canned), 3 oz.	165	Crabmeat (canned), 3 oz.	80	85
Oysters (fried), 6	400	Oysters (shell w/sauce), 6	100	300
Ocean perch (fried), 4 oz.	260	Bass, 4 oz.	105	155
Fish sticks, 5 sticks or 4 oz.	200	Swordfish, (broiled), 3 oz.	140	60
Lobster meat, 4 oz. with 2 tbsp. butter	300	Lobster meat, 4 oz., with lemon	95	205
Duck (roasted), 3 oz.	310	Chicken (roasted), 3 oz.	160	150

Meats

Loin roast, 3 oz.	290	Pot roast (round), 3 oz.	160	130
Rump roast, 3 oz.	290	Rib roast, 3 oz.	200	90
Swiss steak, 3½ oz.	300	Liver (fried), 2½ oz.	210	90
Hamburger (av. fat, broiled), 3 oz.	240	Hamburger (lean, broiled), 3 oz.	145	95
Porterhouse steak, 3 oz.	250	Club steak, 3 oz.	160	90
Rib lamb chop (med.), 3 oz.	300	Lamb leg roast, (lean only), 3 oz.	160	140
Pork chop (med.), 3 oz.	340	Veal chop (med.), 3 oz.	185	155
Pork roast, 3 oz.	310	Veal roast, 3 oz.	230	80
Pork sausage, 3 oz.	405	Ham (boiled, lean), 3 oz.	200	205

For This		Substitute This		
Pie	*Calories*		*Calories*	*Calories saved*
Apple, 1 piece (1/7 of a 9″ pie)	345	Tangerine (fresh), 1	40	305
Blueberry, 1 piece	290	Blueberries (frozen, unsweetened), ½ cup	45	245
Cherry, 1 piece	355	Cherries (whole), ½ cup	40	315
Custard, 1 piece	280	Banana, small, 1	85	195
Lemon meringue, 1 piece	305	Lemon flavored gelatin, ½ cup	70	235
Peach, 1 piece	280	Peach (whole), 1	35	245
Rhubarb, 1 piece	265	Grapefruit, ½	55	210
Pudding (flavored), ½ cup	140	Pudding (dietetic, non-fat milk), ½ cup	60	80
Potatoes				
Fried, 1 cup	480	Baked (2½″ diam.)	100	380
Mashed, 1 cup	245	Boiled (2½″ diam.)	100	145
Salads				
Chef salad with oil dressing, 1 tbsp.	180	Chef salad with dietetic dressing, 1 tbsp.	40	140
Chef salad with mayonnaise, 1 tbsp.	125	Chef salad with dietetic dressing, 1 tbsp.	40	85
Chef salad with Roquefort, Blue, Russian, French dressing, 1 tbsp.	105	Chef salad with dietetic dressing, 1 tbsp.	40	65
Sandwiches				
Club	375	Bacon and tomato (open)	200	175

For This		Substitute This		
Sandwiches (Cont'd)	*Calories*		*Calories*	*Calories saved*
Peanut butter and jelly	275	Egg salad (open)	165	110
Turkey with gravy, 3 tbsp.	520	Hamburger, lean, (open), 3 oz.	200	320
Snacks				
Fudge, 1 oz.	115	Vanilla wafers, (dietetic), 2	50	65
Peanuts (salted), 1 oz.	170	Apple, 1	100	70
Peanuts (roasted), 1 cup, shelled	1375	Grapes, 1 cup	65	1310
Potato chips, 10 med.	115	Pretzels, 10 small sticks	35	80
Chocolate, 1 oz. bar	145	Toasted marshmallows, 3	75	70
Soups				
Creamed, 1 cup	210	Chicken noodle, 1 cup	110	100
Bean, 1 cup	190	Beef noodle, 1 cup	110	80
Minestrone, 1 cup	105	Beef bouillon, 1 cup	10	95
Vegetables				
Baked beans, 1 cup	320	Green beans, 1 cup	30	290
Lima beans, 1 cup	160	Asparagus, 1 cup	30	130
Corn (canned), 1 cup	185	Cauliflower, 1 cup	30	155
Peas (canned), 1 cup	145	Peas (fresh), 1 cup	115	30
Winter squash, 1 cup	75	Summer squash, 1 cup	30	45
Succotash, 1 cup	260	Spinach, 1 cup	40	220

TABLE B*
Food groups

Group 1. Milk	Group 2. Vegetables	Group 3. Fruit
Each serving has 170 calories, 12 gm. carbohydrate, 8 gm. protein, 10 gm. fat.	Raw, these vegetables may be eaten as desired; cooked, 1 cup is one serving. They contain little carbohydrate or protein and few calories.	Each serving has 40 calories, 10 gm. carbohydrate.

Milk		Serving	Asparagus	Sauerkraut		Apple (2″ diam.)	Serving: 1 small

Group 1. Milk

Each serving has 170 calories, 12 gm. carbohydrate, 8 gm. protein, 10 gm. fat.

Serving

Milk
Whole 1 cup
Skim* 1 cup
Evaporated ½ cup
Powdered, whole ¼ cup
Powdered, skim (non-fat dried milk*) ¼ cup
Buttermilk
From whole milk 1 cup
From skim milk* 1 cup

* Add 2 Fat servings to your meal when you use one cup of skim milk or buttermilk made from skim milk.

Group 2. Vegetables

Raw, these vegetables may be eaten as desired; cooked, 1 cup is one serving. They contain little carbohydrate or protein and few calories.

Asparagus	Sauerkraut
Broccoli	String Beans,
Brussels	young
Sprouts	Summer
Cabbage	Squash
Cauliflower	Tomatoes
Celery	"GREENS"
Chicory	Beet
Cucumbers	Chard
Eggplant	Collard
Escarole	Dandelion
Lettuce	Kale
Mushrooms	Mustard
Okra	Spinach
Pepper	Turnip
Radishes	

For these vegetables, 1 serving equals ½ cup.

Each serving has 36 calories, 7 gm. carbohydrate, 2 gm. protein.

Beets	Pumpkin
Carrots	Rutabaga
Onions	Squash,
Peas, green	winter
	Turnips

Group 3. Fruit

Each serving has 40 calories, 10 gm. carbohydrate.

Serving

Apple (2″ diam.)	1 small
Applesauce	½ cup
Apricots, fresh	2 medium
Apricots, dried	4 halves
Banana	½ small
Berries: Straw., Rasp., Black.	1 cup
Blueberries	⅔ cup
Cantaloupe (6″ diam.)	¼
Cherries	10 large
Dates	2
Figs, fresh	2 large
Figs, dried	1 small
Grapefruit	½ small
Grapefruit Juice	½ cup
Grapes	12
Grape Juice	¼ cup
Honeydew Melon (7″ diam.)	⅛
Mango	½ small
Orange	1 small
Orange Juice	½ cup
Papaya	⅓ medium
Peach	1 medium
Pear	1 small
Pineapple	½ cup
Pineapple Juice	⅓ cup
Plums	2 medium
Prunes, dried	2 medium
Raisins	2 tbsp.
Tangerine	1 large
Watermelon	1 cup

To season your food, you can use many things. Some suggestions are: chopped parsley, mint, garlic, onion, celery salt, nutmeg, mustard, cinnamon, pepper, and other spices, lemon, saccharine, and vinegar. You may use all of these freely.

Other foods you need not measure are: coffee, tea, clear broth, bouillon (without fat), unsweetened gelatin, rennet tablets, sour pickles, unsweetened dill pickles, cranberries, and rhubarb.

---

* This table has recently been revised to include information on fats and cholesterol and is available from the American Dietetic Association, Inc., by whose permission it is reproduced here in slightly modified form.

TABLE B *(cont'd)*

Group 4. Bread		Group 5. Meat		Group 6. Fat	
Each serving has 68 calories, 15 gm. carbohydrate, 2 gm. protein.		Each serving has 73 calories, 7 gm. protein, 5 gm. fat.		Each serving has 45 calories, 5 gm. fat.	
	Serving		*Serving*		*Serving*
Bread	1 slice	Meat or Poultry		Butter or	
Biscuit (2" diam.)	1	(medium fat)		margarine	1 tsp.
Muffin (2" diam.)	1	*beef, lamb, pork,*		Bacon, crisp	1 slice
Corn bread (1½"		*liver, chicken,*		Cream, light	2 tbsp.
cube)	1	*etc.*	1 oz.	Cream, heavy	1 tbsp.
Cereals		Cold cuts		Cream cheese	1 tbsp.
Cooked	½ cup	*(4½" × ⅛")*		Avocado *(4"*	
Dry (flake or puff		*salami, minced*		*diam.)*	⅛
types)	¾ cup	*ham, bologna,*		French dressing	1 tbsp.
Rice, Grits, cooked	½ cup	*liverwurst,*		Mayonnaise	1 tsp.
Spaghetti, Noodles,		*luncheon loaf*	1 slice	Oil or cooking fat	1 tsp.
etc., cooked	½ cup	Frankfurter		Nuts	6 small
Crackers		(8-9 per pound)	1	Olives	5 small
Graham (2½"		Egg	1		
square)	2	Fish			
Oyster	½ cup	*Haddock, etc.*	1 oz.		
Saltines (2" square)	5	*Salmon, Tuna,*			
Soda (2½" square)	3	*Crab, Lobster*	¼ cup		
Round, thin (1½"		*Shrimp, Clams,*			
diam.)	6-8	*Oysters, etc.*	5 small		
Flour	2½ tbsp.	*Sardines*	3 medium		
Vegetables		Cheese			
Beans, Peas, dried,		*Cheddar type*	1 oz.		
cooked (lima,		*Cottage*	¼ cup		
navy, split peas,		Peanut Butter	2 tsp.		
cowpeas, etc.)	½ cup				
Baked beans, no					
pork	¼ cup				
Corn	⅓ cup				
Parsnips	⅔ cup				
Potatoes, white	1 small				
mashed	½ cup				
sweet or Yams	¼ cup				
Sponge Cake, plain					
(1½" cube)	1				
Ice Cream (omit 2					
Fat servings)	½ cup				

TABLE C
Protein requirements by age and weight

Age		Weight (lbs.)	Grams of Protein Per Day
Less than 6 months		14	14
6 months–1 year		20	20
1–3 years		28	23
4–6 years		44	30
7–10 years		66	36
Men:	11–14 years	97	44
	15–18 years	134	54
	19–22 years	147	54
	23–50 years	154	56
	Over 51 years	154	56
Women:	11–14 years	97	44
	15–18 years	119	48
	19–22 years	128	46
	23–50 years	128	46
	Over 50 years	128	46
	Pregnant		Add 30
	Breast Feeding		Add 20

Source: Adapted from the National Research Council recommended daily dietary allowances, revised 1974, Food and Nutrition Board, National Academy of Sciences.

10
Smoking

IT HAS BEEN ARGUED THAT A BALANCED DISCUSSION OF SMOKING
would include the good it does by providing jobs in the tobacco industry. Curiously, no mention is made of morticians, physicians, nurses,
respiratory therapists, and others who derive a considerable degree of
their work from the death and disease caused by smoking. At any rate,
the same argument maintains that government support of the tobacco
industry, such as subsidies for tobacco farmers, should be encouraged
or at least not withdrawn once in place. In this view, a job is such a
good thing that the effect of the job on society should be overlooked.
Fortunately there seems to be some sort of limit on this kind of thinking.
Otherwise, the Mafia might receive a subsidy as well. After all, organized crime keeps people off welfare and does an excellent job of keeping them gainfully employed.

So much for a balanced discussion. From here on the news is all
bad. These are a few of the effects of smoking:

■ *A two to three times greater chance of dying from a heart attack.* Since
  heart disease is our leading killer (675,000 Americans will die of a
  heart attack this year), smoking actually causes more deaths
  through heart disease than through lung cancer.

■ *Twenty-five times the chance of developing lung cancer.* If you can
  manage exposure to asbestos as well, you can increase your chances
  of getting cancer to about *70* times that of a nonsmoker. And don't

forget an increased chance at cancer of the larynx (voicebox), lip, mouth, pancreas, and bladder.

■ *Emphysema is a sure thing.* Destruction of lung tissue is a direct effect of smoking, so every smoker develops emphysema to some degree. How much depends on how much you have smoked. If you live long enough, your emphysema will get to the point where just getting up to go to the bathroom will leave you out of breath and exhausted. If you tend to underestimate the latter, try breathing through a straw sometime. Get one that has a small enough diameter that it makes you work to breathe while sitting down. Now get up and try to move around and do something, still breathing through the straw. Get the picture? This is called suffocation.

■ *Dead and sick babies.* Miscarriages are at least twice as common when the mother smokes heavily. Smoking mothers have 55 percent more congenitally deformed babies. Low weight at birth is associated with increased chances of death and disease in a child and children born to smoking mothers weigh about 200 grams less than the average. Infants whose mothers smoke are more likely to be admitted to the hospital during the first year of life for pneumonia or bronchitis. Lead accumulates in the blood of unborn children whose mothers smoke.

■ *A deadly interaction with oral contraceptives.* The death rate for smokers on the Pill is about six times that for nonsmokers, according to studies by the Population Council. This is far more than if the risk of smoking was simply added to the risk of oral contraceptives.

■ *The menopause occurs earlier.* While studying the relationship between heart attacks and the menopause, investigators unexpectedly discovered that smokers experience the menopause at significantly younger ages than nonsmokers do.

■ *The country loses over 27.5 billion dollars each year.* This is the price a UCLA study puts on the death and disability due to smoking. It amounts to over $450 for each of the 60 million smokers in America. And that doesn't count the money it costs for the cigarettes themselves.

Undoubtedly you knew at least some of the above. Surveys indicate that both smokers and nonsmokers know that smoking is disastrous to health. Studies indicate that such knowledge is important in keeping nonsmokers from beginning and in getting smokers to think about stopping and making an effort to stop. But it seems to have little effect on actual chances for success in stopping. This is an indication of the degree to which smokers are addicted. People who knowingly continue to damage their health and that of their children clearly have a problem. It is particularly distressing that knowledge that one's smoking damages the health of others, especially children born or unborn, has little effect. Indeed, these studies indicate that the desire to be a good example for those who are important to you does not contribute even to making an effort to stop, let along actually stopping. Obviously smokers are heavily dependent on this habit.

Be clear in your mind that smoking is not just a nasty habit, something that is done to keep hands and mouth occupied, something that lets you look cool when you don't know what to do or say. If you are a smoker, you are just as addicted as any junkie who ever knocked over a liquor store. Since this addiction is to nicotine, a stimulant, it has been suggested that smoking lets you function at a "higher" level— or, somewhat paradoxically, that smoking calms the nerves. At least until it kills you.

Bad news again. A Columbia University study on how smoking affects behavior sheds some light on this. The subjects were heavy smokers, nonsmokers, and heavy smokers who were deliberately and successfully reducing the amount they smoked ("restrained smokers"). They were *not* told that the study had anything to do with smoking. They were told that the purpose of the experiment was to determine how annoying aircraft noise was to humans. During three separate sessions in which they were exposed to simulated aircraft noise, they were not permitted to smoke, or they were permitted to smoke low nicotine or high nicotine cigarettes to whatever extent they desired. The subjects were then asked to estimate the degree to which they were annoyed by the aircraft noise. The results were as follows:

■   When heavy smokers were permitted no access to cigarettes or only low-nicotine cigarettes, they were more than twice as annoyed as nonsmokers.

■   When heavy smokers were given high-nicotine cigarettes, they reported an annoyance level similar to that of nonsmokers.

■   Restrained smokers remained more than twice as annoyed regardless of whether they were permitted low- or high-nicotine cigarettes.

Thus cigarette addicts are rather easily irritated unless there is access to their usual amount of nicotine. And even when the addicts do have access to abundant nicotine, their mental state only begins to approach that of nonsmokers. Smoking does not provide a stimulant that allows them to function at a "higher level." It does have a calming effect in the sense that it relieves some of the agitation and irritation of being in withdrawal. It has no such effect on someone not addicted. The results for "restrained smokers" indicate that their mental state—continually annoyed—is appropriate for someone undergoing self-induced withdrawal. This and other experiments indicate that when allowed to smoke, smokers only return to a level of mental functioning comparable to that of a nonsmoker.

You can see the effects of this addiction every day. Smokers who are undergoing withdrawal are a pretty nasty group. They need a cigarette in the morning in order to face the world. Caught in areas where smoking is prohibited, they become agitated and lash out against those who are violating their "rights." And pity the smoker who is trying to cut down. No wonder this is such a miserable existence. Being an addict in withdrawal has never been fun.

The best evidence supports the view that smokers behave as typical addicts. Indeed, an English study indicates that cigarettes are more addicting than alcohol or barbiturates. If smokers are given what they crave, they function at near normal levels. If the addicting substance is not used, they go into withdrawal. The smoker gets nothing out of smoking. It does not calm the nerves, it does not improve mood or performance. The smoker smokes only to avoid withdrawal.

Knowing that you *should* stop smoking is not enough. To stop, you must *want* to stop and have confidence in your ability to stop. Here are some things that should make you want to stop:

- *You stink.* So do your clothes, car, office, home. To the extent that you expose them to your smoke, so do your spouse and kids. If they smoke, tell them that they stink all by themselves.

- *You are ugly.* Dermatologists report that women who smoke develop more facial wrinkles and do so sooner than those who don't.

- *You are tough to love.* Kissing a smoker may not be exactly like kissing a dirty ashtray, but it's close enough.

- *You have little sense of taste or smell.* Smoking decreases these senses. You don't know what you've been missing.

- *You spend the vacation money.* A two-pack-a-day habit costs over $400 per year for the cigarettes alone. That's plenty for a week at a resort, several new suits, round-trip air fare to London, or numerous other treats.

- *You are a fire hazard.* According to the National Fire Protection Association, smoking is the major cause of fatal residential fires.

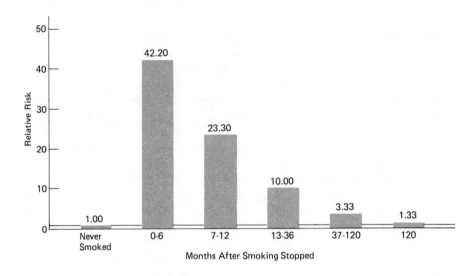

You can get back most of what you have lost through smoking. Naturally the longer you wait to quit, the more irreparable the damage. Yet your body has a remarkable ability to come back if you will give it a chance. The figure above shows the results of one investigation into the risk of lung cancer after quitting the noxious weed. Note that smokers who have just quit have very high risks of cancer. It is not uncommon for doctors to see heavy smokers soon after they have quit and to diagnose lung cancer at that time. Undoubtedly many of these persons had developed symptoms which scared them into quitting. The moral is clear: If you wait until you have symptoms, it is too late to quit.

Far too late. Less than five percent of persons with lung cancer live for five years, most are dead within one year. Relying on chest x-rays to pick it up "early"? Too bad. By the time they can be seen on an x-ray, it is too late. The story is much the same for the other cancers, heart disease, and emphysema caused by smoking: Treatment results range from poor to abysmal, and attempts at "early" detection do not help.

Quitting

If you want to stop and think you can, chances are very good that you will succeed. If your spirit is willing but you fear that the flesh is too weak, take heart. Over 30 *million* Americans have quit. It does not require superhuman willpower, but you must persist. If at first you don't succeed, and so on. If one method does not work, try another. But don't look for any method to do it *for* you—at best it will help *you* to stop.

There are many methods. Most seem to "work" permanently for about 20 percent of the people who try them. The good news is that it is not the same 20 percent for each method. If one doesn't help, another may. Recently there has been a report of a program which has a better than 50 percent success rate by combining the "fast-puff" and suggestion methods. There is considerable activity in this field so new developments may occur at any time. A call to your doctor or public health department will help you find the best method in your area.

A few general comments on choosing a method. Don't look for a drug to cure you—there isn't any. The high-priced methods may work a little better because anyone who will pay the price really wants to stop. Finally, give it a try on your own before you look for outside help.

Here is a procedure that can help you to stop:

- *Pick a day to stop.* Get definite as to when you are actually going to do something. Make it about one month in the future.

- *Start cutting down before your day to stop.* Addiction to nicotine cigarettes is *real*—so make it a little easier to stop by reducing the dosage of nicotine. One good way to reduce is to pick "nonsmoking hours" and then extend these hours gradually.

- *Make it more difficult to get at your cigarettes.* Wrap them in paper, put them in a box or a locked desk drawer, in an inconvenient pocket of a coat, and so on.

- *Switch to cigarettes low in tar and nicotine.* This will help only if you don't change your method of smoking. Many smokers who switch to low tar and nicotine cigarettes smoke more of them, smoke them further down toward the butt, and/or take more puffs in an effort to satisfy their nicotine addiction. This is probably more unhealthy than their previous habit. Switch cigarettes only as part of a conscious plan to decrease nicotine and make sure the switch does that.

- *Smoke only half the cigarette.*

- *Chart your progress.* Know how much, when, and where you smoke. See Section V.

- *Use substitutes.* Mints, gum, and so forth replace the oral activity provided by smoking.

- *On your day to stop, treat yourself to something.* Have a big dinner, go to a movie or a play. Get rid of the ashtrays and other smoking equipment. Exercise—a long walk is especially good. Brush your teeth immediately after eating. Allow yourself something you want—even a cocktail or extra cup of coffee.

- *Don't worry about gaining weight.* After you have kicked the habit, you can work on this. And the odds are everwhelmingly in favor of returning to your original weight.

- *Expect to feel down for a few days.* This is part of becoming unaddicted. If you need the help of your physician, don't hesitate to get it.

- *Read this chapter three times each day.* It will remind you of all those good reasons to stay off the butt.

Finally a word concerning pipe and cigar smoking. Because they usually do not inhale, the increased risk of lung cancer to pipe and cigar smokers is small in comparison to that of cigarette smokers. However, pipe and cigar smokers have a greater risk of lip cancer and nearly the same risk for cancer of the mouth, larynx, esophagus, and stomach. So while switching to a pipe or cigar is better than doing nothing, it still leaves you with an increased risk to your health.

11
Alcohol

LIKE ALL DRUGS, ALCOHOL IS A POISON. THAT IT IS A MILD POISON is attested to by the fact that a large portion of the population uses it regularly in small amounts without clearly demonstrable ill effect. (Perhaps "direct ill effect" would be better—auto accidents involving alcohol will cause significant death and disability in this group). As mentioned in Chapter 8, there is even some evidence that light use of alcohol may have some beneficial effect on heart disease. However, the usual "beneficial" effects are sedation, relaxation, a sense of power, a mild euphoria. A sobering thought: The euphoria you feel is probably due to your brain being deprived of oxygen. "Drunk" feelings are experienced in other situations in which there is a lack of oxygen. For example, persons who survive drowning often report euphoria just before becoming unconscious. Somehow it seems fitting that inebriation should be equivalent to drowning slowly.

An even more sobering thought is the cost of alcoholism to society. A UCLA study concluded that alcohol abuse costs us over 44 *billion* dollars every year. That's nearly 5,000 dollars for each and every alcoholic.

Alcohol affects virtually every tissue in the body but is especially damaging to liver, brain and spinal cord, and stomach. The nausea, heartburn, abdominal pain, lack of coordination, slowed reflexes, and other problems that most of us have suffered at one time or another attest to the acute toxic effects of alcohol. The fact that we recover does not mean that there is no real damage, but rather is testimony to the

143

body's considerable power to heal itself. In early stages damage is reversible, but with repeated insult it becomes permanent and untreatable. Poor nutrition in many alcoholics aggravates the situation further. The slow death of an alcoholic is never pretty—bloody vomiting, staggering, bloated abdomen, and dementia are common.

Fast deaths due to alcohol will turn your stomach as well. The dismembered bodies of drunk drivers and their victims are all too common sights on our highways. Investigation by the U. S. Department of Transportation reveals that fully one-half to three-fourths of drivers causing fatal accidents are drunk. The more violent the crash, the more likely the driver had been drinking. Studies by Haddon and others show that high blood alcohol concentrations are common in fatally injured pedestrians as well as those killed by drowning, falls and other nonhighway accidents.

If a little alcohol may be good and a lot is definitely bad, how much is too much? In my opinion, if you are averaging more than two cocktails or beers per day, you have crossed the line and alcohol is a problem. You may not be an alcoholic in the usual sense, but alcohol is decreasing your chances at a long and healthy life. Before you reassure yourself that your habit is still on the safe side, consider this: To my knowledge, there has never been a documented case of someone *over*estimating the amount of alcohol consumed. Traditionally, physicians are taught to *double* whatever the patient tells them about alcohol consumption as a way of coming up with a more realistic estimate of alcohol intake. So if you think you may be borderline and might have a problem, you probably do.

Discussions of whether alcoholism is a disease are usually unproductive. Perhaps this is because this is not really the question being considered. Most people are dealing with a different issue than whether there is a genetic or biochemical defect, or even where to put this problem in terms of psychiatric or behavioral disorders. They want to know whether the alcoholic is sick and deserves sympathy and medical treatment, or a no-good bum who needs the law laid down. Neither choice is correct and thinking of alcoholism as a disease may be misleading. Clearly the important question is what can be done to prevent and treat alcoholism, but this does not mean that prevention and treatment must be medical. Certainly it does not mean that the alcoholic should be regarded as an innocent victim unable to participate in treatment. In the final analysis, alcoholism is treated successfully only when the alcoholic takes responsibility for solving the problem. As with other addictions, treatment is really a matter of helping the alcoholic to help himself—or herself.

There are a variety of successful methods of treatment. Some involve physicians but many of the most successful do not. Some involve the temporary use of drugs but most do not. Some insist that absolute abstinence is necessary while others set reduction of drinking to acceptable limits as the goal. Individual therapy, group therapy, behavior therapies of different types all have been used. The common element in all of these, and the most important aspect of alcoholism treatment, is that the focus is on changing behavior, not on treating the problem as a "medical" problem with a "medical" solution. Nothing is more useless than to approach the problem as one that doctors and hospitals can or should be able to solve. Nothing is more futile than treating the medical complications of alcoholism when the alcoholic's behavior remains the same.

A discussion of the methods by which alcoholic behavior may be changed would fill several volumes, but there are a few principles that should be known to all. First, alcoholics seldom change their behavior on their own. The family is especially important in helping an alcoholic to change, but friends, colleagues, employers, and interested groups such as Alcoholics Anonymous may also play major roles. Second, helping an alcoholic is not an easy job and knowing how to help is very important. Neither haranguing nor pitying benefits the alcoholic. Indeed, emotionally charged confrontations contribute to the problem— the alcoholic needs these to sustain his or her detrimental behavior. In what might be called the alcoholism game, the alcoholic creates a crisis by drinking (and losing a job, having an accident or something of that nature), is condemned for this, pleads to be forgiven, and finally is forgiven. When the emotion of the foregiveness scene wanes, the game is played again. And again. And again for as long as the condemning-forgiving person(s) will play or until the alcoholic (or someone else) dies from the game. As long as the game is played, alcoholism is reinforced. Not playing the game is very difficult for family and friends. Few people can learn to do this on their own. Help from an outside source is usually needed in order to stop playing and start helping.

Thus the cardinal principle for you to remember is this: Get help. Whether you are an alcoholic or someone whose life is being affected by another's alcoholism, don't try to go it alone. Fortunately there are groups ready to help you in almost every community. Alcoholics Anonymous is the largest private group and its record of success is second to none. Al-Anon and Alateen stand ready to teach families of alcoholics how to help the alcoholic while protecting themselves. Most public health departments have alcoholism programs or will provide referrals to programs in the area. Your family physician may help you directly or make sure that you find help. A growing number of industries are sponsoring programs of their own. Many clergy have had special training in dealing with alcoholism.

You can do something about alcoholism. Just get the help you need.

12
Accidents

ACCIDENTS ARE THE GREAT KILLER OF THE YOUNG. EACH UNNEC-
essary death seems doubly tragic—the beautiful child who dies in agony
after drinking drain cleaner, the debutante mangled beyond recognition
in the wreck of her car, the young man at the height of his physical
prowess maimed forever by an accident on the job. For people between
the ages of one and 44, accidents are the leading cause of death. Between the ages of one and four, fatal accidents are about equally dis-
tributed between home and the automobile. For the 40 years after that,
the automobile has no equal as a grim reaper. But automobiles are
hardly our only problem. Approximately 15 percent of all accidental
deaths are on the job—an alarming percentage, considering that only
a portion of the population will spend only a part of its time in the
workplace. Since a large number of jobs have little or no risk, those
recognized as having hazards are probably very hazardous indeed.

The most important single factor in accidents is the use of alcohol.
Over 50 percent of drivers who cause accidents in which they are killed
have been drinking, usually heavily. A North Carolina study found that
over half the fatal accidents occurring during recreational and sporting
activities (swimming, boating, fishing, hunting, etc.) were related to
the use of alcohol. Other studies indicate that alcohol plays a major
role in injuries to pedestrians as well as those due to falls or drowning.

The automobile is involved in almost half of all fatal accidents as
well as over two million disabling injuries each year. It has been the

Number One cause of accidental death for decades. This massacre is largely of our own choosing and we have the tools to do something about it. Lowering the speed limit to 55 miles per hour was a major reason why automobile deaths declined from about 55,000 in 1973 to about 45,000 in 1974. Seat belts could save about 50 percent of those dying in auto crashes. Air bags might be more effective than seat belts, according to information now available.

In the home, poisons, falls and fire are a devastating trio. Accidents in the home account for almost two-thirds as many deaths (26,000 per year) and more than twice the disabling injuries (4.1 million) as the automobile. Although young children are the victims for the most part, many adults find that creating a fire hazard is as easy as falling off a ladder. As if you needed another reason to stop, smoking is the major cause of fatal residential fires.

If you are looking for a hazardous job, you can't beat mining, but you may want to consider construction and heavy industry. Accidents on the job will account for more than 14,000 deaths and 2.5 million disabling injuries this year.

Can Accidents Be Prevented?

Perhaps the most disturbing aspect of this whole business is that most accidents are so clearly preventable and we have known how to prevent them for so long. Decreasing speed limits reduces deaths. Vigorous campaigns against alcohol and driving can reduce deaths. Seat-belt laws can reduce deaths. Air bags can reduce deaths. Home-safety campaigns can reduce deaths. Poison control centers can reduce deaths. Occupational safety programs can reduce deaths.

What are we waiting for?

The answer involves a most basic question: Can and should people's behavior be modified? Time and time again those who would rather do nothing have argued that people cannot and should not change their ways and that accidents are inevitable. Nevertheless, behavior can be modified. And it has been modified without resorting to oppressive methods or loss of fundamental freedoms. But our approach has been incredibly haphazard and uneven. We have lowered speed limits, but we do not have a seat-belt law as many European countries do. (Of course, we lowered speed limits to save energy, not lives.) Mines are safer than they were 50 years ago but are far from being as safe as they could be. Poison control centers are more common but the most fundamental aspect of poison control, education of the public, has been neglected.

So it is a question of will rather than way. We are not waiting for any fundamental discovery or new drug or new technology. We are waiting for ourselves.

Can Accidents Be Treated?

Enormous strides have been made in the treatment of accidents in this century. It appears that these advances have had more of an effect on reducing disability from survivable accidents than in reducing deaths due to accidents. It also appears that in the last two decades we have leveled off considerably in our ability to make new inroads on the death and disability due to accidents. Most of the improvement that has occurred is due to the fact that more can be done once the patient is in the hospital. Now we have turned our interest to what happens *before* the patient gets to the hospital, and interest in emergency medical systems has soared. Again, our preoccupation with the notion that treatment would be more effective if it began sooner (which is not at all illogical) has led to the investment of hundreds of millions of dollars in sophisticated ambulance systems. There is hardly a more dramatic or exciting idea than that of the highly trained paramedic rushing to save lives through a combination of his or her own skill and advanced technology. (Indeed, the drama has been sufficient to sustain at least one highly rated television series.) Unfortunately, there is not much evidence that these systems have had a great deal of impact. The reason may be that most accidents either will be fatal regardless of how quickly help is available or will be survived as long as help arrives within a reasonable time. Thus there will be a relatively small number of accidents in which even a very quick response by an ambulance is critical.

What Should You Do About Accidents?

Secure for yourself the benefits of prevention. If you drink, don't drive. Wear your seat belts. Get a car seat that protects younger children and make the older kids wear their seat belts. Keep your speed down. Support driver education programs. Know your poison control center number. Speak out concerning the hazards of your job. Conduct the home safety inspection described below.

In some emergencies, what happens in the first few minutes is all that counts. It is impossible to provide emergency services in this short a time span. Impossible, that is, unless these emergency procedures are provided by the public. You can learn what to do about poisons while you're contacting the poison control center or the emergency room. (See the Oral Poisoning chart, page 152.) You can learn the technique of cardiopulmonary resuscitation (CPR) and other first aid techniques through your local Red Cross Chapter. Prepare yourself so that you and your family will have the best possible chance should an emergency arise. This is a far better bet than hoping that a super duper ambulance will arrive in time.

Home Safety Inspection

The Kitchen

■ Are oven cleaners and other caustic materials, such as drain cleaners, locked up or placed out of reach?

■ Are pot handles routinely kept away from the edges of the stove?

■ Are the electric cord extenders on appliances such as coffee makers removed from the socket immediately after use?

■ Are ant poisons and insect sprays out of reach?

■ Are electric irons kept away from children?

The Bathroom

■ Are razor blades discarded safely?

■ Are all medicines kept locked or out of reach?

■ Are all prescription drugs left over from an illness flushed down the toilet?

■ Are bathroom cleansers locked up or out of reach?

The Living Room

■ Are electric cords in good repair?

■ Is the fireplace adequately screened?

■ Are containers that hold combustible liquid used in the fireplace kept out of reach?

■ Are fire extinguishers appropriately located in the house and ready to use?

■ Is there a fire alarm system?

■ Are electric sockets not in use covered?

■ Is there a guardrail around space heaters, Franklin stoves, and similar devices?

■ Are children instructed in a fire exit plan?

■ Beware of poisonous plants such as poinsetta leaves, daffodil bulbs, and castor beans.

The Nursery

■ Does the crib have no more than two and one-half inches between slats so the baby's head cannot become wedged between them?

■ Are all cords (from Venetian blinds, mobiles, etc.) that could become tangled around the baby's neck kept away from the area of the crib?

■ Are crib mattresses and bumpers of the correct size and fastened so that the baby's head cannot be wedged between them and the crib frame?

The Bedroom

■ Are cosmetics and perfumes kept out of the reach of children?

■ Is shoe polish kept out of reach?

The Dining Room

Are children kept away from dangling tablecloths when a hot meal is on the table?

The Children's Room

■ Do toys have sharp edges?

■ Do toys have small parts that can easily be removed and swallowed by young children? Have old broken toys been discarded?

■ Are windows in rooms above the ground floor closed or protected so that children cannot fall?

■ Is there a fire escape from which children can easily fall?

■ Is model glue kept away from toddlers?

The Yard and Garage

■ Are children kept away from rotary lawnmowers when in use?

■ Do rotary lawnmowers have protective shields?

■   Are solvents in the garage kept away from children's reach?

■   Are pesticides, fertilizers, and snail bait stored away from children?

■   Are turpentine and paint products stored away from children and in their original containers? (*Caution:* Never use soda bottles.)

■   Is your yard free from poisonous plants (such as oleander, scotch broom, etc.)? Your local nursery will usually be glad to help you with plant identification and safety if you have any questions.

■   Is there an old refrigerator or freezer in which children could play?

Oral Poisoning

Although poisons may be inhaled or absorbed through the skin, for the most part they are swallowed. The term *ingestion* refers to oral poisoning.

Most poisoning can be prevented. Children almost always swallow poison accidentally. Keep harmful substances, such as medications, insecticides, caustic cleansers, and organic solvents like kerosene, gasoline, or furniture polish, out of the reach of little hands. The most damaging are strong alkali solutions used as drain cleaners (Drano), which will destroy any tissue with which they come in contact.

Treatment must be prompt to be effective, but while speed is important, accurate identification of the substance is equally so. *Don't panic.* Call the doctor or poison control center immediately and get advice on what to do. Attempt to identify the substance without causing undue delay. Always bring the container with you to the emergency room. Life-support measures take precedence in the case of the unconscious person, but the ingested substance must be identified before proper therapy can be instituted.

Suicide attempts cause many significant medication overdoses. Any suicide attempt is an indication that help is needed. Such help is not optional, even if the patient has "recovered" and is in no immediate danger. Most successful suicides are preceded by unsuccessful attempts.

Home Treatment

All cases of poisoning require professional help. Someone should call immediately. If the person is conscious and alert and the ingredients swallowed are known, there are two types of treatment: those in which vomiting should be induced, and those in which it should not. Vomiting can be very dangerous if the poison contained strong acids, alkalis, or petroleum products. These substances can destroy the esophagus or damage the lungs as they are vomited. Neutralize them with milk while

```
┌─────────────────────────────────┐        ┌──────────────┐
│ Is the patient awake and alert? │  no →  │     See      │
│                                 │        │  physician   │
└─────────────────────────────────┘        │     now.     │
                │                           └──────────────┘
              yes
                ↓
┌─────────────────────────────────┐        ┌──────────────┐
│ Are ingredients known?          │  no →  │     See      │
│                                 │        │  physician   │
└─────────────────────────────────┘        │     now.     │
                │                           └──────────────┘
              yes
                ↓
┌─────────────────────────────────┐        ┌──────────────┐
│ Do the ingredients include a    │        │  Give milk   │
│ strong acid, a strong alkali,   │  yes → │ and contact  │
│ or a petroleum product?*        │        │  physician   │
└─────────────────────────────────┘        │     now.     │
                │                           └──────────────┘
               no
                │
                ↓
┌──────────────┐   ┌────────────────────────────────────────┐
│   Induce     │   │ Give milk and contact physician now if  │
│  vomiting    │   │ the patient has swallowed any of these. │
│ and contact  │   │ Acids: battery acid, sulphuric acid,    │
│  physician   │   │ hydrochloric acid, bleach, hair         │
│    now.      │   │ straightener, etc.                      │
└──────────────┘   │ Alkalis: Drano, drain cleaners, oven    │
                   │ cleaners, etc.                          │
                   │ Petroleum: Furniture polish, gasoline,  │
                   │ kerosene, oils, barbeque lighter fluid, │
                   │ perfume, etc.                           │
                   └────────────────────────────────────────┘

┌──────────────────────────────────────────────────────────┐
│ Poison control center telephone number _____   │
│                                                            │
│ Emergency room telephone number _____        │
└──────────────────────────────────────────────────────────┘
```

contacting the physician. If you don't have milk, give the person some water or milk of magnesia.

Vomiting is a safe way to remove medications and suspicious plants. It is more effective and safer than using a stomach pump and can be induced by anyone. Vomiting can usually be achieved immediately by stimulating the back of the throat with a finger (don't be squeamish!). In a child, two to four teaspoonfuls of *syrup* (*not* extract) of ipecac, may be used, followed by as much liquid as the child can drink. Vomiting follows usually within twenty minutes but, since time is important, using your finger is sometimes quicker. Or you can try both. Mustard mixed with warm water also works. If there is no vomiting in 25 minutes, repeat the dose of syrup of ipecac. Collect the vomitus so that it may be examined by the physician.

Before, after, or during first aid, contact a physician. Many communities have established poison control centers to identify poisons and give advice. These are often located in emergency rooms. Find out if such a center exists in your community and, if so, record the telephone number on the chart. Quick first aid and fast professional advice are your best chance to avoid a tragedy.

If an accidental poisoning has occurred make sure that it doesn't happen again by conducting a home safety inspection.

What to Expect at the Doctor's Office
Significant poisoning is best managed at the emergency room. Treatment of the conscious patient depends on the particular poison and whether vomiting has been achieved successfully. If indicated, the stomach will be evacuated by vomiting or by the use of a stomach pump. Patients who are unconscious or have swallowed a strong acid or alkali will require admission to the hospital. With those who are not admitted to the hospital, observation at home is important.

13

Drugs

THE MOST WIDELY USED DRUG IN AMERICA IS NOT ALCOHOL OR Valium or even the nicotine in cigarettes—it's caffeine. Coffee, cocoa, tea, and soft drinks all contain caffeine. Tea and cocoa also contain theophylline and theobromine respectively, chemicals which are closely related to caffeine. In addition to the stimulation of the nervous system for which these drugs are best known, they also cause the kidneys to produce more urine (diuresis), stimulate the heart, dilate the heart's arteries, increase respirations, relax the smooth muscle in the walls of the intestines and in the bronchial tree, increase stomach secretions, and stimulate skeletal muscles.

With all this going on, it is difficult to make simple statements as to whether the use of caffeine is good or bad. No doubt a certain amount of psychic dependence develops in those who regularly use caffeine-containing beverages. At least in the abstract, it would seem best not to be dependent on any drug, no matter how mild the dependency and even if it is psychic rather than physical. (Most addiction is psychic rather than physical.) On the other hand, it is possible (but not likely) that caffeine has had significant benefit by increasing users' productivity and sense of well being. Certainly, it would seem better for your dependence to be on caffeine than on a depressant (alchohol, barbiturates, narcotics, etc.) or stimulant with their devastating ill effects (nicotine in cigarettes).

Caffeine's effect on the stomach and heart are the principal concerns with regard to health. In experimental animals, caffeine can produce stomach irritations and ulcers, but the doses given were very large. It is doubtful that caffeine by itself produces many ulcers in people, but it certainly is not beneficial and may contribute to their formation—as well as produce a lot of heartburn. If you have any stomach problems, you should avoid using caffeine.

While one Boston study indicated that use of caffeine significantly increased the risk of heart attack, most studies have not supported this. Studies such as these may not be able to demonstrate conclusively a comparatively small increase in risk. It has been shown that 250 mg of caffeine (the equivalent of two to three cups of coffee) causes a substantial increase in blood pressure and heart rate. Most physicians (including myself) feel strongly that caffeine can contribute to abnormal heartbeats as well. It seems likely that these effects increase risk in someone prone to heart attack. Thus, while it seems unlikely that caffeine by itself causes heart attacks, it may be the last straw for someone on the brink of one. Tea may be more of a problem than coffee, since theophylline is a more potent stimulator of the heart than caffeine.

The implication of all this is to use common sense. Moderation is always wise. If these beverages upset your stomach or give your heart the flip flops, don't drink them. If you are overweight, smoke, and never exercise, then you are already on the brink. Those 10 cups of coffee or tea a day may help you over the edge.

Two last notes: People who are habituated to caffeine may experience headaches temporarily when the caffeine is discontinued. Conversely, caffeine is often added to headache remedies such as the infamous "APC" (aspirin-phenacetin-caffeine) despite evidence that caffeine may actually decrease the pain-relieving capacity of aspirin.

Finally, caffeine will not reverse the effects of alcohol, although it may still stimulate the nervous system. Thus you may become a more alert drunk, but you will still stagger, have trouble seeing, have slowed reflexes, and so forth. Never give coffee or anything else by mouth to semiconscious or unconscious persons in an attempt to revive them. It won't do any good even if it gets to the stomach and there is an excellent chance of getting it into the lungs. There it may cause an aspiration pneumonitis, a serious condition which can be fatal.

Marijuana

Our ignorance of the effects of long-term marijuana use is great. Research has been hampered because the drug is illegal and Federal permits to conduct research have been difficult to obtain. Data currently available would indicate that marijuana may be somewhat less toxic than alcohol, at least with short-term or intermittent use. The person who is stoned is generally less compromised than someone who is drunk but still is in no shape to drive. Hangovers are rare. Marijuana does not have the harmful effects of alcohol on the liver and stomach, again at least in the short-term situation. Marijuana may be of some use in the treatment of glaucoma.

What happens with long-term, heavy use is less clear. First, smoking a joint is likely to be as bad for your lungs as smoking a cigarette. Second, heavy use leads to apathy and a deterioration of social relationships—divorce, loss of job, and similar problems. This may be linked to the atrophy (shrinking) of the brain, which has been reported to be associated with long-term, heavy use. A number of studies have suggested that damage to the nervous system is likely with chronic use of this drug. Third, it has been reported that genetic damage results from prolonged pot use, but the evidence for this is rather weak. Further study is required on this point as well as virtually all other aspects of marijuana use.

At this point it seems that, despite some obvious dissimilarities, a reasonable rule for marijuana is much like that for alcohol. If you are smoking more than two joints per day, you probably have a problem. Dropping out can be done for good reasons and bad, and it may have good effects or bad. Just be sure that it's what you really want and that you are not just stuporously sliding that way because it is the path of least resistance.

Vitamins and Food Supplements

Despite the facts that these are big business in America, that there have been thousands of pages written about them, and that a sizeable cult has grown up around their use, they still may be dealt with very briefly.

The chance that choline, vitamin E, or anything else will keep you from aging is zero. If you are eating anything close to a balanced diet, the chance that you are suffering from a lack of any vitamin or nutrient is very nearly nil (see Chapter 9). With the exception of large amounts of vitamins A and D, the chance that you are harming yourself by taking them is also small. If you feel that they help and want to spend your money for them, have at it. Surely they do a great deal of good for many people, and just as surely most of this good is due to the placebo effect (see Chapter 3). But why quibble? For centuries the placebo effect was the most potent weapon of physicians and only rarely did anyone try to put them out of business.

Sleeping Pills

If a wake up cup of coffee is acceptable, why not something for people who have trouble sleeping? The best reason is that drugs do not work very well and hardly seem worth the risk they entail. The heavily promoted "sleep aids" that are available without a prescription may produce some sedation, but really work only when the placebo effect is pronounced. (See Chapter 3 for an explanation of the placebo effect.) The more powerful drugs that are obtainable with a prescription are more likely to really zonk you, but do not produce a natural sleep. They interfere with what is called rapid eye movement (REM) sleep, and this has the effect of making the sleep less restful. As a consequence, you will often feel more fatigued than ever and conclude that you need more of the drug. Obviously this type of circular pattern can only lead to trouble.

Most people who complain of inability to sleep are actually getting an appropriate amount for their age. (The amount of sleep needed normally decreases with age.) The difference is usually that their sleep pattern is disturbed—they are cat napping at various times—and that they are worried about not sleeping. They may feel that they should be asleep as soon as they hit the bed. In addition, the elderly may not be aware that it is natural for them to sleep for shorter periods of time.

If you are having a sleep problem, give the following program a try. It is the regimen that physicians prescribe most for this problem. If it doesn't work, see your doctor. But don't expect too much—remember that drugs are seldom the answer.

To help with your sleep:

- Avoid alcohol in anything but the smallest amounts. It disturbs REM sleep just like the other drugs. It may cause rebound agitation and fatigue.

- Try to establish a regular bedtime, *but* do not go to bed if you feel wide awake. Try to find a bedtime that you associate with sleepiness.

- Relax on retiring. Read, watch television, or listen to soothing music. Often it is best not to do this in bed so that the bed becomes associated with sleep only. (I find that trying to read something I should read but don't want to puts me to sleep instantly.)

- Avoid caffeine in the two hours before bedtime. Remember that soft drinks and chocolate have significant amounts of caffeine, as do coffee and tea.

- Eat or don't eat, depending on what works for you. Eating seems to have different effects on different people. Foods such as milk, meat, and lettuce contain a natural sleep inducer called L-tryptophane, a constituent of protein. However, a single glass of milk probably does not contain enough L-tryptophane to explain the effect of the traditional glass of warm milk at bedtime. Whatever the reason, a glass of milk or a snack does seem to help many people.

- Get rid of the dripping faucet. Try to do something about those little sounds or lights in the night that annoy you. Sleep masks, ear plugs, darker window shades, and soundproofing the bedroom may help on occasion.

- Do what's necessary in the beginning. As you start out, take a nap after lunch if this is necessary to improve your performance during the rest of the day. But remember that you must gradually reduce this or accept less sleep at night. If you're sleeping for a couple of hours during the day, common sense tells you that you're going to want to stay up longer during the night.

- Exercise regularly. Exercise is conducive to sleep and especially to those deeper stages which are associated with restfulness. But avoid exercising within two hours of bedtime. This has been shown to interfere with sleep with one very important exception. The most effective and healthy sleep inducer known is—you guessed it—sex.

Tranquilizers

First it was Miltown, then Librium, and now Valium. All tranquilizers, these have been the most frequently prescribed drugs in the last two decades. Valium seems to be destined to be the most frequently prescribed drug of all time by a large margin. And for some very good reasons. Valium usually produces a pleasant sedation with few side effects. It is sometimes useful as a sleep medication, as a muscle relaxant, and is a superb anticonvulsant when given intravenously. Serious reactions such as hepatitis are rare.

But it is also the sales leader for some bad reasons. The use of Valium is a symptom itself, an indication that our society has come to believe that pills can solve problems. Many of us seem to believe that it is no longer necessary to suffer any discomfort and that drugs should be able to keep us in a perpetual state of euphoria and tranquility. Expecting chemicals to be the answer to our problems, we fail to work toward a real solution. We may find ourselves trapped in a cycle that reinforces dependency on the drug. As we fail to find answers to our problems, symptoms become worse and we use more drugs to suppress the symptoms. This renders us even less likely than before to find answers, allows the symptoms to continue, and so on. The problem with reliance on these drugs is not so much what the drugs do to us directly, but what dependency on them prevents us from doing for ourselves.

Stimulants

These drugs are on their way out. They consist mostly of the amphetamines and closely related chemicals once thought to be useful as appetite suppressants. They are not. Realizing this, and that they have few legitimate medical uses, the Federal Drug Administration has begun steps to severely limit their availability. Soon our old friend caffeine will be the only stimulant available except under special circumstances.

Narcotics and Barbiturates

These drugs have legitimate medical uses as pain relievers, sedatives, and anticonvulsants. They are also the drugs often involved in addictions that destroy the life of the user. They can be deadly under the wrong circumstances or in the wrong dosage. Cocaine ("coke") is in vogue as a "safe" narcotic, but this foolishness can be fatal. Advice on them is relatively simple: Never seek to use them on your own. If they are prescribed by a competent physician, use them only in the manner prescribed and discontinue their use as soon as possible.

Hallucinogens

One of the most disturbing developments of recent years is the widespread availability of an easily made hallucinogen referred to as PCP or "angel dust." Often this chemical is added to marijuana cigarettes. It cannot be stated too strongly that this is a very dangerous drug that has the capacity to disturb thought processes for days, weeks, months, or even years after the drug has been taken. These disturbances are severe and may be indistinguishable from psychoses. They can cause convulsions and death. In short, we still do not know how dangerous these drugs are, but it appears that they have the ability to do severe and perhaps permanent damage to the mind—if they don't kill you.

14
Contraception

EVERY WOMAN MUST DECIDE TO ABSTAIN FROM SEX, HAVE BABIES, or use a contraceptive technique. Ideally, the male partner participates in this decision, but through a peculiar quirk of nature he does not participate in the most direct consequences. This chapter is concerned with the *medical* considerations involved in making decisions about contraception and childbearing. These decisions have a major effect on your health, both directly and indirectly, be you male or female. Directly, childbearing and every form of contraception has a definite risk. Indirectly, the threat to health of an ever-increasing population is equally real.

Few women will pursue one course of action for all their childbearing years. Abstention will be a reasonable choice for only a few, but for most it is neither a practical nor healthy suggestion. The vast majority of women will employ some form of contraception except for specific periods when they are attempting to get pregnant or are not engaging in sexual intercourse. If you are sure that you do not want any more children, tubal ligation or vasectomy are the safest methods for ensuring this. Here are brief descriptions of the most popular forms of contraception:

■ *Oral Contraceptives.* Birth-control pills use hormones to prevent pregnancy and must be taken on a daily basis. When used safely, they are very effective in preventing pregnancy. However, they may cause blood clots and these clots have been fatal on occasion. They may also contribute to high blood pressure. There are also less dangerous but annoying side effects, such as weight gain, nausea, fluid retention, migraine headaches, vaginal bleeding, and yeast infections of the vagina.

■   *Intrauterine Device (IUD).* This device is inserted into the uterus by a physician and remains there until removed or expelled. If the IUD is expelled, it may not be noticed, and in such cases some pregnancies have resulted. The IUD may also cause bleeding and cramps. In rare instances they are associated with serious infections of the uterus, although the type with which this most frequently occurred (the Dalkon Shield) has been removed from the market.

■   *Diaphragm.* A diaphragm is a rubber membrane that fits over the opening to the uterus in the vagina. It must be inserted before intercourse and retained in place for several hours thereafter. There are no side effects or complications from diaphragms. They are always used with a contraceptive foam or jelly.

■   *Contraceptive Foams and Jellies.* These compounds contain chemicals that kill or immobilize the male's sperm. In the past they have been used by themselves, but now are almost always used in conjunction with a diaphragm. Side effects are unusual and consist of some irritation to the walls of the vagina. Their effect will last for only about 60 minutes and many people find these preparations inconvenient or just plain messy.

■   *Condoms.* These are enjoying a resurgence of popularity. If used correctly, they are 90 percent effective in preventing pregnancy. There are no side effects, they are inexpensive and widely available, and they give some protection against venereal disease. However, remembering to use them seems to be a problem and they do result in decreased sensitivity, although newer condoms claim little loss—or even enhancement—of sensitivity.

■   *The Rhythm Method.* Intercourse is avoided during the time when ovulation is expected. This method requires fairly regular periods and a willingness to carefully take daily temperatures in order to predict the time of ovulation. Under the best of circumstances, it is only moderately effective.

■   *Coitus Interruptus.* This means that the male withdraws from the vagina just before ejaculation. Since there are sperm present in the secretions of the penis *before* ejaculation occurs, and since withdrawal at just the right time is a tricky business, this method really simply reduces the chances of pregnancy by reducing the number of sperm deposited in the vagina.

■ *Douche.* Douching after intercourse also decreases the number of sperm in the vagina, and therefore decreases the chance of pregnancy somewhat.

The accompanying table of expected pregnancies gives the relative risk of pregnancy for unprotected intercourse and the most popular forms of contraception. The second table, on risks, gives the risk to life for these.

A number of facts are central to your decision about what contraceptive method to use—or whether to use one at all:

■ Unprotected intercourse is by far the most hazardous choice.

■ The least hazardous techniques require the availability of abortions.

■ Except for oral contraceptives, the hazard of each contraceptive technique depends mostly on the probability of pregnancy.

■ There is a substantial difference between "theoretical" and "average experience" risk. That is, how faithfully you use the method counts a great deal.

As far as your health is concerned, it would seem clear that you should consider "mechanical" forms of contraception (IUD, condom, diaphragm with foam) and assure yourself of access to facilities to interrupt an unwanted pregnancy. You may find that mechanical methods simply are not for you. You may have ethical or religious objections to abortion—or to contraception, for that matter. The objective here is not to promote any particular method, but to ensure that your decision is an informed one. To risk your health unknowingly is the truly tragic choice.

You may accept an increased risk to health for the best of reasons— your own reasons. It is one of the most intensely personal decisions, and the rest of us should respect your right to make up your mind. Ideally, your choice would depend only upon the feelings of you and your spouse.

Unfortunately, the consequences of childbearing go far beyond the immediate family. As explained in Chapter 2, environment and the standard of living have a major influence on health, far outweighing the contribution of medical care. It is most unlikely that the demands

Expected pregnancies

Number of pregnancies expected for 100 women using contraceptive methods in a year. (The "average experience" group includes women who were using the method inconsistently or incorrectly.)

	Used correctly	*Average experience*
Birth control pills	0.340	4-10
Condoms and foam	1	5
IUD	1-3	5
Condom	3	10
Diaphragm and foam	3	17
Foam	3	22
Coitus interruptus	9	20-25
Rhythm	13	21
No protection	90	90
Douche	?	40

Source: Robert A. Hatcher, Gary K. Stewart, Felicia Guest, et al., *Contraceptive Technology, 1976-1977.* New York: Irvington, 1976. Reprinted by permission.

Risks of pregnancy versus contraceptives

	Deaths per 100,000 women
Pregnancy	16
Oral contraceptive users	0.3-3
Mechanical methods (death resulting from 20 percent becoming pregnant)	3
Mechanical methods and abortion for pregnancy	0.6
Unprotected intercourse and abortion	2.6

Source: Robert A. Hatcher, Gary K. Stewart, Felicia Guest, et al., *Contraceptive Technology, 1976-1977.* New York: Irvington, 1976. Reprinted by permission.

of an ever-increasing population on an ever-decreasing supply of resources should not adversely affect the environment and the economy.
It is most unlikely that advances in medical science will be able to
counter these adverse effects. It is likely that economic and environmental factors can overwhelm the protective effects of a beneficial
lifestyle. For example, in Los Angeles the death rate due to cancer of
the lung is several times that in Chicago, despite similar percentages
of smokers in the population. The higher degree of air pollution in Los
Angeles is the most likely cause for this difference.

In 1900, the population of the United States was 76 million. In
1950 it was 152 million. Today it is approximately 222 million. The
Bureau of Census estimates that by the year 2000 it could be 287
million. The energy crisis may become just one of many crises—the job
crisis, the housing crisis, the food crisis, and so on and on. Attempts to
produce more jobs, housing, and food inevitably consume resources
and produce waste. This brings us closer to what may well be the last
crisis—too few resources, too much pollution. Unlike some developing
nations, the United States has never been forced to formulate a national
policy concerning population control. It seems obvious that it would
be advantageous for each of us to consider this issue now before our
options become limited and our crises become impossible to solve.

In curious contrast to population control, methods of contraception
have always been a public issue. Not only have specific methods been
illegal, but until recently even giving information about birth control
was illegal in some states. Again, the purpose here is not to argue for
or against any method, much less discuss the ethical or moral aspects
of contraception. But from the point of view of public health, the
banning of contraceptive methods or information must be regarded as
a detrimental step. In the current debate on abortion, then, you must
consider the fact that this procedure is a part of the safest approach to
contraception. Even if you oppose abortion, a decision that every other
woman must accept an increased risk to health should not be taken
lightly.

15
Immunizations

HISTORICALLY, INFECTIOUS DISEASES HAVE BEEN THE MOST SIGNIFI-
cant wasters of human life; but now they are controlled by many
methods, including improved nutrition of the population, improved
sanitation, improved housing, and, more recently, the development of
immunizations and antibiotics. Immunizations are one of the most
significant contributions of medical science to the control of disease.
Smallpox has virtually been eliminated from the face of the earth in
the past decade by the worldwide campaign of the World Health Organization. Polio, which used to cripple 20 thousand a year in the early
1950s, now affects only a handful of people a year in this country,
thanks to immunization campaigns.

With regard to immunizations we are now in a critical period in
this nation's history. Many people have become complacent about immunization because of the rarity of the diseases that immunizations
have aided in eliminating. In addition, the recent swine influenza de-
bacle has undermined the confidence of many in immunizations and
raised questions in the minds of many parents. There have always been
problems in the use of immunizations. However, the risks of the vaccines are usually minimal when compared with the risks of the disease.

Avoiding an illness often presents many practical problems. Since
the bacteria and viruses responsible for causing infectious illness may
be spread by contact with people, with animals, or with airborne drop-

lets, avoidance is often impossible. On the other hand, protection by the use of immunizations is a practical solution.

The principle of immunization is to develop your body's defense system to a point where it is capable of foiling any attack by a particular agent. To accomplish this, a small dose of the modified infectious agent is given. For some immunizations, the virus has been modified in a laboratory so that it causes a very mild infection. Other immunizations use a dead virus that is chemically the same but cannot infect. Others inject just a part of the viral organism. The body's defense system builds up an immunity to this part, which in effect creates an immunity to the whole infecting agent. Still another method of immunizing involves substituting a related virus that causes a much milder infection. This technique is used for smallpox, wherein the individual is inoculated with cow pox in order to prevent infection with smallpox.

The practice of immunization dates back several thousand years to attempts by a Chinese monk to prevent smallpox. Immunization methods were developed long before the nature of the infecting agents was known. Jenner, who is credited with the modern development of immunization in the late eighteenth century, borrowed the idea from English farmers who had been utilizing cow pox to protect themselves from smallpox for centuries. Jenner merely performed a study validating what the farmers had been doing for years.

Immunizations have been developed to combat some of the most devastating illnesses affecting human life. Remember, however, that immunizations are only one of the ways of defending against illness. Persons in good health are less likely to be devastated by infectious disease than persons in poor health. Most infectious diseases, such as tuberculosis, have been steadily decreasing in frequency because of improved nutrition, sanitation, and medical care.

Modern virological techniques allow the manufacture of vaccines effective against many illnesses. But all immunizations carry with them the possibility of side effects due to the immunization itself. No immunization is 100-percent effective or 100-percent safe.

If you have questions about a particular immunization, your physician or health department should be willing to explain in detail the current risks, benefits, and recommendations for that immunization. If you are not satisfied with the explanation, you may turn to any of the following groups:

■   The United States Department of Health, Education and Welfare, Public Health Service, Center for Disease Control, Atlanta, Georgia 30333

- Advisory Committee on Immunization Practices, United States Public Health Service

- Council on Environmental Health, American Medical Association, Chicago, Illinois

- The Academy of Pediatrics, Committee on Infectious Diseases, Evanston, Illinois

For the most part, the diseases for which immunizations are recommended occur in childhood. The following table gives the schedule for "baby shots." Adults who have had these need only to maintain their immunity to tetanus by having booster injections every ten years. (If you suffer a particularly dirty wound, especially a puncture wound, you should have a tetanus booster if it has been more than five years since your last one.) Diptheria, rabies, and influenza immunizations may sometimes be advisable. These diseases and immunizations are discussed below.

If you failed to receive some or all of your baby shots, determining which immunizations you now need depends upon your age, your possible exposure to these diseases in the future, and whether you received partial immunization in the past. You will need the help of your physician to determine the appropriate approach. Usually it is felt that

Immunization schedule

Age			
2 months	DPT (diphtheria, pertussis, tetanus)	and	Oral polio virus
4 months	DPT	and	Oral polio virus
6 months	DPT	and	Oral polio virus
15 months	Measles		
18 months	DPT	and	Oral polio virus
4–6 years	DT (diphtheria, tetanus)	and	Oral polio virus
10–12 years	Rubella (only for females whose blood test shows no immunity to rubella)	and	Oral polio virus

adults should be immunized against tetanus but not against polio, pertussis, or measles. Recommendations with respect to immunization against diphtheria and mumps are highly variable but usually mumps is not recommended and diphtheria is recommended only if exposure to the disease is likely. Rubella immunization should be considered only in women of childbearing age whose blood tests indicate no immunity to this disease.

Tetanus (Lockjaw)

Nature of the illness. Tetanus is a dangerous illness. The tetanus bacteria and its spores are found everywhere. They are present in dust, soil, pastures, and human and animal waste. Symptoms consist of severe muscle spasm, often of the neck and jaw muscles, causing lockjaw. The symptoms are caused by toxin produced by the bacteria. The tetanus bacteria grows only in the absence of air, so wounds that are created by punctures or sharp objects, possibly introducing bacteria underneath the skin, are the wounds with the greatest likelihood of causing tetanus. After tetanus develops, it may be treated with antibiotics and tetanus immune globulin, but mortality may still be as high as 40 percent. Tetanus can and should be prevented by immunization.

Nature of the immunization. Tetanus is one of our best immunizations. The tetanus immunization is a toxin that is produced by the tetanus bacterium and modified in the laboratory so that it has very little of its toxic potential. Of all the vaccines available, tetanus comes closest to 100-percent effectiveness after the initial series of shots. Local reactions are rare and usually cause only mild discomfort for a short time. Severe local reactions can occur if too many shots are received, a phenomenon that was frequently seen in military recruits who received unneeded immunizations. Tetanus shots are needed only every ten years unless a particularly dirty wound is suffered. Maintain your own records of immunizations—do not rely solely on the physician, health department, or clinic where the immunizations are given.

Diphtheria

Nature of the illness. At this time, there are about 300 reported cases of diphtheria each year in the United States and probably far more than that are not reported. Diphtheria affects the throat, nose, and skin and is contagious. Complications of diphtheria include paralysis (in approximately 20 percent of patients) and heart damage (in approximately 50 percent). Diphtheria can be treated by a combination of penicillin and serum injections. However, despite treatment, approximately 10 percent of persons who acquire diphtheria will die from it. Only immunization can successfully prevent diphtheria.

Nature of the immunization. Diphtheria immunization has been available since 1920. A portion of the toxin (the chemical product of the bacteria that causes damage) is altered with formalin to render it harmless. This modified toxin, known as a toxoid, stimulates the body's defense system to produce an antitoxin. Immunity persists for many years after several inoculations. Although the person may come in contact with bacteria and even become infected, the toxin will be neutralized by the antitoxin within the person's body and the infection will cause no harm.

Reactions to diphtheria toxoid are extremely uncommon. Generally, they are limited to a slight swelling at the injection site. This reaction can be decreased in older children and adults by giving lower concentrations of toxoid, known as "adult-type" diphtheria toxoid.

Diphtheria toxoid should be begun (in combination with pertussis and tetanus) at the age of two months. The primary schedule consists of three immunizations given several months apart in the first year of life. A booster shot should be given one year later. An additional booster shot should be given when the child enters school. Adults should have boosters every 10 years if they are at high risk for exposure to diphtheria (hospital workers, etc.).

Rubella (German Measles)

Nature of the illness. Rubella, as well as rubella immunization, provides us with a set of very difficult decisions. Rubella is a mild illness, usually with a mild fever and a mild rash. Many people do not even know they have had the illness. The danger from rubella lies in the risk to a developing fetus during early pregnancy.

In 1964, during the last rubella epidemic in this country, more than 20,000 children were born with deformities caused by the rubella virus. The deformities included heart defects, blindness, and deafness. While many fetuses escape these devastating effects, the huge number who have suffered greatly make efforts at eliminating this disease worthwhile.

Nature of the immunization. The purpose of a rubella immunization program is to prevent pregnant women from becoming infected. Before rubella immunization became possible in 1969, over 80 percent of women had already been infected and therefore were not at risk of producing an infant deformed by rubella. Women who have had rubella infections can become reinfected with rubella a second, third, or even fourth time, but it is doubtful that these reinfections pose any threat to the fetus. It is presently assumed, though not proven, that only the initial infection with rubella can damage the fetus.

A rubella immunization program was undertaken in this country in 1969 for several reasons. The most compelling reason was that rubella epidemics run in seven- to ten-year cycles and the next epidemic was expected soon. In order to avert the epidemic, widespread community campaigns were conducted. By immunizing at least two thirds of the population, it was hoped that the entire population would be protected (so-called herd immunity). Unfortunately, even in communities in which 95 percent of the population has been immunized, introduction of the virus has been shown to result in infection of the remaining five percent.

It was decided to immunize children over the age of one year, hoping that the mothers would be protected by immunizing the children. This was a unique policy in the annals of immunization practice; for the first time, individuals were being exposed to vaccination and its complications in order to protect other individuals. This may or may not have been a reasonable policy. Supporters point to the fact that the expected epidemic did not occur. However, we are currently not certain how long the protective level of the immunizations will last. Some studies indicate that immunity may eventually be lost. If the protection does not remain sufficiently high to interfere with the production of deformities, then we may be producing a generation of women who will be susceptible at childbearing ages. Remember that in the past, more than 80 percent of the population was immune at childbearing age. Is it possible that the next epidemic will be even more devastating because a large number of women will be susceptible?

Other countries have adopted a different policy and only vaccinate teenage girls who are shown by blood test to have no protection against rubella. Vaccination of males doesn't seem to make much sense, since "herd" immunity does not work. The policy of vaccinating teenage women diminishes the chance that the immunity will fall to such a low level that it will not be protective in the childbearing years.

But there are problems with adopting a policy of late immunization. Side effects from the immunization are much more common at this age. Particularly troublesome are the joint pains that occur in over ten percent of women receiving the vaccination during adolescence or later. Some of these women have had arthritis for as long as 24 months following immunization. In addition, a few women (between 1 in 500 and 1 in 10,000) experience a peripheral neuropathy (a sensation of tingling created by an inflammation in the nerves of the hands).

An additional risk in administering the vaccine in older women is the possibility of pregnancy at the time of vaccination. Although none have occurred yet, rubella vaccine may possibly cause birth defects if given to pregnant women. Thus far, no congenital anomalies have been reported in women whose *children* were given rubella vaccine. It is probably safe to immunize the children of pregnant women, although it is not advised. A policy of immunizing women of childbearing age requires adequate contraception for two to four months following immunization.

Fortunately, a major rubella outbreak has not occurred since 1964. This has been a worldwide phenomenon both in countries immunizing infants and in countries immunizing only teenage females. It is assumed that the predicted epidemic has in part been avoided by the use of rubella immunization. It seems reasonable to continue to recommend the immunization of women before pregnancy, if a blood test shows no antibodies. We also recommend carefully following future information on rubella immunizations.

Influenza

Nature of the illness. Influenza is a respiratory tract infection caused by the influenza virus that produces muscular symptoms as well. There are many illnesses that may mimic influenza, and the term influenza is applied liberally to many syndromes involving cough, cold and muscle aches.

Nature of the immunization. Influenza virus vaccines are live weakened viral vaccines. They are recommended for both children and adults who have chronic illnesses, particularly respiratory and cardiac diseases. This recommendation is somewhat controversial. More so is the practice of routine immunization of the elderly in good health. The effectiveness of flu vaccines has been challenged by no less an authority than Dr. Albert Sabin, developer of the oral polio vaccine. Certainly its use in healthy persons is not likely to be of benefit.

One of the long-term benefits of the media coverage of the swine influenza controversy of 1976 will be to sensitize the public to the complexities involved in making rational medical decisions. On the other hand, it is our hope that individuals will not be dissuaded from obtaining vaccines with a long history of demonstrated safety and effectiveness in preventing serious illness.

Rabies

Nature of the illness. Rabies is a viral illness that is transmitted in the saliva of wild and domestic animals with rabies. It is fatal if not treated. Animals known to be significant carriers of rabies include skunks, bats, and foxes. Rabies in dogs and cats does occur but has become rare. Rabies is rare in rodents such as squirrels, chipmunks, mice, and rats. Fortunately, there are only one or two cases of rabies in humans reported in this country each year.

Nature of the immunization. Both attenuated rabies vaccine and antirabies serum are available. The complex methods of administering these vaccines will not be discussed here. Immediate cleansing of any animal wound is the first line of defense. Bites from wild animals or unknown domestic animals should be reported to a physician immediately.

In addition to these vaccines that are given *after* a bite, there are vaccines that are used to produce immunity in persons who must be in areas where exposure to rabid animals is more likely. For most of us, the possibility of contacting rabies is very small so that these vaccines should not be used routinely. Side effects and serious reactions do occur with their use.

The bottom line for most adults is a tetanus booster every ten years, with diphtheria boosters for those who are at high risk for exposure to this disease. Rabies immunizations are rarely needed. Influenza shots are overrated and offer little for the overwhelming majority of adults.

16
Mental Health

MENTAL HEALTH IS A DIFFICULT SUBJECT FOR EVERYONE, DOC-
tors included. Giving each psychiatric disease an understandable definition is a formidable task, and formulating a useful definition of mental health is even more difficult. The border between normal and
abnormal behavior is often obscure. Each of us displays traits of mental
illness at one time or another. Even when these problems occur regularly, they do not preclude useful and productive lives. Beethoven was
lonely and experienced emotional outbursts, Lewis Carroll was painfully shy, and Lincoln was plagued with attacks of depression. All of us
are crazy some of the time and some of us are crazy all of the time—
and many of us have significant problems for substantial periods of
time. Mental health is more than the absence of mental illness, but
what must be added is not clear. For the present we will have to settle
for a goal of avoiding illness.

Anxiety and depression are by far the most common problems in
this area. Each may have readily apparent causes. For example, you
may be anxious over the outcome of an operation to a close friend or
relative. If the operation should fail, then it would be natural to be
depressed. (Doctors often use the term "reactive depression" when the
cause of the depression seems obvious.) Thus feelings of anxiety or
depression may be a normal reaction to certain events in life. However,
these feelings may occur without the reason being known, a more
worrisome situation. This type of anxiety has been likened to "fear

without knowing what is feared." Similarly one could say that this type of depression is "feeling down" without knowing why. Anxiety or depression without known cause is likely to interfere with normal functions and to go on for long periods of time. The key word here is "known." Undoubtedly there are reasons for these feelings, but they are hidden from the person experiencing the problem as well as from those trying to help. In general, treatment for these problems is aimed at making these hidden causes known so that the individual may deal with them.

Stress is the great common denominator of our existence. Sooner or later, it gets to us all. It can produce anxiety, fatigue, anger, depression, heartburn, headaches, insomnia, and just about every other mental and physical ailment known to man. How much stress you feel and how you react to it—how you cope with life's stresses and strains—have a lot to do with your mental health. A brief description of the major types of mental problems will be useful as background for the discussion of stress, your feelings and what to do about them.

Neuroses are relatively benign disorders usually involving chronic anxiety and difficulty in coping. Depression is common as well. Symptoms usually occur in response to stress. For example, a physical illness may bring on a period of inability to concentrate, sleeplessness, fatigue, diffuse anxiety, and preoccupation with the body that lasts for weeks or months after the illness itself has passed. It is characteristic that persons with neuroses suffer inwardly but virtually never lose their grip on reality. For the most part, they lead normal lives except during the periods when stress has produced symptoms. Clearly this is an area in which differentiating between normal and abnormal is most difficult. Since we all are anxious or depressed or fatigued at one time or another, the question is one of degree rather than kind.

In contrast, *psychoses* are major disturbances in thinking that interfere with the ability to meet the ordinary demands of daily life. Persons who are out of touch with reality—who may hear voices, believe themselves to be someone else, and so on—fall into this category. Schizophrenia, paranoid states, manic-depressive psychoses, and involutional melancholia are major types of psychoses. Often psychoses are easier to recognize than to describe. A prominent professor of psychiatry, somewhat exasperated by the difficulty in explaining this subject to a group of medical students, finally blurted out that "these are the people who are really crazy." At any rate, a detailed description of the various psychoses will not be attempted here.

Personality disorders are deeply ingrained abnormal patterns of behavior, especially evident in the way the person deals with other people. People in this group tend to blame others for their problems.

They have little or no understanding that these problems originate within themselves. They seem unable to "get along" with the rest of society. There are many types of personality disorders: paranoid, manic-depressive, schizoid, explosive, obsessive-compulsive, hysterical, asthenic, passive-aggressive, inadequate, antisocial. Again, they are separated from normal behavior by the degree to which their symptoms dominate. Often severe personality disorders are difficult to distinguish from psychoses. Therapy is difficult and often unsuccessful.

Transient situational disturbances are the direct result of stress and may take the form of a neurosis or even psychosis. They usually resolve when the stress is over. A type that is very familiar to doctors is the "CCU (Coronary Care Unit) or ICU (Intensive Care Unit) psychosis." Severely ill patients forced to stay for days in the highly abnormal environment of these special units may develop symptoms of paranoia or other psychoses. These rapidly disappear when they are moved out of the unit. The frequency of these disturbances is testimony to the significant stress of hospitalization. Undoubtedly this stress is a major reason that many persons with heart attacks are better treated at home.

Psychophysiologic disorder is a term sometimes used when a problem such as peptic ulcer or migraine headache has a prominent, emotional component. Since we now appreciate that every health problem has an emotional component, this term has become so broad as to lose much of its usefulness. It may help to use this term when the emotional component of an illness predominates.

In general, each of these disorders may benefit from professional help. In contrast, each of us has periods of depression or anxiety that are normal and natural, and in which the role of professionals is much less clear. Certainly the routine reliance upon tranquilizers and other drugs to solve these problems is questionable. This is true despite the fact that tranquilizers have been the drugs most frequently prescribed during the last two decades. Nevertheless, the odds are pretty good that each of us at some time will have a problem with which we could use some help, a problem that has continued for some time and that interferes with work, sleep or family life. That really is the best single rule: If it is interfering significantly with your ability to function effectively, it is time to talk to someone about it.

What Causes Mental Illness?

The causes of mental illness are the subject of endless debate and discussion. Some disorders may appear to run in families, but most of the time it is impossible to say whether this is due to heredity or environment. We have only just begun to learn of the biochemical changes in the brain in some types of mental illness, so knowledge concerning *why* these changes occur is a long way off. Perhaps we are even further from explaining the relationship between biochemical theories and the mass of evidence concerning the effect of environment—family, friends, and community, for example. It seems as if we can all agree that the child of a psychotic parent has an increased risk of mental illness, but we are not sure exactly why.

Given this complex and confusing situation, what can you do for yourself? Years ago the answer might well have been "not much." Prevailing opinion was that people seldom changed their mental outlook without professional help. Without such help you took your chances along life's rough road, hoping that heredity, childhood experiences, brain biochemistry, or all three did not fail you.

Today we are bombarded with the opposite message. Your mental outlook can be changed to give you happiness, freedom from worry, financial success, power, friends, lovers—if you will just buy a book, attend an encounter session, take a course, or add choline to your diet. Information available to you ranges from reasoned, well-written descriptions of documented techniques to absurd collections of demented drivel. It must be admitted that even the best information has never been demonstrated to have had a significant effect when offered through a mass medium—as this book is, for instance. With this humbling thought in mind, it still seems worthwhile to discuss two important concepts.

First, the biggest hurdle in doing something for yourself (or another) is *awareness* that something should and can be done. Certain emotional problems are characterized by denial that anything is wrong. Even when denial is not a part of the illness itself, it remains one of the common ways in which all of us deal with problems. With or without denial, it's just plain hard to get in touch with your feelings at times. It's especially important to understand in which areas of your life you are experiencing satisfaction or dissatisfaction. Dissatisfaction that is not recognized may be a hidden cause of anxiety, depression, or other problems. Later in this chapter there are materials to help you develop a better understanding of your own feelings.

The other concept is that of stress. It is now clear that stress may play a role in producing almost any illness, not just mental illness or those illnesses labeled psychophysiologic or psychosomatic. Likewise, any physical illness itself produces stress, a fact too often overlooked as we concentrate on healing the body. Perhaps the first law of health should be that the mind and body are inseparable. You can't affect one without affecting the other.

None of us can forever avoid stressful situations. Life is just not like that. None of us can so arrange our minds that no situation is stressful. No one can accept the death of a loved one with complete equanimity—indeed, one might suspect mental illness if this were the case. But you can decrease the amount of harm that stress does by recognizing its presence and then doing something about it. You may be maintaining an elevated level of stress unconsciously—that is, you may be uptight and not know it. Also, you can detect a dangerous sequence of stressful events through the Holmes Readjustment Rating Scale (presented later in this chapter). The ability of the Holmes Scale to predict serious illness demonstrates that unusual stress may be as much a risk to your health as high blood pressure.

Can Mental Illness Be Prevented?

This is a controversial area. Some feel that society itself is conducive to mental illness and that changes in society could prevent at least some mental illness. Others believe that encouraging the use of health services by those who feel troubled for any reason will prevent serious emotional problems. A more realistic hope is that a large portion of the population can learn to avoid the hazards of excessive stress. Nevertheless, we still do not have convincing evidence that any approach actually *prevents* mental illness.

Can Mental Illness Be Treated?

Most forms of mental illness may be improved by therapy of one kind or another, but it would be an error to credit therapy with many cures. Most mental illnesses wax and wane, and therapy decreases the frequency with which symptoms interfere with functioning. Whether the loss of symptoms will be permanent depends more on the individual and the severity of the illness than the mode of treatment.

Today drugs play a much greater role than in the past, especially in psychoses. Effective medications are credited for the substantial decrease in the number of patients confined to mental institutions. It should be remembered that drugs alone are inadequate—their use must be a part of an overall treatment plan.

Paralleling the profusion of drugs has been the emergence of new concepts in treatment programs themselves, such as group therapy, work therapy, half-way houses, placement of patients from institutions in private homes, day hospitals, and so on. This indicates a willingness to take a new look at the treatment of mental illness, an important reason for optimism in the area of mental health.

Can Mental Illness Be Detected Early?

There is no known way to detect mental illness before symptoms occur. In fact, a disease of the mind is defined by the types and severity of symptoms. The difficulty of distinguishing between normal and abnormal behavior has already been discussed. Someday it may be possible to detect changes in body chemistry before changes in behavior occur, but it is impossible to predict whether or when this will occur.

What Should You Do About Mental Health?

Despite being a cliché, "Getting in touch with your feelings" is pretty good advice. Getting in touch includes learning to recognize the stress and the potential for stress in your life. This is the necessary first step in ensuring your mental health, but taking it does *not* mean you have a problem or that you need help now. It simply means learning to identify those things that can or do create stress for you. This may save you a lot of grief—as well as anger, frustration, depression, and anxiety.

Finding out what you really feel about things may not be easy despite the enormous number of courses, seminars, retreats, encounters, books—each offering a different "method"—that claim to show you how. Many have been helpful to someone, none have been helpful to all. While their diversity and variability prohibit any recommendations, common sense tells you to avoid those that promise power, wealth, job advancement, and so forth. These are the equivalent of the easy way to lose weight. They are rip-offs.

The purpose of the questionnaires you'll find on the next few pages is to give you something to ponder. Each tells you how to interpret your answers. This interpretation should be taken for what it is: a suggestion based on trends among a large number of people completing the questionnaire. Treat it as an informal opinion—not quaranteed helpful, pertinent, or accurate, but worthy of your consideration. But beware of saying "it doesn't apply to me" too often. You may well be the exception to the rule, but don't use this as an excuse to avoid thinking about your results. Above all, bear in mind that the objective is to get you in touch with your feelings—not to diagnose or pronounce judgment on your mental processes. If this approach helps, great. If not, forget it.

The "Looking for Satisfaction" section that follows is based in part on the Heimler Scale of Social Functioning and developed by Professor Eugene Heimler. Professor Heimler's work indicates that a very useful way of getting in touch with your feelings is to look for signs of satisfaction or dissatisfaction in 10 basic areas of your life. In one of the areas, Finance, questions directly from the Heimler Scale are used. In the other nine areas, you can record your thoughts as to whether you feel satisfied or dissatisfied with this part of your life. Some possible responses are indicated as examples, but use them only if they truly represent your feelings.

A note about the Holmes scale. Dr. Thomas Holmes' theory is that change, regardless of whether it seems to be for better or for worse, causes stress and that this stress can make one more susceptible to illness. He developed his schedule as a way of indicating the stress of life events involving change. Several studies have demonstrated the value of this questionnaire in predicting illness. It is used in calculating your LifeScore. The main reason for its inclusion, however, is to help you consider the subject of stress in your life.

If you have questions about emotional problems, don't think you have to see a psychiatrist. Today there are many sources of competent counseling on emotional problems. Referrals can be made if the psychiatrist's particular skills are needed, but often there are more appropriate ways of approaching the problem. Your own physician is a good person with whom to start. Clinical psychologists and clinical social workers are professionals with special training in this area. Nursing has given increasing emphasis to dealing with the emotional and behavioral aspects of health. Modern training of ministers, rabbis, and priests places a high priority on counseling and mental health. There is a wide variety of programs using many different combinations of personnel. True, there are some that lack the necessary skills or are outright frauds, usually conducted by persons whose training is suspect and who are sponsored by fly-by-night organizations. But if the program is sponsored by reputable organizations and conducted by persons who have degrees from recognized universities, then it is likely to offer competent help.

Remember the main rule: If a problem is interfering with your ability to function, it is time to talk to someone about it. Doctors, nurses, clinical social workers, clergy, psychologists, and others can help—but you must take the first step.

Looking For Satisfaction

1. FINANCE*

Please answer each question according to the way you feel today.
Circle Y to indicate YES (Y) Circle P to indicate PERHAPS (P)
Circle N to indicate NO (N) If you are not sure how you feel, answer
PERHAPS (P).

(This section has two parts. If both are important to your present situation, answer both.)

PART A—EMPLOYED ☐ (Check if more important than Part B)

1. Do you live more comfortably than you did two years ago?	Y P N
2. Are you able to save?	Y P N
3. Do you feel at ease about spending?	Y P N
4. Are you reasonably secure financially?	Y P N
5. Do you *feel* financially secure?	Y P N

PART B—HOUSEWIFE—HOMEMAKER ☐ (Check if more important than Part A)

6. Can you manage on your housekeeping money without a lot of anxiety?	Y P N
7. Do you have any income, other than housekeeping money?	Y P N
8. Do you feel at ease about spending?	Y P N
9. Generally speaking, does being a housewife satisfy you?	Y P N
10. Do you feel financially secure?	Y P N

For the remaining sections, record your thoughts on this area of your life and then indicate your overall satisfaction or dissatisfaction.

2. WORK—JOB OR HOMEMAKER

Examples: Like my fellow workers.
Don't get out of the house enough.

Your thoughts: _____

_____

* Section 1, on Finance, is from the Heimler Scale of Social Functioning (Copyright, Eugene Heimler, 1967).

_____

_____

Overall are you: satisfied ___ dissatisfied ___

3. FRIENDS

Examples: Have close friends.
            Don't enjoy partying.

Your thoughts: _____

_____

_____

Overall are you: satisfied ___ dissatisfied ___

4. FAMILY

Examples: Look forward to getting home to family.
            Seem to share little with wife (or husband).

Your thoughts: _____

_____

_____

Overall are you: satisfied ___ dissatisfied ___

5. PERSONAL LIFE

Examples: Marriage has worked well.
            Can't seem to relate.

Your thoughts: _____

_____

_____

Overall are you: satisfied ___ dissatisfied ___

6. ENERGY

Examples:　Always tired.
　　　　　　Feel I have enough energy to enjoy life.

Your thoughts: _____

_____

_____

_____

Overall are you: satisfied ___ dissatisfied ___

7. HEALTH

Examples:　Basically in good health.
　　　　　　Headaches frequently interfere.

Your thoughts: _____

_____

_____

_____

Overall are you: satisfied ___ dissatisfied ___

8. PERSONAL INFLUENCE

Examples:　Don't get enough respect.
　　　　　　Generally can get along with people

Your thoughts: _____

_____

_____

_____

Overall are you: satisfied ___ dissatisfied ___

9. MOOD

Examples:　Feel good most of the time.
　　　　　　Often worry without reason.

Your thoughts: _____

_____

Overall are you: satisfied ___ dissatisfied ___

10. HABITS

Examples: Out of shape.
My habits seem to irritate others.

Your thoughts: _____

_____

_____

Overall are you: satisfied ___ dissatisfied ___

Interpretation of the "Looking for Satisfaction" Questionnaire

This questionnaire addresses 10 of the most important areas in your life. There are no right or wrong answers, but there are answers that indicate more or less satisfaction in these areas. In Section 1, the "desirable" response to each question is "yes"; by "desirable" is meant that this response indicates satisfaction in this part of your life. In the other sections, your thoughts may be telling you more than is apparent at first.

Interpretation requires only your good common sense and the investment of a little time to give your thoughts some honest consideration. Often the biggest hurdle in making life more satisfying is consciously acknowledging those things with which we are unsatisfied. Hopefully, you made a real attempt to record your thoughts honestly. Don't lose the benefit of those honest responses by giving them inadequate consideration. Give special attention to those responses that are less than you would like them to be. This is the first step in changing them.

Holmes scale

Your "past" Holmes Score is the total of the Holmes Points for events that occurred in the last year. Use this total as your Holmes Score in figuring your LifeScore. Your "future" Holmes Score is the total of Holmes Points for events you expect to occur in the next year. Use this total for your Holmes Score in figuring your New You Score.

(Check all items that apply)	Holmes Points
1. Death of spouse	100
2. Divorce	73
3. Marital separation	65
4. Jail term	63
5. Death of close family member	63
6. Personal injury or illness	53
7. Marriage	50
8. Fired at work	47
9. Marital reconcilation	45
10. Retirement	45
11. Change in health of family member	44
12. Pregnancy	40
13. Sex difficulties	39
14. Gain of new family member	39
15. Business readjustment	39
16. Change in financial state	38
17. Death of close friend	37
18. Change to different line of work	36
19. Change in number of arguments with spouse	35
20. Mortgage over $10,000	31
21. Foreclosure of mortgage or loan	30
22. Change in responsibilities at work	29
23. Son or daughter leaving home	29
24. Trouble with in-laws	29
25. Outstanding personal achievement	28
26. Spouse begin or stop work	26
27. Begin or end school	26

28.	Change in living conditions	25
29.	Change in personal habits	24
30.	Trouble with boss	23
31.	Change in work hours or conditions	20
32.	Change in residence	20
33.	Change in schools	20
34.	Change in recreation	19
35.	Change in church activities	19
36.	Change in social activities	18
37.	Mortgage or loan less than $10,000	17
38.	Change in sleeping habits	16
39.	Change in number of family get-togethers	15
40.	Change in eating habits	13
41.	Vacation	13
42.	Christmas	12
43.	Minor violations of the law	11

Source: Thomas H. Holmes, M.D. *Social Readjustment Rating Scale.* Reprinted with permission.

Interpreting the Holmes Scale

The number assigned to each event is a measure of the stress it places on you. Note that many of these events should be happy ones— change itself may be stressful, even if the change is for the better.

For your "past" Holmes score, Dr. Holmes' research indicated the following:

80% of persons with scores greater than 300 suffered a serious illness within two years.

53% of persons with scores between 250 and 300 and 33% of persons with scores between 150 and 250 suffered similar illnesses.

Common sense says to take it a little easier, make those changes a little more slowly. Take your time in arriving at decisions. You can pace yourself even if you are in a hurry. By recognizing the importance of these changes, you can deal with them more effectively. Think about what they mean to you and get in touch with your feelings about them.

17

Environment

SHE WAS FIVE YEARS OLD. SHE LIVED IN THE WEALTHIEST COUN-
try on earth, during the age of the miracles of modern medicine. In
1977 in these United States, she died of worms.

Did she die because this was some rare organism? No, this worm
is a very common one and is carried by many dogs. Did she die because
she received no medical treatment? No, in fact, she spent the last
months of her life in the hospital. Did she die because this is a very
serious illness for which medical treatment can do little? No, there are
drugs for this illness but usually they are not needed. In the vast
majority of children, it is a mild and self-limited disease.

She died because of the environment. She was poor and that meant
that she did not have enough to eat, and that shelter and clothing were
inadequate. Her main opportunity for recreation was to play with dogs,
and so she did. And as she did she was constantly exposed to the risk
of infection with worms. This combination of factors, her environment,
conspired to turn what should have been a mild illness into a deadly
one.

This tragedy illustrates the enormous influence of environment on
health. Environment factors *do* have the ability to overwhelm the ca-
pacities of modern medicine. You have seen evidence of their effects
before. Recall from Chapter 2 that it was improvement in the environment—improved living standards and public health measures—that
accounted for the vast majority of the increase in life expectancy be-

tween the 1700s and the present. Undoubtedly you believe that you will never be exposed to an environment as unhealthy as that caused by this little girl's poverty or the realities of the world in the 1700s. You may be wrong.

Health and Today's Environment

The effects of the environment on health are complex. Often it is difficult to be specific about what it is in the environment that is good or bad. But there is a good deal of evidence supporting the old-fashioned notion that clean air, clean water, and "elbow room" are good for you. For example, several studies have shown that residents of rural areas are healthier and live longer than city dwellers. This is true despite the fact that there are more physicians and medical facilities in urban areas. Also, while it cannot be stated as a fact, there is some evidence that there is more mental illness in urban than in rural areas. Perhaps humans really do need some elbow room in order to keep their wits about them.

Knowledge concerning the specific elements of the environment is increasing rapidly. This is particularly true with respect to pollution with substances that may cause cancer. Consider the following:

■ Asbestos, which is used in automobile brake linings, insulation, and many industrial processes, may increase the risk of a particular type of lung cancer (mesothelioma) by as much as a thousand fold.

■ Air pollution is known to increase the effects of smoking in causing lung cancer and probably is able to cause cancer independently of smoking. The death rate due to lung cancer in Los Angeles is several times that in Chicago, apparently because of heavy air pollution in the Los Angeles basin.

■ On the basis of the amount of carcinogen (cancer-causing chemical) in the air, it has been estimated that breathing the air of an average-sized American city is the equivalent of smoking more than a third of a pack of cigarettes per day. In heavily polluted cities, it may be equivalent to two packs per day.

■ Solar radiation is directly associated with the incidence of skin cancer. The ozone layer of the atmosphere absorbs most solar radiation. Certain chemicals used as aerosol propellants have the capacity to reduce this layer. This could increase the amount of radiation reaching the earth's surface, which in turn could increase the amount of skin cancer.

■   The radiation of x-rays has been associated with a wide number of cancers. There is considerable evidence that we are not nearly so cautious as we should be with the use of x-rays. "Routine" x-rays taken during annual physicals, dental examinations, and upon admission to the hospital are often not justified. Equally important, the amount of radiation delivered in any particular x-ray depends on the equipment used and the skill of the person using it. For example, in the American Cancer Society's breast cancer screening project, some women received *60 times* more radiation than others.

■   A wide range of pesticides and industrial chemicals have been shown to be capable of causing cancer in animals. There is evidence that some of these, such as vinyl chloride, have already done so in humans. This is an especially troublesome finding since many of these chemicals cannot be broken down in nature. They also become more concentrated as they move up the "food chain." A well-known example is that of PCB, a pesticide that has contaminated many fresh water sources, especially those of the Great Lakes region and the Hudson River Valley. (The Sheboygan, Onion, and Mullet rivers in Wisconsin contain 150 times the "safe" level of PCB.) Virtually all of the fish in these waters contain significant amounts of the chemical. When these fish are eaten, the chemical becomes concentrated in certain portions of the human body. Finally, it can become concentrated and secreted into the milk of a woman who is breast feeding. This means that a child who is being breast fed is getting a large dosage in relation to body size. In studies done to date, fully 99 percent of all women tested had PCB in their breast milk.

■   Pollution of the air and water goes far beyond the threat of cancer. Polluted air is poison to the lungs. It presents a hazard to us all, but especially to those who already have a respiratory illness. As the air pollution index goes up, persons with asthma, emphysema, and other respiratory diseases begin to fill up emergency rooms and doctors' offices. While medicines are of some help for these patients, the most important consideration is removing them from the polluted air. These methods are not always successful and there is a significant death rate associated with rising air pollution. The contribution of air pollution to death and disease is occasionally dramatized by "killer smogs" such as the one that caused 4,000 deaths in London in 1952. A similar episode of intense pollution occurred in Donora, Pennsylvania, in 1948, when 50 percent of that town's 12,300 residents became ill and 20 persons died as a result.

■   The tradition of using our rivers as sewers may expose us to multiple hazards. These include those of kepone, a chemical that attacks the nervous system, causing tremors, weakness, and loss of coordination. So much kepone was dumped into the James River in Virginia that authorities now say that it may be impossible to ever remove it all. Another industry dumped so much mercury in the Shenandoah River that it is impossible to estimate whether or when it will be washed away. Fish in this river contain hazardous levels of mercury despite the fact that the dumping stopped 30 years ago. Significant numbers of fish die each year of mercury poisoning. Needless to say, eating such fish poses a threat of mercury poisoning to humans. Fishing in this beautiful river has been banned.

■ The heavy use of pesticides is boomeranging by creating "super pests" resistant to the effects of these dangerous chemicals. In addition, it appears that the pesticides actually make the plants *more* vulnerable to insect damage by altering plant physiology. Finally, the use of pesticides is associated with the emergence of new pests. In the words of one expert, "We have created monsters out of previously unknown pests." The response to this situation has been to use more pesticides, some farmers using 10 to 20 times the normal amount. It is hard to imagine a worse situation: The more we pollute the environment in an attempt to stop pests, the more damage they do.

How Bad Is the Environment?

The most disturbing fact of all is that we really don't know very much about how badly the environment has deteriorated. We know most about those things that might cause cancer, but even here our ignorance is enormous. Research on the environmental causes of cancer is difficult, but this is not the major reason we are so far behind. Investigation in this area receives less than 15 percent of all federal funds for cancer despite the National Cancer Institute's estimate that 90 percent of all cancer is environmentally caused. Even less is spent on subjects such as mercury contamination or the effects of pollution on health. In the final analysis, we know so little because we have been willing to spend so little to learn.

The reasons for this are not obscure. Major polluters are major businesses. Attempts to find out something about the environment, much less do something about it, often run into stiff opposition from those who have a financial interest in not knowing. This includes unions who fear loss of jobs if environmental standards are enforced. Overt efforts to prevent investigation and preservation of the environment may not be the worst of it. It now appears that a major portion of the data upon which the safety of pesticides was judged was, in fact, fraudulent. It may well turn out that levels of pesticides and other chemicals previously thought to be safe are not safe at all.

What Does This Mean to You?

Despite the inadequacy of our current knowledge, there seems to be little doubt that we have the capacity to re-create the Middle Ages in terms of environment and health. The environment will always retain its capacity to become the dominant factor with regard to health. It *is* possible to create an environment that can overwhelm the capacity of lifestyle and medical care to preserve health.

Technology can provide some solutions. It is possible to clean up automobile emission, to burn industrial fuel more thoroughly, and so on. But in the long run there is a Catch 22 of technology: Every technological solution brings on another technological problem. For example, General Motors has announced that it has a device that can convert virtually all auto emissions to water and carbon dioxide. But the device requires a substance called rhodium. To equip all General Motors vehicles with such a device would consume the entire world's output of rhodium.

More important, it is unlikely that technology can keep up with the problems created by an ever-expanding population. For example, in the area of Washington, D.C., there has been a continuing effort for over 25 years to clean up the Potomac River. During the last five years, many millions of dollars have been spent on improved sewage treatment facilities and approximately one *billion* will be spent in the next few years. Yet it now appears that the water of the Potomac may never be safe to swim in or to drink regardless of how much is spent. The reason: rain-run off from building sites, roads, and suburban lawns (so called "nonpoint sources") is so contaminated with debris, dirt, and chemicals (fertilizer, pesticides, asbestos, and the like) that it is rapidly becoming the largest cause of pollution. Sewage treatment facilities, of course, can do nothing about this pollution. Combine this fact with the likelihood that in the near future the demand for water will be so great that it will exceed the entire river flow on occasion. Now you have a problem for which technology has no answer: An increasing population creates more demand for water at the same time it increases the pollution in the water.

In the long run, we will have to learn to use less and to use it better. Our health in the future will depend on our ability to conserve and recycle, to eliminate waste, to stop being the throw-away society before we throw away our future.

The ultimate determinant of our ability to conserve the environment is population. There can be no healthy solution to the problem of an ever-increasing number of persons competing for ever-decreasing resources. Our health depends not only on whether or not we contaminate ourselves with poisons and chemicals that cause cancer, but also on whether there is enough food, clothing and living space to go around. Historically, there has been no better predictor of ill health than an increasing birth rate. The present provides us with ample evidence as well. There is no better generalization than that the poorest nations have the highest birth and death rates and the richest nations have the lowest birth and death rates. Within our society there is a similar pattern: The poorest American families have the most children while the richest have the fewest.

SECTION

IV

YOU AND THE ENEMY — WHAT TO DO ABOUT MAJOR DISEASES

THESE DISEASES ARE THE MAJOR KILLERS AND CRIPPLERS OF OUR time. Together with accidents and alcoholic cirrhosis of the liver (discussed in Section III), they account for more than 85 percent of all deaths. Just as important, they are diseases about which you can do something. With a few of these problems, you have been urged to do something that is ineffective and dangerous.

After a brief description of the disease, you will find information about its cause, prevention, treatment, and whether it can be detected before it causes symptoms. All of this is designed to help you answer the most important question: What should be done to protect yourself against this disease? The answers play an essential part in your LifePlan.

18
Heart Disease

HEART DISEASES ARE DIVIDED INTO THREE MAJOR CATEGORIES. some, called cardiomyopathies, affect only the heart muscle itself, and these are relatively rare. A second category affects the valves necessary for the pumping action of the heart. Rheumatic fever and congenital defects are the most important causes of valve damage. While problems with valves are not rare, the decrease in rheumatic fever has caused them to be much less frequent. Finally, there are diseases of the arteries that supply blood to the heart muscle. These include atherosclerosis, or "hardening of the arteries." As usual, there are a whole host of confusing medical terms and abbreviations for this problem—among them: arteriosclerotic coronary vascular disease (ASCVD), ischemic heart disease (IHD), atherosclerotic heart disease (AHD), and coronary heart disease (CHD). Coronary artery disease (CAD) is the term used in this book. As can be seen from the table on the next page, this is by far the most important cause of death in heart disease. It is this type of heart disease with which we will be concerned for the most part.

Many physicians consider hypertensive heart disease (heart disease due to high blood pressure) to be separate from CAD. Certainly there are cases in which a person who dies with high blood pressure has a large heart but no evidence of CAD. On the other hand, about 90 percent of persons with high blood pressure will have evidence of CAD at autopsy. Whether high blood pressure creates a unique kind of heart disease or merely contributes to CAD remains controversial. For the

Heart disease, the no. 1 killer in America	
	Deaths (1974)
Coronary artery disease	671,140
Rheumatic heart disease	13,440
Hypertensive heart disease	11,690
Cardiomyopathies	5,190
All other forms of heart disease, including congenital heart defects	45,020

sake of simplicity, we will regard high blood pressure as contributing to CAD.

The basic problem in atherosclerosis is the accumulation of materials on the inside of the arteries so that the flow of blood is blocked. An adequate supply of blood is critical to all body tissues, of course, but it is especially important in the heart, which is the hardest working muscle in the body. If an artery is so clogged that a portion of heart muscle dies, this is termed "myocardial infarction," or simply "MI" in medical jargon. In plainer language, this is a heart attack. When an artery is clogged so that the flow of blood is insufficient but not so poor as to cause death of the muscle, then there is "ischemia," meaning that the blood flow is not providing adequate amounts of oxygen. Ischemia in almost any tissue results in pain, the most direct way of letting us know that something is wrong. Heart pain due to ischemia is called "angina pectoris," or simply "angina."

CAD also may prevent the heart from pumping properly so that circulation of blood to the rest of the body is impaired. This problem is known as "congestive heart failure," or "CHF." CHF may be caused by any kind of heart disease and it is not necessary to have had a heart attack or to have angina in order to have CHF.

What Causes Heart Disease?

High blood pressure, smoking, obesity, lack of exercise, decreased HDL cholesterol, increased LDL cholesterol, and increased triglycerides (fats) in the blood are strongly associated with an increased risk of heart disease. (The difference between HDL and LDL cholesterol is explained on the next page.) For this reason, they're usually referred to as *risk factors*. Exactly how risk factors may cause heart disease is not known at present, but this does not decrease their importance to you. You can still do something about each one of these risk factors even though you don't know exactly how they do their dirty work.

A strong family history of heart attacks at an early age probably increases your own risk of heart attack. However, it is likely that a large part of the risk attributed to family history in the past is actually due to some combination of the risk factors mentioned above, not just to heredity. Still, it is likely that some risk attaches to a strong family history of heart attacks over and beyond these other risk factors. It is very difficult to know exactly how large this risk is, but it is probably small in comparison to other factors. Whatever its magnitude, it should rank at the bottom of your list of concerns since you cannot change your family history. Concentrate on those things you can affect, for there is a good chance that these can more than compensate for an unfavorable family history.

There is considerable interaction among risk factors and they have a nasty tendency to gang up on you. Blood pressure tends to go up as weight goes up. People who seldom exercise are often overweight, and people who are overweight often have elevated LDL cholesterol, decreased HDL cholesterol and elevated triglycerides. Smoking is the most independent of the risk factors. Having an ideal weight and a low blood pressure will not save you from the effects of smoking.

One of the most important recent developments in medicine is that of making a distinction between the two types of cholesterol. While a detailed discussion of the biochemistry involved is beyond the scope of this book, you should know that the total cholesterol in the blood can be separated into two different portions, depending on the type of molecules to which it is attached. An increase in the amount of the cholesterol attached to low density lipoprotein (LDL) is associated with an increased risk of CAD. In contrast, an increased amount of cholesterol attached to high density lipoprotein (HDL) is associated with a decreased risk of CAD. These new facts help explain why total cholesterol as used in the past sometimes did not seem to be a very good predictor of CAD. It also goes a long way toward explaining why women have decreased risk of heart attacks during their childbearing years, since they usually have more HDL cholesterol and less LDL cholesterol than men. (It also seems to explain why dogs do not have very much heart disease—they too have high levels of HDL cholesterol.) Perhaps the most important development as far as your health is concerned is that exercise appears to have the ability to change the relative amount of cholesterol types in a beneficial way. That is, it appears that exercise increases the amount of HDL cholesterol. Thus exercise that is safe, inexpensive, and available to all may be able to do what expensive and dangerous drugs have not.

Interestingly enough, alcohol does not seem to be significantly correlated with an increased rate of death due to heart disease. One explanation may be that moderate amounts of alcohol (one to two cocktails per day) are actually beneficial while large amounts have a detrimental effect. The Honolulu Heart Study reported such a relationship and also suggested that this might be due to an increase in HDL cholesterol and a decrease in LDL cholesterol associated with moderate alcohol use. Other physicians, somewhat more cynical (or realistic, depending on your outlook), simply say that alcoholics die of other things before they get a chance to die of heart disease.

As you might expect, initial indications are that smoking and being overweight are associated with decreased HDL cholesterol and increased LDL cholesterol.

Damage to heart valves by rheumatic fever is called rheumatic heart disease. Rheumatic fever usually occurs from two weeks to six months after a streptococcal infection, usually a strep throat. Exactly how rheumatic fever is caused is not known. It does not appear to be due to an infection by the streptococcal bacteria themselves. Most likely it is an abnormal immunologic reaction to a preceding streptococcal infection. Nevertheless, treatment of the streptococcal infection with antibiotics is important in preventing rheumatic fever. If the streptococcal infection is untreated, rheumatic fever occurs in from .4 to 3 percent of cases, depending on the type of infection. If rheumatic fever occurs, from 40 to 75 percent of cases eventually develop damage to their heart valves (rheumatic heart disease). Therefore, rheumatic heart disease occurs in from .2 to 2 percent of persons with untreated streptococcal infections. The lower figure appears to be closer to the actual risk.

Can We Prevent Heart Disease?

All indications are that a change in lifestyle that results in a lowering of the risk factors will go a long way toward preventing heart disease. Many studies show that lifestyle has more influence on heart disease than heredity or geographic location. The degree of protection afforded by beneficial lifestyle seems to be very significant. The evidence for this is discussed in detail in Chapters 8, 9, and 10. As the next two tables show, Americans have made changes in their lifestyle and these changes have been paralleled by very significant drops in death rates due to heart disease and stroke. In addition to the changes in these tables, it seems clear that the number of persons exercising reg-

**Change (per person) in use of certain
products from 1963 to 1975**

Product	Change
All tobacco products	22.4% decline
Fluid milk and cream	19.2% decline
Butter	31.9% decline
Eggs	12.6% decline
Animal fats & oils	56.7% decline
Vegetable fats & oils	44.1% increase

**Decline in death rate due to heart
disease and stroke from 1963 to 1975**

	Decline	
Age	*Heart disease*	*Stroke*
35–44	27.2%	19.1%
45–54	27.4%	31.7%
55–64	23.5%	34.1%
65–74	25.3%	33.2%
75–84	12.8%	21.9%
85+	19.3%	29.4%

ularly has increased dramatically. Keep these figures in mind the next
time you hear someone say that antismoking or other health-informa-
tion campaigns do not work.

Those who are looking for a pill to do for them what they will not
do for themselves are in big trouble. One of the more remarkable
fallacies of our time is that there are drugs that safely lower cholesterol
and/or fats in the blood and, therefore, lower the risk of heart attacks.
In the best study done to date, the Coronary Drug Project conducted
by the Veterans Administration, some of these drugs actually *increased*

the chance of death due to heart attack while others had no significant effect at all. If you are using any of the drugs listed below *to lower cholesterol or fats*, then it is time you had a real heart-to-heart talk with your doctor.

Generic Name	*Brand Name*
Thyroxine (Thyroid Hormone)	Choloxin, Euthroid
Nicotinic Acid (Niacin)	Nicobid, Nicocap, Nicotinex, Nico-400
Clofibrate	Atromid-S
Conjugated Equine Estrogens	Femest

Prevention of rheumatic heart disease depends on prevention of rheumatic fever. Treating a streptococcal infection with penicillin or other antibiotics reduces the chance of subsequent rheumatic fever by about 90 percent. Strep throats and scarlet fever account for the majority of streptococcal infections. A throat culture is the best way to tell whether a sore throat is due to streptococcus. This often will be required in scarlet fever as well, although sometimes the appearance of the rash and the throat is so characteristic that the diagnosis can be made on these alone.

Can We Treat Heart Disease?

Drugs are fairly effective in relieving angina and certain abnormalities of the heartbeat (arrhythmias). Other drugs are also quite helpful in relieving the shortness of breath and swelling of the ankles that occurs in congestive heart failure. In other words, medicines can relieve some of the symptoms of these diseases and sometimes this relief is very dramatic. On the other hand, there is little evidence that these drugs actually change the course of the diseases a great deal. We can make someone feel better, but we cannot cure the disease. A major disappointment has been the coronary care unit (CCU), which was originally believed to have the potential of reducing the mortality due to heart attacks by 50 percent. It now appears that these expensive units have little effect on the mortality due to heart attacks or congestive heart failure. Several studies have shown that the CCU was no better than the standard hospital ward in decreasing deaths. At least one study indicates that *home* treatment is superior to hospital treatment, at least for one group of patients—elderly men with uncomplicated heart attacks. This is understandable. The CCU is a dangerous place that exposes patients to a great deal of stress. (See Chapters 4 and 16). It can treat effectively some of the complications of heart attack (abnormal heartbeats) but does not do anything about the basic disease itself. It appears that most of the deaths prevented in the CCU nevertheless occur within a year after the patient leaves the hospital.

The surgical treatment of CAD, called coronary artery bypass grafting (CABG) is an attempt to relieve the problem by simply providing another route for blood around the obstruction in the artery. A vein is taken from the leg and attached to the artery above and below the clogged portion of the artery. This procedure often is successful in relieving angina when drugs have failed. Needless to say, the surgery itself is quite major and carries considerable risk. The most disturbing part of the CABG business is that this procedure was promoted for almost 10 years before any careful studies of it were available. Unlike drugs, surgical procedures are not required to be tested before they are used on the public. Before CABG was studied, it was common for its promoters to suggest that it increased life expectancy in almost all types of coronary artery disease. It now appears that this is true for only a small group of persons with this disease. Now consider this: Even with this information, we are spending about a *billion* dollars a year on CABG. If we had operated on the basis that CABG increases life expectancy for everyone with detectable coronary artery disease, we would have spent about 75 *billion* dollars. One billion or 75 billion, it's an incredible amount to spend on a procedure of uncertain value.

Open-heart surgery to repair damaged heart valves is a different matter. These procedures are clearly of benefit in rheumatic heart disease and other valvular heart diseases. They do not cure, however. Replacement valves do not function quite as well as normal valves. They eventually wear out and are associated with a number of complications. Each surgical procedure carries substantial risk, especially when it is repeat surgery to replace a worn out artificial valve.

Heart transplants are best regarded as a medical curiosity and last-chance procedure that has provided some very expensive headlines but no breakthrough in the treatment of heart disease.

Can We Detect Heart Disease Before It Causes Symptoms?

For CAD the answer is "yes and no." The original definition of CAD required the presence of some symptoms such as angina or heart attack. Therefore "asymptomatic" CAD would have been a contradiction in terms. The requirement for symptoms made a good deal of sense in view of the fact that it was known that the vast majority of Americans middle-aged or older had some atherosclerosis of their coronary arteries ("hardening" of the arteries of the heart). For example, a study of young soldiers killed in the Korean War showed that 77 percent of them had atherosclerosis of their coronary arteries. Their average age was 22. A large autopsy study of Americans of all ages killed in accidents showed that 75 percent of these persons had at least one of the three main coronary arteries more than 25 percent blocked by atherosclerosis. Thus in its original usage the term CAD differentiated not so much between those who had atherosclerosis and those who didn't as between those who had symptoms due to their atherosclerosis and those who didn't.

The advent of electrocardiograph stress testing and coronary arteriography led to a change in the definition of CAD. The electrocardiographic stress test essentially consists of taking a continuous electrocardiogram during progressively harder exercise. The coronary arteriogram is an x-ray procedure by which the inside of coronary arteries may be seen. CAD is now thought of as significant blockage of a coronary artery or arteries. The amount of blockage required varies somewhat but at least 50 percent of blockage of one artery is typical. If you are living, have not had a heart attack, and do not have any symptoms, then coronary arteriography is the only way by which a diagnosis of CAD can be made at present. Unfortunately, coronary arteriography is a complex procedure with a significant chance of causing disability and/or death itself. It is not acceptable as a screening procedure. The electrocardiographic stress test also has some chance of causing disability and/or death, but it is considerably less than that of coronary arteriography. Unfortunately, the results of electrocardiographic stress testing in persons without symptoms do not correlate very well with meeting the requirements for the diagnosis of CAD by coronary arteriogram. As many as 47 percent of persons with "abnormal" stress tests *do not* have CAD by coronary arteriography, and as many as 62 percent of persons with "normal" electrocardiographic stress tests *do* have CAD by coronary arteriography. Clearly, both of these procedures have features that prohibit their use as routine tests on persons without symptoms of heart disease.

All types of valvular disease, including rheumatic heart disease, may cause heart murmurs that can be picked up on physical examination before they cause symptoms. However, the vast majority of heart murmurs are not indications of disease, especially in children. This and other factors combine to severely limit the usefulness of the physical examination as a means of screening for valvular diseases of the heart. Indeed, a study of one such large scale screening effort indicated that it did more harm than good, because the detection of murmurs *not* caused by heart disease still convinced some children and their parents that there was a heart problem. These families then acted as if the child were sick with a serious heart problem. The effect of the screening program was to give heart disease to some children who had none.

What Should You Do About Heart Disease?

Prevention of both CAD and rheumatic heart disease is effective. Treatment of CAD may decrease symptoms, but is largely ineffective in changing the course of the disease. Surgery does produce good results in many patients with rheumatic heart disease and other diseases of the heart valves, but the surgery is hazardous and painful and the relief it affords is not permanent.

Detection of CAD before it causes symptoms is fraught with difficulties. More importantly, it makes little difference to detect CAD before it causes symptoms because you already know what you want to do before it is detected: Alter your lifestyle to give yourself the best possible chance of preventing the disease rather than hoping drugs or surgery can cure it. Drugs and surgery have narrow applications—and only in those who have symptoms or disability due to CAD. As for valvular disease, attempts to detect it before it causes symptoms may do more harm than good.

The most rational approach is to change risk factors to give yourself the best shot at health and long life. Stop smoking, start exercising, watch your weight, and perhaps avoid foods rich in cholesterol and saturated fats. All the cholesterol tests, electrocardiograms, and stress tests in the world will not tell you anything more than this.

A blood pressure check once a year is the most important thing that your doctor can do for you. Skip your annual physical and use the time to read Chapters 8, 9 and 10.

19

Cancer

CANCER IS NOT ONE DISEASE BUT MANY. THE IMAGE OF A SINGLE, invincible disease that can strike down any person at any age is basically the creation of those who would like you to continue to contribute to find "the cure." With literally hundreds of different kinds of cancer, each with its own peculiar characteristics and quirks, the chance of finding a medicine or procedure to cure all cancers is virtually nil. Yet, despite the fact that no expert in the cancer field thinks that a single cure will ever be found, we are continually reminded of the need to find a cure for "it" in our lifetime.

The common denominator linking all these diseases is the phenomena of cells out of control. Cancer cells grow without restraint, invade adjacent tissues, and spread (metastasize) to other parts of the body. These cells lose their ability to function as normal cells, although some may actually overproduce some substances normally found in the body. For example, some thyroid cancers will produce thyroid hormones and cancers of the ovary sometimes produce sex hormones. Cancers may also produce toxic substances, and these have been blamed for the anemia and weight-loss that often accompanies this group of illnesses. Still, it is relatively rare for toxic substances to be the main problem with most cancers. They do most of their damage by invading and replacing normal tissue.

Medically, the term tumor simply means swelling. The vast majority of tumors are not malignant (cancerous). These tumors are called benign, but sometimes can cause serious problems simply by creating pressure on other structures. This is common with benign brain tumors since the skull is rigid and cannot expand to relieve pressure. Benign tumors are more likely to produce normal tissue substances than malignant ones. For example, a thyroid tumor that produces thyroid hormones is much more likely to be benign than malignant.

The history of cancer in the country should teach us some valuable lessons, although those who make public health policy—you and your representatives in government—seem reluctant to learn them. The next two figures, showing age-adjusted cancer death rates for males and females, give the death rates for the most important types of cancer. These curves can be divided into three groups: (1) Clearly going up—lung cancer, with women beginning to reap the "rewards" of equality in smoking. (2) Clearly going down—cancer of the stomach and uterus for reasons that are not known for certain (see below). (3) Not clearly going anywhere—everything else. The overall result is that the death rate due to all forms of cancer is going *up*. Why? Because an epidemic of a disease caused by lifestyle and environment—lung cancer—far outweighs the effects of "the war on cancer" and everything else med-

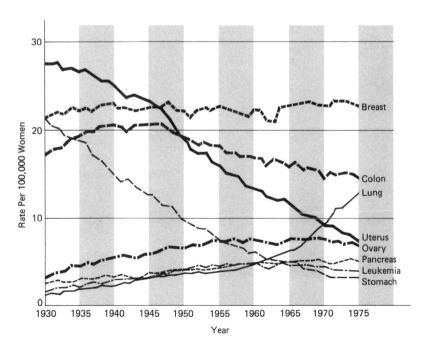

Sources: U.S. National Center for Health Statistics and U.S. Bureau of the Census, by courtesy of the American Cancer Society.

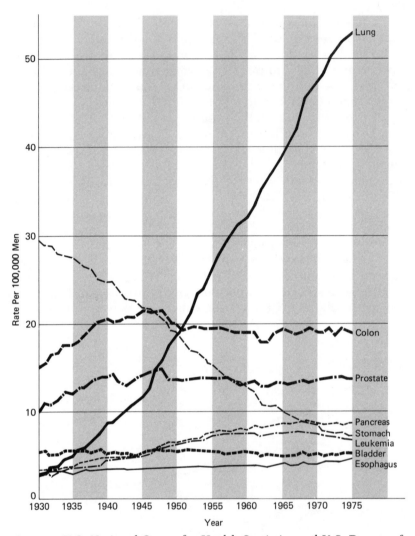

Sources: U.S. National Center for Health Statistics and U.S. Bureau of the Census, by courtesy of the American Cancer Society.

icine has to offer. Pause a moment in memory of the millions who have died of a preventable disease while billions have been spent to find a "cure."

In the following discussion we are going to confine ourselves to those cancers that are not rare and that may be prevented or may be treated effectively. These account for approximately half of all cancers. Most others can not be prevented, detected, or treated satisfactorily.

What Causes Cancer?

The diversity of the diseases called cancer is most apparent when one considers the hundreds of things that are known to produce cancer in laboratory animals. This includes everything from acids to x-rays. An important group of these causes are chemicals, and the term "carcinogen" usually indicates such a chemical. However, it may be used for any agent that causes cancer. By the same token, anything that causes cancer may be called "carcinogenic." The accompanying table lists some chemicals and the human cancers with which they have been linked. Many other industrial chemicals, pesticides, food dyes and additives, and chemicals used in cosmetics have been shown to cause cancer in laboratory animals. How this relates to human cancer is a subject of great and continuing controversy. At present it can only be said that these findings cast an ominous shadow for the future, since (1) these chemicals are in widespread use and (2) the effects of carcinogens often are not seen for years after exposure begins.

Several carcinogens have been found in tobacco smoke, but which one(s) are doing most of the damage is a subject of controversy. It is likely that these chemicals are absorbed into the body and spread to

Chemicals believed to cause cancer in humans

Chemical	Type of cancer
Asbestos	Lungs
Diethyl stilbestrol	Vagina
Benzidine	Urinary bladder
Vinyl chloride	Liver
Certain tars, soots, and oils	Skin, lungs
Estrogens	Uterus
Nickel compounds	Lungs, nasal sinuses
Chromium compounds	Lungs
Aniline dyes (2-Napthylamine)	Urinary bladder
Azo dyes (Amino azotoluene)	Liver
Arsenic	Skin
Benzene	Leukemia
Aflatoxin	Liver

many tissues. Smoking is associated not only with cancers of the respiratory system (lip, mouth, larynx, and lung) but also with cancer of the esophagus and of the bladder.

Viruses have long been known to cause certain cancers in animals, but to date only one type of human cancer, Burkett's lymphoma, may be said to have a viral cause. As one of the highest priorities in the "war on cancer," research into viral causes of cancer has been supported with millions upon millions of taxpayers' dollars. While new scientific knowledge has been gained, it is a major disappointment that this has produced little that can be applied usefully to human cancer. In truth it must be said that as of now it would be difficult to prove that any cancer victim has benefited from this research.

Cancers of the stomach and intestine may vary markedly between countries with very different diets. This has spurred the search for a dietary cause of cancer. To date, it has not been confirmed that any diet will cause or prevent cancer. Certain food additives in very large doses cause cancer in experimental animals, but the implications with respect to humans are not clear. Recall from the two figures you just saw that the only cancer that is clearly causing fewer deaths in both sexes is that of the stomach. There is evidence that the food preservatives BHT and BHA contributed to this *decrease* in stomach cancer. The question of food additives is discussed more fully in Chapter 9.

Radiation, both from x-rays and from the sun, has long been known to cause cancer. Yet at one time some doctors used x-ray treatments to reduce the size of tonsils and adenoids and to treat acne and ringworm of the scalp (tinea capitis). Now, 15 to 30 years later, we are seeing the effect: An increase in cancer of the head and neck, especially of the thyroid gland. In fact, the incidence of thyroid cancer in young adults has increased two to four times. Undoubtedly these doctors believed that the amount of radiation was too small to cause harm. From the days of Madame Curie (who discovered radium and also died from cancer caused by radiation) to the present there has been a continuing debate as to how much is necessary to produce a malignancy. It now appears that the effects of small amounts of radiation have been underestimated. For example, the radiation involved in an x-ray to detect breast cancer (xeromammogram) has been estimated to *increase* the risk of breast cancer by .01 to .6 percent. If such tests were done on *all* women every year, they would help kill more women than they would help cure. There is even some evidence that relatively small amounts of x-rays given to either parent at any time in their life may increase the chance of leukemia in their children later on. This should not be regarded as proven, however.

The influence of familial factors is seen in several cancers. A history of breast cancer in mother or sister increases the individual's risk for this disease. Jewish women are slightly more likely to develop cancer of the uterus than non-Jewish women.

There are a number of factors that increase the risk of cancer by unknown mechanisms. The most important example is the increased risk of uterine cancer when sexual activity began at an early age or has been heavy and with many different partners.

A confusing factor in the search for causes of cancer is the fact that the various causes may interact to *multiply* their effect. For example, asbestos exposure alone may increase the chance of lung cancer only two times, but exposure in a heavy smoker increases the chance *70* times. That an interaction is sometimes required to produce cancer can be seen in the strange case of the virus that causes Burkett's lymphoma. This cancer is found almost exclusively in Africa and is only rarely reported in this country. However, the virus that causes Burkett's lymphoma appears to be the same virus that causes infectious mononucleosis. Why do Americans get mono while Africans get cancer? It seems clear that something in addition to the virus must be present before it can cause a cancer.

Can We Prevent Cancer?

Yes! At least 25 percent of all cancer deaths may be prevented. Two Nobel Prize winners have estimated that more than 75 percent of all cancer deaths could have been prevented. There are more than 10 types of cancer that are known to be preventable or for which the possibility of prevention has been seriously weighed.

Lung cancer accounts for about 23 percent of all cancers, and the vast majority of this is caused by cigarette smoking. Mesothelioma, one of the less frequent types of lung cancer, may be caused by asbestos, which is used in brake linings, fire-proofing materials, and insulation.

Smoking is also associated with a greater risk of cancer of the lip, mouth, larynx, esophagus, and bladder. If stopping the use of tobacco were the only preventive measure taken, this step alone would reduce the amount of cancer by about 25 percent.

Cancers of the liver are among the less frequent types. However, many of these cancers occur either in persons with cirrhosis (due to alcohol abuse, for the most part) or in persons exposed to vinyl chloride in their jobs. It is very likely that much cancer of the liver could be prevented if exposure to vinyl chloride and alcohol abuse could be limited. Alcoholism is also associated with increased rates of cancer of the larynx, esophagus, stomach, and pancreas.

Prolonged exposure to the sun over many years is associated with increased risk of the most common types (basal cell, squamous cell) of skin cancer. However, the deadliest type of skin cancer (melanoma) does not appear to be associated with exposure to the sun. Also, limiting exposure to the sun may not be a very practical alternative for many persons (farm laborers, etc.) because they really have no alternatives in terms of their work. Application to the skin of chemicals to block the sun's rays (sunscreens) is not known to be of benefit when exposure cannot be avoided.

High risks of cancer of the cervix (uterus) are associated with sexual activity beginning at an early age, with frequent sexual activity with many different partners, and with being Jewish. Again, the proposal to prevent some of the cancers of the cervix by limiting sexual activity may not be very practical.

Thyroid cancer resulting from x-rays was mentioned above. While these types of treatment are no longer used (so far as we know), we should all be well warned concerning the hazards of radiation and avoid unnecessary x-rays.

Cancer of the colon appears to be less frequent in certain societies in which there is more fiber and/or less meat in the diet. However, the connection between either of these substances and cancer is far from clear. For more information, see Chapters 9 ("Diet") and 3 ("Making Health Decisions").

There are ominous indications that the cancer risk in environment is substantial and growing. Consider this:

- The risk of death due to lung cancer in Los Angeles is substantially higher than in Chicago. The most likely reason is the air pollution in Los Angeles. (The percentage of smokers is about the same in both cities.)

- The concentration of asbestos is rapidly rising in our water sources, in the air, and in the earth. In some instances the contamination is due to industrial pollution, as in the case of the Reserve Mining Company's contamination of Lake Superior. A more widespread threat appears to be the asbestos that contaminates the environment as automobile brake linings become worn.

- It appears that we have the capacity to destroy the ozone layer in the atmosphere. This layer blocks much of the sun's radiation and prevents it from reaching the earth's surface. As it deteriorates, our radiation exposure increases.

- A large number of pesticides and other industrial chemicals appear to be capable of causing cancer. As of yet, we do not know how much of a threat this poses (see Chapter 17).

This may have an ironic twist to it: As the amount of cancer rises, the percentage of that which is preventable will also rise. Perhaps the first strategy of the war on cancer should be to put nothing into the environment that causes more cancer.

Can We Treat Cancer?

The effectiveness of cancer treatment is a subject of constant debate. Is a treatment effective if it extends life for a year but the patient still dies of the disease? Is that year worth living considering the pain and disability the treatment itself frequently causes? These questions can be resolved only on a case-by-case basis. The answers depend more on the patient's own values than anything else. Suffice it to say that most people will pursue the slimmest hope and that doctors find it nearly impossible to say that nothing can be done. With the exceptions discussed below, treatment must be considered to offer little chance of cure. One must remember, however, that cancers vary enormously in their prognosis. Most patients with lung cancer will be dead within six to twelve months of the discovery of the tumor, whereas most patients with breast cancer will survive for more than five years. This is true regardless of the type of treatment or whether there is any treatment at all.

With few exceptions, surgical removal of a cancer that has not spread is the only method by which cures are achieved. The likelihood that the cancer has spread before surgery is performed depends on the characteristics of the particular cancer and just plain luck. For example, cancer of the lower lip grows slowly and is often noted and removed before spread has occurred. Ninety-five percent of persons with this cancer will be cured. This is almost never the case in cancer of the pancreas, a silent disease that produces symptoms only in its last stages. Less than 10 percent of those who have cancer of the pancreas will be alive one year after its discovery.

The thought that surgery would be more successful if performed earlier is logical. Surprisingly, there is little scientific evidence to indicate that we can discover cancers earlier or that we will be able to do so in the foreseeable future. The desire to be successful with treatment has led to an unfortunate emphasis on annual physicals and other procedures that are not effective. Those procedures that may be of help are discussed in the next section.

The treatment of cancer with radiation or with drugs has produced cures in only a few types of cancers. Hodgkin's disease and certain other lymphomas (these are cancers of the lymph glands) are treated effectively with radiation or drugs or a combination of the two. A relatively rare tumor of the uterus, choriocarcinoma, appears to be susceptible to the use of drugs. These therapies are very hazardous in themselves. It is usual for them to cause at least some amount of disability and it is not uncommon for the patient to die of a complication of the therapy itself. Rather than cure, the use of radiation and drugs usually results in some temporary relief from the disease, or remission. Remissions vary greatly depending on the type of cancer and the individual in whom they occur. Perhaps the most dramatic examples are those induced in childhood leukemias. Before the drugs were available, children with leukemia usually succumbed within four months. Now the average survival time is approximately two and a half years. However, only a small percentage will live as long as five years.

Can We Detect Cancer Before It Causes Symptoms?

A Pap smear is an effective way of detecting cancer of the cervix. If such a cancer is present, a single Pap smear will reveal it in 80 to 95 percent of cases.

Ninety percent of breast cancers are discovered by self-examination (palpation) of the breast. Many of these cancers were detected by chance rather than through monthly, regular self-examination. Waiting for your doctor to detect a lump at your yearly exam stacks the odds against you. Do not rely on xeromammography (x-ray) of the breast alone, even if it has been recommended to you. One large study found that in women under age 50, 61 percent of cancers were found by palpation alone, while only 19 percent were detected by xeromammography alone. In women over age 50, about 40 percent of breast cancers were detected by palpation alone and an equal number were detected by xeromammography alone. As explained above, xeromammography has the serious drawback of radiation exposure. Self-examination should be your first line of defense against breast cancer. Xeromammography should be used only in women at high risk for breast cancer—that is, those with a history of breast cancer in themselves, their mothers, or their sisters.

Many tumors of the thyroid can be felt with the fingers (palpation). Periodic palpation by a physician has not been demonstrated to be of value in the general population, but appears to be very valuable in persons who received x-ray treatments to head or neck and are at high risk for thyroid cancer. Self-examination of the thyroid can be taught, but again its value has not been demonstrated.

Beyond these procedures, we must be much more cautious about saying what it is that we can detect at an early stage. Skin cancers may be detected by regular inspection and knowing what to look for, although there is no hard and fast evidence that this has a significant effect on the number of deaths or disability due to skin cancer. The same is true for self-examination of the testes.

Yearly or twice-yearly rectal examinations for cancer of the prostate and cancer of the bowel have been advocated. While logical in some respects, the value of such examinations has not been demonstrated. The evidence available does support the recommendation of a proctosigmoidoscopic examination (looking into the rectum and lower bowel through a tube) once after the age of 50. Having such an examination before the age of 50 or on a frequent basis after the age of 50 has not been demonstrated to be of help. Testing the stool for hidden blood every year after the age of 50 can be recommended because it is so inexpensive (about 13¢) and safe, although its value has yet to be demonstrated. A major drawback is that many minor problems (hemorrhoids, stomach irritation from aspirin) may cause some blood in the stool.

X-rays to detect lung cancer must be condemned as a totally ineffective method of detecting early cancer of the lung and as an unnecessary exposure to radiation.

There is no evidence that other tests to detect cancer that are so persistently advocated by some have anything to offer. They may very well cause harm. Certainly the annual physical has been vastly overrated as a means of dealing with cancer. It has not been demonstrated to be of benefit, much less to justify its cost and risk.

What Should You Do About Cancer?
It should be clear from the above that prevention is by far your best bet. If you don't smoke, and if you avoid the chemicals listed in the table you saw earlier in this chapter, you will cut the risk of cancer in half. You will be virtually assured of not having lung cancer, cancer of the liver (assuming you're not already dying of cirrhosis), and several relatively rare tumors. Your risk of bladder cancer will be reduced. Best of all, you will enjoy a number of other benefits, especially if you stop smoking. See Chapter 10 for a discussion of the more than 20 serious medical problems you will avoid by not smoking.

Any excess radiation increases the chance of a malignancy. On the other hand, in most x-rays the radiation can be limited to a relatively small amount and the x-ray may be very valuable in treating illness. If the x-ray is really needed, then it should be done. Otherwise, it should be avoided. "Routine" x-rays done for annual physicals, dental examinations, work permits, and on admission to the hospital are to be avoided unless you already have a particular problem that requires them to be performed. Keep track of the x-rays you have had by recording them in your PHR. This will help you to:

■ Avoid "repeats" because you don't know whether, when, or where you had a particular type of x-ray

■ Better understand the number of x-rays and the amount of radiation you are receiving, and

■ Ask specific questions about the need for a particular x-ray such as, "Why do I need this x-ray when I had the same one six months ago?"

Whenever you do have an x-ray, insist that you be provided with a gonadal shield to limit the amount of radiation to ovaries or testes.

There are several things you can do to detect cancer. Monthly breast self-examination is by far the most important. This is described below. You may choose to examine your own skin, thyroid, and testes. Although these examinations have not been shown to be effective, they are safe and the price is right. Your physician, nurse, or public health agency can teach you how.

The doctor's office has some specific procedures that are worth considering. Although a Canadian study found no evidence that screening with Pap smears resulted in a decrease in cancer deaths, an American study came to the opposite conclusion. A Pap smear every year or two after the age of 25, or after sexual activity becomes regular, seems prudent. (This is especially important if any of the factors discussed on page 210 are present.) The physician can examine your breasts at the same time. Proctosigmoidoscopy should be done once after age 50; doing it more frequently has not been shown to be of value. A test for hidden blood in the stool should be performed every two years after age 40 and yearly after age 50. Rectal examinations are of unknown value and must be regarded as optional at best. Xeromammography (breast x-rays) should be considered after the age of 40 in women who have a mother or sister who has had breast cancer. Otherwise, the value of screening with x-rays has not been shown, although this may eventually prove to be useful after age 50. If you received x-ray treatments to the head or neck for tonsils, adenoids, acne, or ringworm, then a yearly thyroid examination is a must.

If you prefer to wait for medical science to find a cure, then buy as much life insurance and health insurance as you can. At least then your family won't have to suffer financially.

How To Do A Breast Self-Examination
Most lumps in the breast are not cancer. Most women will have a lump in a breast at some time during their life. Many women's breasts are naturally lumpy (so-called "benign fibrocystic disease"). Obviously every lump or possible lump cannot and should not be subjected to surgery.

Cancer of the breast does occur, however. Regular self-examination of your breasts gives you the best chance of avoiding serious consequences. Self-examination should be monthly, just after the menstrual period.

The technique is as follows:

■ First, examine your breasts in the mirror, first with your arms at your side and then with both arms over your head. The breasts should look the same. Watch for any change in shape or size, or for dimpling of the skin. Occasionally a lump that is difficult to feel will be quite obvious just by looking.

■ Next, while lying flat, examine the left breast, using the inner finger tips of the right hand. Press the breast tissue gently against the chest wall. Roll the tissue between your fingers and the chest wall by moving your fingers in a circular pattern. Do not pinch the tissue between the fingers, for all breast tissue feels a bit lumpy when you do this. The left hand should be behind your head while you examine the inner half of the left breast and down at your side when you examine the outer half. Do not neglect the part of the breast underneath the nipples or that which extends outward from the breast toward the underarm. A small pillow under the left shoulder may help.

■ Repeat this process on the opposite side.

Any lump detected should be brought to the attention of your physician. Regular self-examination will tell you how long it has been present and whether it has changed in size. This information is very helpful in deciding what to do about the lump, for even the doctor often has difficulty with this decision. Self-examination is an absolute necessity for a woman with naturally lumpy breasts, since she is the only one who can really know whether a lump is new, old, or has changed size. For all women, regular self-examination offers the best hope that surgery will be performed when, and only when, it is necessary.

20
Stroke

STROKE OCCURS WHEN CIRCULATION TO A PART OF THE BRAIN BE-
comes inadequate. The brain tissue then dies and a part of the brain's
functioning is lost. Strokes may affect any area of the brain. They may
cause a problem with memory, reasoning, or personality. The vast
majority of strokes affect the control of the body's muscles and sensation is often affected as well. If loss of muscular control is complete,
then there is paralysis. If the loss is only partial, then there is weakness
and this is termed "paresis." The vast majority of strokes are said to
be "localized." This means that the paralysis, paresis, or loss of sensation is confined to one part of the body. Because of the way the brain
is structured, these problems are usually confined to one side of the
body. For example, it would be common for a stroke to cause a weakness of the left arm and left leg, but it would be unusual for a single
stroke to cause weakness in both arms and both legs without other
severe symptoms. A stroke so massive as to affect the entire body
usually results in coma and death. Thus a feeling of generalized weakness and fatigue should not be a cause for concern about stroke.

Transient ischemic attacks (TIA's) are the subject of considerable
interest and controversy today. They occur when blood flow is insufficient, but not so poor as to cause the death of brain tissue. In many
ways, TIA's resemble mild, temporary strokes. Common symptoms are
temporary clumsiness and numbness in hand or foot, or slurring of

speech. Unfortunately, some types of TIA's can produce nonspecific symptoms such as dizziness. The controversy concerning TIA's stems from the notion that TIA's should be looked for intensely and treated vigorously in order to prevent a stroke. Unfortunately, there is little evidence that we can effectively prevent strokes in most persons suffering TIA's. Moreover, symptoms such as dizziness are so generalized and nonspecific that the diagnosis of TIA is often difficult. We would do a great deal of harm to suggest that everyone with dizziness be considered to be possibly having a TIA. Persons under the age of 40 with dizziness almost never have a TIA as the cause and it is a relatively rare cause even in elderly persons. However, if an episode has a good chance of being a TIA, it should be brought to the attention of a physician.

What Causes Stroke?

The villain is usually atherosclerosis, or "hardening of the arteries"—the same problem that's responsible for most heart attacks. As in the heart, the vessels simply become so clogged up that they cannot carry an adequate amount of blood. In general, the same factors associated with atherosclerosis of the vessels of the heart are also "risk factors" for stroke. (These are reviewed in Chapter 18.) There is some evidence that blood pressure is of particular significance in stroke and has more impact in this disease than in heart disease.

In some strokes, the blood vessel in the brain actually ruptures. This is called cerebral hemorrhage. It is now believed that most cerebral hemorrhages occur in blood vessels that have already been damaged by atherosclerosis. However, high blood pressure seems to increase the risk of cerebral hemorrhage above and beyond its role in causing atherosclerosis.

Cerebral hemorrhage may also occur in a vessel that has a weak portion called a "berry aneurysm." Berry aneurysms are really congenital defects and are present from birth. Autopsy studies reveal that they are quite common (occurring in perhaps 10 percent of the population), but that the vast majority of them never result in any bleeding in the brain.

If blood clots form in the heart, they may break off and float into a blood vessel in the brain. This is called a cerebral embolism. If the clot is large enough, it blocks the flow of blood and causes a stroke. Usually such blood clots form only when there has been some previous damage to the heart, such as a heart attack or rheumatic heart disease. Occasionally they form when a particular type of irregular heartbeat, atrial fibrillation, has been present for a long period of time.

Can We Prevent Stroke?

Since the risk factors for stroke are essentially the same as those for coronary artery disease, prevention consists of altering these risk factors. As discussed in Chapter 18 and illustrated in the tables on page 199, there is good reason to believe that changes in lifetstyle have played a major role in reducing the death rate due to stroke. This death rate dropped by approximately 30 percent between 1963 and 1975. You can give yourself significant protection against stroke by controlling your risk factors—high blood pressure, weight, exercise, smoking, and diet.

Determining whether or not treatment of TIA's will prevent stroke is complicated by the difficulty in making the diagnosis. Generally it is agreed that the presence of TIA's greatly increases the chance of stroke. A wide variety of drugs that interfere with blood clotting (heparin, coumadin, aspirin, and others) have been used in an attempt to decrease this chance. There is no convincing evidence that these drugs reduce the number of deaths or strokes, although a recent study found some evidence of benefit from aspirin. The number of TIA's may have been reduced, but this is far from clear.

Surgery also has been used to remove deposits clogging arteries. This is called endarterectomy, and it is usually considered only when the involved artery is in the neck (carotid or vertebral artery). Only a small minority of patients with TIA's will have such a problem. Even in this situation, the benefit of surgery is far from clear-cut. At present it must be said that only one type of TIA—transient blindness in one eye—is associated with a high probability that endarterectomy will help. Surgery offers little for the vast majority of persons who experience TIA's.

Can We Treat Stroke?

Not really. Drugs that dilate vessels or prevent clotting have frequently been tried, but without demonstrable success. There is little evidence that we can change the course of the disease once the stroke has occurred. It is, however, very important to remember that most strokes go through a typical pattern in which symptoms tend to get better with time. Therefore, physical therapy and rehabilitation are important for preventing the very real problems that inactivity itself can cause, as well as to allow individuals to function at the highest possible level. Most stroke victims eventually are able to care for themselves and return to useful lives.

Can We Detect Stroke Before It Causes Symptoms?

There are no tests that will detect an impending stroke. Only when TIA's precede the stroke is any warning given.

What Should You Do About Stroke?

In general, the same principles discussed under heart disease are applicable here as well. The main emphasis must be on prevention. "Early" detection and treatment offer very little in comparison to prevention. As for possible TIA's, a localized weakness, temporary blindness in one eye, or difficulty in speaking, especially in an older person, is certainly a valid reason for consulting your physician. But for the complaint of dizziness, especially in young people, concern over TIA's is seldom of benefit.

21
Diabetes

EVERYBODY KNOWS ABOUT DIABETES—AND A GOOD DEAL OF WHAT they know is wrong. In no other disease is misinformation more abundant or promoted more vigorously by people who should know better. We are continually implored to consider whether we could be one of "10 million Americans who have undetected diabetes." We seem to be an especially ignorant lot since "half the Americans with diabetes don't know they have it." Before you accept this information, you should get the facts about diabetes. Start by knowing that diabetes can be used to mean any of three diseases and three nondiseases. That's right. Diabetes is frequently used to indicate three conditions in which there is probably no disease at all. And for the health of the average American, it is far more important to avoid the diagnosis of one of these nondiseases than it is to detect one of the real diseases early.

One of the three nondiseases, *prediabetes* is of least interest. It is essentially a theoretical concept and is used to indicate persons who might develop diabetes at some point but who at present have no indication of any kind of the disease. Its main use is to pump up the number of people who are "threatened" by diabetes. For example, it is sometimes said that "up to 10 percent of the population will develop diabetes if they live long enough." Such statements are meaningless, as you shall see.

The second nondisease, *latent diabetes*, refers to a situation in which blood sugar becomes "abnormal" as a result of some "stress." Drugs such as cortisone will produce such a stress and at one time it was advocated that persons should be tested with cortisone to see if they had "latent diabetes." Mercifully, this is seldom the case now. The term may be useful in denoting the condition in which blood sugars become abnormal during the stress of pregnancy.

The nondisease of which you must be most wary is *chemical diabetes*. Something of a medical Frankenstein's monster, this nondisease was concocted of equal parts of good intentions and ignorance. Unlike the original monster, this one is hardly an outcast. It won instant acceptance and endless promotion by those whose livelihood depends on the notion that it is a rampant killer disease that can be controlled if just detected and treated in time. Perhaps the most popular deception of the century is that there are many diseases we could treat much better—perhaps even cure—if we will just detect them soon enough. Yet to date there is only one disease—hypertension—that unequivocably fills the bill.

Chemical diabetes is considered to be "asymptomatic diabetes" by those who believe that it should be detected and treated. In other words, they consider it to be diabetes that just hasn't yet produced any symptoms. The argument for promoting the concept of chemical diabetes and screening programs to detect it is relatively straightforward: An abnormal blood sugar means that diabetes is present even if it is not causing any symptoms. Earlier treatment might prevent some of the complications of diabetes, such as blindness and kidney disease. Even if treatment doesn't help, at least it won't hurt because it can be treated with drugs, oral hypoglycemics, which are safe and can be taken by mouth (and therefore don't hurt like insulin injections).

Now bid a warm welcome to the facts:

■ The significance of abnormal blood sugars is often not clear. There is a long and embarrassing history of trying to define diabetes according to blood sugars. Blood sugars taken at random had to be discarded when it became clear that they depended mostly on what and when the patient had eaten. These were followed by blood sugars taken two hours after meals, so-called post-prandial blood glucoses. These, too, were found to have too wide a range of variability to be useful. Finally, we have gone to glucose tolerance tests (GTT's), which at least give more reproducible results when repeated in the same person. Traditionally, such tests are performed on college students in order to determine what's normal and abnormal. Unfortunately, this ignores the fact that blood sugars change with advancing age. The result is that from 77 to 100 percent of elderly persons will have "abnormal" GTT's. Thus if you insist on using this laboratory test to define diabetes, you are faced with the prospect of attributing this disease to virtually all elderly persons—despite the fact that the vast majority have no symptoms that can be attributable to diabetes and never will.

■   It has not been demonstrated that treating persons with "chemical diabetes" helps prevent the major complications of diabetes such as blindness and kidney disease. Actually, there is scant evidence to indicate that persons so treated benefit in any way at all.

■   There is abundant evidence that oral hypoglycemics are hazardous drugs and that people may suffer from their use. All have side effects, some of which may be fatal. One of these drugs, phenformin, has been removed from the market because of its association with a serious and often fatal reaction, lactic acidosis.

The punch line to all this is that almost all of those millions of Americans with "undetected diabetes" have the nondisease of chemical diabetes. This means you are being urged to contribute to the discovery of a "disease" that is: (1) causing no symptoms, (2) defined on the basis of an abnormal laboratory test, and (3) one whose treatment has no known benefit but definite hazards.

Of the three diseases called diabetes, diabetes insipidus, or "water diabetes," is the least common. It may be caused by problems with the pituitary gland or the kidneys themselves. Knowledge of this disease is not important unless you have it and it will not be discussed here.

Diabetes mellitus, or "sugar diabetes," is divided into two types: juvenile or juvenile-onset diabetes and, adult or adult-onset diabetes. These names are taken from the period in life in which each characteristically presents. However, age is no absolute determinant of these diseases. It is not unusual for juvenile diabetes to occur in a young adult, and occasionally a disease that seems to be more like adult diabetes will occur in a young person. Although they share a common name and are best known for their problems with the body's handling of sugar, they are distinct in many ways and are best thought of as two separate diseases.

Juvenile diabetes is what most people are thinking of when they talk of diabetes, even though it accounts for less than 20 percent of those who are diagnosed as having diabetes. In the days before insulin became available, this was a uniformly fatal disease that killed in a relatively short period of time. Its victims usually died in ketoacidosis, or diabetic coma. During ketoacidosis, blood sugar levels rise to extremely high levels and juvenile diabetes was thought to be exclusively a problem in control of blood sugar. With the advent of insulin, death due to ketoacidosis became a rarity. From a disease that often killed in a matter of months, juvenile diabetes became one that could be controlled for many years. But much to everyone's disappointment, insulin did not *cure* juvenile diabetes. It soon became apparent that juvenile diabetes is not a disease simply of insufficient insulin, but rather a complex disease whose major manifestations are due to its attack on blood vessels. In juvenile diabetes it is the destruction of blood vessels that causes blindness, loss of limbs, kidney failure, and difficulty in dealing with infections.

Adult-onset diabetes mellitus presents a much different picture. In this disease, which occurs late in life, insulin is seldom needed to control the elevated blood sugar. Often a controlled diet alone is sufficient. At one time oral hypoglycemics were prescribed to lower the blood sugar in this disease. Even if adult diabetes is untreated, ketoacidosis, blindness, and amputation are rare. However, neuropathies—problems with the nerves leading to numbness or pain—are actually more frequent and may occur before the blood sugar is elevated to any great degree.

Oral hypoglycemics have been largely discontinued in treatment of adult-onset diabetes for the reasons listed above. In addition, most adult diabetics are obese, so weight loss, exercise, and proper diet often provide as good, if not better, control of the disease. If you get nothing else out of this chapter, remember this: oral hypoglycemics have a capacity to do harm and should be used only if necessary. Many physicians, myself included, prefer to use insulin if diet alone is inadequate. This is an infrequent occurrence and usually diet is sufficient by itself.

What Causes Diabetes?

As we have seen, a simple lack of insulin is not the answer. Indeed, in the early stages of juvenile diabetes, insulin levels are actually higher than normal. Although we are making progress in understanding the complex biochemical changes in diabetes, it must be said that as of now we do not know exactly what these changes are or why they occur.

Diabetes mellitus is generally regarded as a hereditary disease, but there is no agreement on exactly how it is passed on from generation to generation. The picture is further confused by different approaches to the definitions of diabetes. Some investigators have focused on juvenile diabetes while others have maintained that chemical, adult, and juvenile diabetes are all the same disease. Juvenile diabetes really has the strongest inheritance pattern and the appearance of this disease in a close relative definitely increases your risk of getting it. This is probably also true for symptomatic adult diabetes, but remember that virtually all elderly persons will have abnormal GTT's, so many of the diagnoses of adult diabetes must be questioned. The risk of diabetes

Risk of diabetes

With this family history:	Your chance of getting diabetes is:
Juvenile diabetes in one parent	1 in 8
Juvenile diabetes in two parents	1 in 4
Juvenile diabetes in one brother or sister, parents normal	1 in 8
Juvenile diabetes in one brother or sister and one parent	1 in 4
Juvenile diabetes in one brother or sister and both parents	1 in 2

mellitus in any one person cannot be precisely defined, but the accompanying table gives some approximations based on several sources.

Can Diabetes Be Prevented?

As far as we know, juvenile diabetes cannot be prevented, although it is sometimes said that the onset can be delayed if weight is controlled to near ideal levels. This is mostly a reflection of the fact that most diabetics at one time or another are overweight. However, most juvenile diabetics are not overweight at the time the diagnosis is made.

Adult diabetes seems to be different. The vast majority of adult diabetics will be overweight when the diagnosis is made. As was mentioned above, most of the time adult diabetes can be controlled with the patient's diet and weight alone. Frequently, blood sugar will return to normal as weight is lost. However, other manifestations of this disease, such as nerve problems, may not be helped even if the blood sugar returns to normal. It seems likely that diet and weight control can delay and perhaps even prevent the onset of this illness, but this is far from a certainty.

What is certain is that you can prevent giving yourself a disease when you don't have one. While "chemical diabetes" is not a disease, adult-onset diabetes without symptoms may be. But surely this diagnosis alone has little meaning—it simply says that your blood sugar is higher than "normal." (Obviously, the first thing to do is to make sure that "normal" was defined appropriately for your age group.) It does little good to make this diagnosis because:

■ Appropriate therapy is diet and exercise to maintain ideal body weight. This is the kind of program you should be on anyway.

■ If you are overweight, you already know you need to shed some pounds—so the preceding comment goes double for you.

■ Going beyond diet and exercise through the use of drugs, either insulin or the oral hypoglycemics, is virtually never indicated in the absence of symptoms.

Remember that the oral hypoglycemics are dangerous and that insulin must be administered by injection. And of course insulin may produce its own very serious reactions. It is conceivable that the blood sugar could be so high (four or five times normal) that the need for drug therapy should be considered even in the absence of symptoms, but the notion that just any blood sugar outside "normal" limits should be treated with a pill or a shot is nonsense. If such a suggestion is made, you should get a detailed explanation of the reasons for it—and a second opinion as well.

Can Diabetes Be Treated?

Treatment is only for control, not for cure. And we control the blood sugar (usually) but not necessarily other parts of the disease. Therefore, ketoacidosis can be prevented for the most part but not the blood-vessel problems that can cause blindness, loss of limbs, and kidney failure. It should be pointed out also that this is a chronic disease, and that almost all of the therapy will be in the hands of the patient. Therapy is only effective when the patient understands the relationships among insulin, diet, exercise, and other factors (such as stress) that affect the blood sugar level.

By now you are well aware that the treatment for adult diabetes most often is diet and control of body weight. As a rule, the use of drugs should be considered only if diet and exercise fail to control symptoms as well as blood sugar.

Can Diabetes Mellitus Be Detected Before It Causes Symptoms?

We have already discussed the difficulty of defining diabetes by means of laboratory tests and especially the GTT. It is true, however, that virtually all persons who develop juvenile diabetes and most of those who develop adult diabetes will have abnormal blood sugars and sugar in the urine prior to developing symptoms. The primary difficulty is that the vast majority of those who have "abnormal" blood sugars and GTT's will never develop any symptoms. A urine test for sugar has some advantages:

- It is quite inexpensive

- You can do it yourself.

- In most people blood sugar must be substantially elevated before sugar appears in the urine, so that minor elevations of blood sugar are not detected.

However, these advantages still do not make this a test which can be routinely recommended. (See below.)

What Should You Do About Diabetes?

For the reasons given above, the question of early detection should be considered seriously only for juvenile diabetes. Should we do a blood sugar or a glucose tolerance test on everyone who has a family history of juvenile diabetes? Or should we simply wait for the first symptoms and treat at that time? The symptoms that first bring the juvenile diabetic to the physician are likely to be those of ketoacidosis—frequent urination, thirst, and weight loss. The first episode of ketoacidosis is usually detected and treated before serious illness results. But it seems logical that at least once in a great while there will be a death resulting from ketoacidosis that might have been prevented by a diabetes detection program. On the other hand, there is clearly a disability connected with being labeled a diabetic, and many have argued that this damages a young person so much that he or she is better off not knowing about diabetes until it is absolutely necessary to treat with insulin. The substantial cost involved in doing simple blood-sugar tests, let alone GTT's, is a serious drawback to a large-scale screening program. To date screening programs have cost significant amounts, have labeled asymptomatic persons as sick, and have *not* demonstrated that they are of benefit.

In this situation, the following becomes the crucial (and complex) question: Will earlier control of blood sugar retard the progression of the disease? Unfortunately, fewer controversies in medicine are as old and sustained as this one. Suffice it to say that it has not been demonstrated clearly that any early detection program will be significant in slowing down this disease. My own approach to this problem is as follows:

If you have no family history of juvenile diabetes, diet and exercise should be your only concern. If you do have a family history, then you have a choice. You may do nothing more than diet and exercise. The chance that you will be hurting yourself if you pursue this course is very small. Or you can take advantage of the fact that when blood sugar is high, some of it comes out in the urine. You can test your own urine cheaply and easily by purchasing Tes-Tope, Clinistix, Clinitest Tabs, Diastix or similar products at the drug store. Each test of the urine with these products will cost three to five cents. Once every month or so will be enough. Don't make yourself sick with the testing by assuming it's just a matter of time before you develop diabetes. Approach it as you would a blood-pressure test: not sick, just smart. You should also know that some people have sugar in the urine when the blood sugar is not very high, so don't panic if your urine shows some sugar. But if the urine does show sugar, then it is well worth the cost of the blood test to see what the level of blood sugar is. If you should have frequent urination, thirst, and weight loss, then you can test your own urine without waiting to visit the doctor. Ketoacidosis does not occur without at least some sugar in the urine.

22
Tuberculosis

TUBERCULOSIS (TB) IS BEST KNOWN AS A SLOWLY PROGRESSIVE disease of the lungs. It can, however, affect virtually any part of the body. It is felt that in most cases infection first occurs in the upper portion of the lungs and from there may spread to other tissues. However, in dark-skinned individuals—blacks, Indians, and others—a majority of cases may have tuberculosis in tissues outside the lungs and have little or no evidence of any infection within the lungs.

Practically everything about TB is slow. The disease may progress so slowly that symptoms do not appear for many years after infection first occurs. Making the diagnosis may take up to three months, because it can take that long for a tuberculosis culture to grow enough to be called positive. Eradication of the disease may take as long as two years and usually is treated for at least one year.

TB has been decreasing for at least the last 75 years. In 1900 more than one out of every 10 deaths was due to TB; but today it causes only one out of every 1,000 deaths. It is important to know that only a small part of this dramatic decrease is due to use of antibiotics or other types of medical treatment. TB is basically a disease of poor living conditions. As our standard of living and public health measures have improved, TB has decreased. More than 90 percent of the decline in mortality due to TB occurred before drugs against TB were available. Today it is most prevalent in those areas where living conditions remain poor. However, it is still true that virtually anyone may be exposed to TB and develop the disease. Eleanor Roosevelt died of tuberculosis despite the fact that she had never been exposed to poor living conditions. Undoubtedly she had contracted the disease many, many years before her death, which again illustrates how slowly the infection may progress.

What Causes Tuberculosis?

A peculiar type of bacteria, mycobacterium tuberculosis, is responsible for TB. Just as it grows and spreads slowly in the body, it also grows only slowly and under special conditions in the laboratory. Obviously, this hinders identification of the disease—it may take several months for a culture to show that mycobacterium tuberculosis is present.

Can Tuberculosis Be Prevented?

TB is effectively prevented by improving living conditions. Unfortunately, prescriptions cannot be written for this, and so the remedy is more a question of economics and politics than of medicine. The next best approach is to treat all known cases, limit exposure to known cases as far as possible, and perform skin tests for TB on those who may have been exposed.

In some countries the use of an antituberculus immunization with Bacillus Calmette-Guerin (BCG) vaccine is the rule. At one time the use of BCG vaccine was hotly debated. Its opponents claimed it was ineffective and made detection of TB difficult because it causes TB skin tests to become positive. Today BCG is generally regarded as about 80 percent effective, but of benefit only in areas where the threat of TB is high and exposure of children is common.

Can Tuberculosis Be Treated?

Treatment for TB is effective. However, it is prolonged (one to two years), requires two or three drugs, and must be closely supervised, since the drugs may have serious side effects. Healing leaves scars, so that some damage remains after the infection is cured.

Can Tuberculosis Be Detected Before It Causes Symptoms?

A tuberculosis skin test, either the PPD or the Tine Test, is a low cost, safe, and effective way of determining whether there has been contact with the TB bug. A positive test establishes only that there has been contact and does not necessarily mean that there is active tuberculosis. The diagnosis of active tuberculosis is usually made by characteristic findings on chest x-ray and confirmed with a sputum culture. Thus a two part procedure is necessary: Skin tests are done first and then those with positive tests are given chest x-rays and other tests to determine whether there is an active infection.

At one time it was common to treat all persons with positive skin tests with a one-year course of a drug known as izoniazid, or INH. The value of this approach was always questionable since it was known that the positive skin test did not necessarily mean that there was an active infection, and because it was not clear that the one drug alone would be adequate therapy if there was an active infection. It was justified on the basis that INH was thought to be a very safe drug with almost no side effects. However, when it was further studied it became clear that virtually nobody who had been given the INH prescriptions was actually taking the drug. This was understandable since the patients involved were asked to take the drug for at least a year for an illness they could not really feel or see and which did not make them sick. Nevertheless, with the best of intentions, major efforts were made to get people to take their INH and were at least partially successful.

However, when people actually began to take their INH faithfully, it was discovered that INH may cause a severe and sometimes fatal form of hepatitis. Whether persons with positive TB skin tests should be treated or followed carefully is still a subject of controversy. (The latter seems more rational to me.) Nevertheless, this episode teaches a valuable lesson: Claims that a drug "never causes any problems" must be treated skeptically, since patients seldom take drugs exactly as directed and doctors seldom search out problems with drugs.

What Should You Do About Tuberculosis?

Some physicians feel that skin tests may be omitted in areas where there has been little or no TB for years. Often it is difficult to define exactly where this applies, and it seems better to err on the side of too many skin tests rather than too few. Anyone who may have been exposed to TB certainly needs to have a skin test every year or two for the first 10 years after the suspected exposure. After the first 10 years, the skin test can be done much less frequently, every five to 10 years. If you have no definite history of exposure to tuberculosis but live in an area in which tuberculosis still occurs, then skin tests every five to 10 years is a reasonable approach.

23
Arthritis

ARTHRITIS MEANS INFLAMMATION OF A JOINT. INFLAMMATION is more than pain alone—it involves swelling, warmth, and redness. Doctors are fond of reminding medical students and patients—and anyone else who will listen—that pain alone does not necessarily indicate arthritis. Yet the most common type of arthritis, osteoarthritis, is remarkable for the lack of symptoms other than pain and stiffness. Nevertheless, it is important to understand that in this chapter we are discussing arthritis, and not the myriad problems that may cause pain in the area of a joint.

Most of us will develop osteoarthritis to some degree as we get older. Because of this, many have suggested that this should not be considered a disease but rather a part of the aging process. It truly seems to be a "wear-and-tear" problem, with the joints that bear the most weight (knees, hips, back) usually being the most affected—although the joints of the fingers are often involved as well. The principal problem with osteoarthritis is pain. It seldom damages the joint enough to cause severe impairment of motion.

Rheumatoid arthritis is in many ways the basis for our concept of arthritis. Involved joints are hot, red, swollen, and painful. If untreated, chances are that the joints will be damaged so that loss of motion will occur. This is a chronic disease that has no cure, but it can be treated effectively. Often the joints of the hands and wrist are most severely affected, but any joint may be involved. Sometimes there are bumps under the skin, rheumatoid nodules, especially around the elbow. Rarely lung or heart problems may occur in this disease.

Recently there have been striking developments with respect to ankylosing spondylitis, an arthritis of the spine that causes loss of flexibility of the back and neck. While not rare, it was thought that this was one of the less common types of arthritis. Now we know that this disease is associated with a gene found in about eight percent of the population. Approximately one out of five persons with the gene will have this type of arthritis. Most of these people will have a mild form of the disease and are unlikely to experience the total loss of flexibility of the spine seen in advanced cases. But many will have stiff backs and all would likely benefit from treatment to halt or slow the progression of the disease.

There are many other types of arthritis, but they are all less common, cannot be prevented, and do not require rapid treatment. Therefore, you need not concern yourself with their prevention or early recognition. Gout is discussed in Chapter 30.

What Causes Arthritis?

As noted, osteoarthritis seems to be a part of the natural process of aging. The cause of rheumatoid arthritis is unknown but seems to be inherited to some extent. There is also some evidence that the damage in rheumatoid arthritis is caused by the body's immune response reacting against the body's own tissues. The evidence seems strong that ankylosing spondylitis is an inherited problem. There is, however, great variation in the severity of the disease in those who carry the gene.

Can Arthritis Be Prevented?

There is no known way to prevent these three diseases.

Can Arthritis Be Detected Before It Causes Symptoms?

The changes in osteoarthritis are occasionally seen on x-rays of joints that are not painful, but it is doubtful whether the chance of seeing such change is worth the expense or radiation exposure involved.

The blood test for rheumatoid arthritis may be positive in normal persons or negative in those with rheumatoid arthritis. Therefore, it is not practical to diagnose rheumatoid arthritis before symptoms appear.

The test for detecting the gene associated with ankylosing spondylitis is sophisticated, expensive, and not widely available. The presence of the gene establishes only the tendency toward ankylosing spondylitis and does not tell whether or not the disease will be mild or severe—or even whether you will in fact get it. A more reasonable approach is the detection of mild ankylosing spondylitis as detailed below.

Can Arthritis Be Treated?

None of these diseases can be cured but all may be treated. In osteoarthritis, the objective of treatment is usually control of pain, since loss of motion is rare. Aspirin is usually the drug of choice, although other drugs may be used occasionally.

In preventing rheumatoid arthritis, the objective is to suppress the inflammation that causes pain and destruction of the joints. Aspirin is again the mainstay of treatment but there are several other drugs that are useful. Cortisone-like drugs are effective, but if used for long periods, their side effects may be more harmful than the disease itself. Their long term use must be avoided if possible. Response to therapy varies widely, but most patients with rheumatoid arthritis lead normal and useful lives.

Preservation of flexibility is the objective in treating ankylosing spondylitis. There are exercise programs designed to preserve this flexibility, and anti-inflammatory drugs such as aspirin may also be used. Rarely, potent and dangerous drugs called antimetabolites may be used. Therapy usually is effective in retarding the advance of this disease.

What Should You Do About Arthritis?

The amount of pain will tell you whether you need to see your doctor about osteoarthritis. Use your aspirin first—that is what he will recommend anyway. Any hot, swollen joint is reason enough for a visit to the physician, especially if there is a history of rheumatoid arthritis in your family. Rheumatoid arthritis always requires the doctor's help.

A group of doctors at Stanford University Hospital has recently developed a series of questions to detect the possibility of ankylosing spondylitis. If you have back pain, answer the following:

- Has the back pain ever gone on for three months or more?

- Has the back been stiff, especially in the morning?

- Did the discomfort begin before the age of 40?

- Did the problem begin slowly?

- Has the discomfort been improved with exercise?

If you answered "yes" to four of these questions, the chance that you have ankylosing spondylitis may be as high as one in 15. If you answered "yes" to all five, the chance appears to be about one in five. If stiffness or pain is a continuing problem, check with your doctor.

24

Gout

PERSONS WHO SUFFER FROM GOUT ARE IN VERY GOOD COMPANY. Michaelangelo, Alexander the Great, Issac Newton, Charles Darwin, Martin Luther, John Calvin, Benjamin Franklin, Alexander Hamilton, Ben Jonson, Samuel Johnson, and Charles IV of England are among those distinguished persons who have suffered with this disease. Perhaps misery loves company, but the pain of a gout attack is little helped by knowing that Ben Franklin had the same problem.

A rather simple chemical called uric acid is the culprit in gout. We all have uric acid in our blood but persons with gout have too much and in the wrong places. When there is too much uric acid, it tends to crystalize out of solution. These crystals are found most notably in joints and in the kidney, but can form in almost any tissue. Sometimes uric acid deposits, called tophi, can be seen and felt in and under the skin. Deposits in joints may become irritating and the body may react against them. This produces the hot, swollen, tender, and painful joint that is the hallmark of a gout attack. An attack may occur in almost any joint, but for some reason gout has a strong preference for the big toe. About 90 percent of persons with gout will have an attack in the big toe at one time or another. Other sites frequently involved are the instep, ankle, heel, knee, and wrist. In the kidney, damage may be caused by fine, diffuse deposits throughout the kidney tissue or by the formation of kidney stones.

Gout clearly tends to run in families, but exactly how it is inherited is unknown. It is impossible to say exactly how much the risk of gout is increased if you have a history of it in the family. The occurrence of gout seems to be an interaction of several factors, including sex, diet, and weight.

Gout is almost entirely a disease of middle-aged men; only about five percent of persons with gout are women. It is unusual for gout to occur in children and young adults or after the age of 65. Most gout sufferers will be overweight at the time of their first attack.

The role of diet in this problem has always intrigued physicians. Since uric acid is formed from the breakdown of nucleic acids, it has been suggested that foods rich in these substances should be restricted. Moderate restriction seems to be of little benefit, however, and severe restriction seems likely to cause more harm than good. A more useful relationship exists with obesity and alcohol consumption. It has been frequently noted that many persons with gout who reduce their weight to an ideal level and avoid alcohol lose all symptoms of the disease. This includes a return to normal levels of the uric acid in the blood. Frankly, we don't have a very good explanation for this phenomenon.

Can Gout Be Prevented?

While there is no known way to absolutely prevent gout, it may well be that controlling your weight and avoiding alcohol may prevent or delay the occurrence of the disease in persons who have a tendency toward it. This is based on the observation that many persons are overweight and using alcohol freely when they have their first attack and that they may lose all signs of the disease when the weight is reduced and alcohol is avoided. This is much like the situation with adult diabetes (see Chapter 21).

Can Gout Be Treated?

Medicines are available both for treating the acute attack and for lowering the level of uric acid so as to prevent future attacks. They are usually effective. As with all medicines, they may have side effects and some of these may be quite serious.

Can Gout Be Detected Before It Causes Symptoms?

Determining the level of uric acid in the blood is simple enough. Interpreting that level is not so simple. The chances of developing gout depend on how high the uric acid level is. Most elevations of uric acid above "normal" are very mild and most persons with "abnormally' high uric acid levels will never have a problem with gout. However, as the elevation increases to quite high levels, the chances get to be very great that there will be a problem with gout. It is also true that gout may occur in persons whose uric acid level is within normal limits. In light of these facts, if joint problems were the only concern in gout, then there would never be a question of trying to detect the disease before the first attack. While it would be desirable to avoid the suffering associated with attack, the attack itself would cause no permanent damage and treatment would be initiated at that time. The real problem is the possibility of kidney damage *before* there is an attack in a joint. To the best of our knowledge this is an extraordinarily rare occurrence, so a mass testing program for uric acid elevations is not warranted.

What Should You Do About Gout?

It's the same old sweet song: Keep your weight down and use alcohol in moderation. This is especially true if you have a family history of gout. But remember that lack of a family history does not protect you against this disease.

25

Venereal Disease

ANY DISEASE THAT IS TRANSMITTED PRIMARILY THROUGH SEX-
ual contact may be termed a venereal disease. While there are a number
of such diseases, "VD" usually refers to syphilis and gonorrhea.

Gonorrhea is a bacterial disease which usually produces a localized
infection. This infection produces pus, so that a discharge, either from
the penis or from the vagina, is characteristic of gonorrhea. In males
the most common sites for infection are the urethra (the tube leading
from the bladder to the end of the penis), the throat, and the rectum.
In females the infection usually begins in the vagina and the cervix of
the uterus. The uterus and fallopian tubes are often affected and this
is sometimes referred to as pelvic inflammatory disease, or PID. (PID
may also have causes other than gonorrhea.) The throat and the rectum
may also be sites of infection. Less frequently, the liver and the joints
may be involved. In addition to the pain and the fever of acute infection
gonorrhea creates, it may permanently damage involved organs
through the process of infection and subsequent scarring. Sterility and
strictures (narrowing) of the urethra, rectum, or fallopian tubes may
result. Children may develop eye infections if the mother has gonorrhea
when she gives birth. Such infections may cause blindness.

Unlike gonorrhea, syphilis does not stay localized but spreads
throughout the body. It has three distinct phases. Primary syphilis may
result in a small, painless ulcer (chancre) on the genitalia (occasionally
on the mouth or hands), which appears from 10 to 90 days after sexual

contact with an infected person. If untreated, the chancre will heal in approximately four to six weeks. The patient is highly infectious during the primary stage. In about 30 percent of all male cases, there is no chancre and thus no sign of this phase. In females, even if the chancre is present, it is often unnoticed. Secondary syphilis occurs shortly after the first stage, although it occasionally occurs simultaneously with the chancre. This stage is a rash that may have small bumps or flat, red lesions, or it may, in fact, take almost any form except blisters. It is especially likely to involve the soles, palms, and face. The tertiary stage occurs years later. This is the stage in which people die or go insane. Tertiary syphilis may affect virtually any part of the body, but death usually comes from involvement of the heart or nervous system.

Can Veneral Disease Be Prevented?

Avoidance of contact with infected persons is the only completely effective method of prevention. Persons who have many transient sexual relationships clearly are more likely to have the disease. Human nature is such that these considerations—or even the presence of a discharge—are often ignored. A male having a single intercourse with gonorrhea-infected female has about one chance in four of developing the disease whereas a female having intercourse with an infected male is nearly certain to develop the disease. Even for males the odds aren't that good, for after three such encounters, the male has better than a 50-50 chance of developing the disease.

The use of condoms will decrease the odds of spreading gonorrhea, but this is far from being 100 percent effective. For males, urinating immediately after intercourse may reduce the chances of infection slightly. Vaginal douches offer little protection for the female.

The chances of becoming infected with syphilis are far more difficult to determine because they depend on the stage of the disease and because detecting the disease is more difficult.

Giving antibiotics to persons likely to be exposed to a venereal disease has been advocated. This has been the policy of the armed forces on occasion. Unfortunately, this has not been shown to be effective and may have contributed to the rise of resistant strains of gonorrhea. Because of the rise of these resistant strains, work on developing a vaccine for gonorrhea is receiving renewed attention. There is a vaccine for syphilis—but only for rabbits! At present, humans have no vaccine that will prevent these diseases.

Can Venereal Disease Be Treated?

The fact that both gonorrhea and syphilis have been effectively treated with antibiotics in the past is responsible in part for the current epidemic of these diseases. The notion that the problem can always be cured with an antibiotic has contributed to a decline in discrimination with respect to sexual partners. Now we face the real possibility of a strain of gonorrhea that is resistant to all known antibiotics. It is a mistake to throw all caution to the wind with the assumption that the cure will be there when you need it.

Can Venereal Disease Be Detected Before It Causes Symptoms?

Both males and females may have gonorrhea without symptoms. Aside from the risk that they may eventually develop a full-scale attack of gonorrhea, these persons are particularly effective spreaders of the disease. A culture from the cervix of the uterus or from the penis will sometimes, but not always, detect the presence of the disease. Having a culture made is worthwhile only for persons who have large numbers of sexual contacts. In several Western European countries where prostitution is legal, such cultures are performed routinely on prostitutes and this has helped to control the spread of the disease.

There are a number of blood tests that indicate exposure to syphilis (VDRL, FTA). However, since the test does not become positive for from three weeks to three months after exposure, any negative test during that period must be repeated when the three months has elapsed. If there has been no definite exposure, then it is common to occasionally do blood tests anyway. Often this is required for employment, marriage licenses, and so on.

What Should You Do About Venereal Disease?

Don't rely on condoms, douches, or urinating immediately after intercourse to protect you. You will have to use some discretion if you want to give yourself the best chance of avoiding infection. If you are a female with many sexual partners, you should consider having a culture for gonorrhea done even in the absence of symptoms. See that your children are prevented from having eye infections through the use of the appropriate eye drops at birth. Most important, if there are any symptoms that suggest gonorrhea or syphilis, you should seek medical care promptly.

If there has been any exposure to syphilis, then a blood test is mandatory. If there has been no definite exposure, then occasional blood tests are a reasonable approach. These should be no more frequent than every four to six years.

26

Glaucoma

THE FLUID THAT FILLS YOUR EYEBALL IS CONTINUALLY CIRCU-lating. Special cells within the eye, called ciliary cells, produce the fluid, which is then drained off through minute openings located in the angle formed by the iris and cornea (anterior chamber angle). Pressure in the eye may become abnormally high if: (1) too much fluid is made (this is rare); (2) the anterior chamber angle is narrow so that the openings are blocked (narrow-angle glaucoma); or (3) the openings themselves are too small (wide-angle glaucoma). Elevated pressure within the eye eventually damages the eye, especially the optic nerve, causing blindness.

Wide-angle glaucoma accounts for at least 90 percent of all glaucoma. It is an inherited disease, although the heredity pattern is not perfectly clear. There are usually no symptoms until visual loss begins to occur. The first loss is an enlarged blind spot, but this is usually not noticed. Later, peripheral vision is lost so that "tunnel vision" is often the symptom noticed. Although the tendency toward wide-angle glaucoma is inherited, it usually does not occur before the age of 40. About two of every 100 persons over the age of 40 has some degree of wide-angle glaucoma, although not all of these will go on to have loss of vision.

Narrow-angle (or angle-closure) glaucoma results when the angle between the lens and iris is too narrow. This defect tends to run in

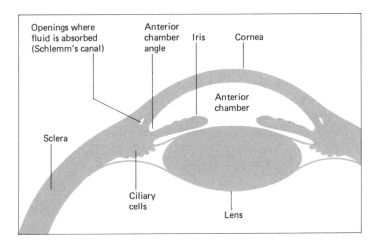

families also. Often the course of the disease is much like that of wide-angle glaucoma, with symptoms of vision loss only after the age of 40. However, if the pupil is dilated and the iris should suddenly close the angle and block the openings for fluid drainage, then acute glaucoma occurs. In acute glaucoma, there is sudden onset of blurred vision and pain in the eye. There may be nausea and vomiting. Such an attack should be treated as quickly as possible even though it will spontaneously subside hours or days after it began.

Some cases fall in between the chronic and acute types (subacute glaucoma). In these there may be complaints of blurred vision and seeing halos around lights. This is due to fluid under high pressure being forced into the cornea.

Can Glaucoma Be Prevented?
There is no known way to prevent the disease.

Can Glaucoma Be Treated?
Almost all cases of glaucoma can be successfully treated in that further damage to the eye can be prevented, but lost vision cannot be restored. In wide-angle glaucoma, drugs are preferred, with surgery used only when pressure in the eye cannot be controlled by drugs alone. Surgery is indicated in narrow-angle glaucoma although drugs usually are used to lower the pressure within the eye prior to operation. Both eyes are usually treated even if only one has developed elevated pressure since the other is very likely to do so in the future.

Can Glaucoma Be Detected Before It Causes Symptoms?

Measuring the pressure in the eye is called tonometry. It can be done with a simple instrument called a Schiotz tonometer. The procedure is quick and easy, and should be widely available. A very few cases will be missed with this instrument, but they can be detected through applanation tonometry and/or tonography. These last two procedures are more involved and require expensive equipment, and consequently they are usually found only in the offices of ophthalmologists and optometrists. Needless to say, they cost more than Schiotz tonometry.

What Should You Do About Glaucoma?

Since this disease cannot be prevented, does irreversible damage without warning, and can be detected before damage has begun, this is one of the few times when a screening test does make sense. You should have tonometry at least once every four years after the age of 40. If you have a family history of glaucoma, you should have it every year after age 30. Schiotz tonometry is adequate unless you have previously had eye surgery or are very nearsighted. In these instances, applanation tonometry is more accurate.

27

Anemia

ANEMIA MEANS A DECREASE IN THE NUMBER OF RED BLOOD CELLS, the cells that carry oxygen to the tissues of the body. While the number of red blood cells may actually be counted and this number used in the diagnosis of anemia, most often the term "blood count" refers to the hematocrit, the percentage of blood that is red blood cells, or the amount of hemoglobin, the substance within red blood cells that actually carries the oxygen. The following table gives a range of the normal hematocrit and hemoglobin for both sexes at various ages.

Hematocrit and hemoglobin values at various ages

Age	Hematocrit %		Hemoglobin Grams/100cc	
Birth to 1 week	44-64		14-24	
1 week to 1 month	35-49		11-20	
1 month to 2 years	30-40		10-15	
2 years to puberty	31-43		11-16	
	Men	*Women*	*Men*	*Women*
After puberty	40-54	37-47	14-18	12-16

Anemia owes its popularity to its connection with the problem of fatigue. It is true that persons who are anemic may complain of fatigue. But it is also true that persons who complain of fatigue are seldom anemic. Anemia is a relatively rare cause of fatigue. (So is "low thyroid," another old standby. See Chapter 28.) Among persons seen for fatigue in a university clinic, less than four percent actually had anemia.

On the other hand, blaming fatigue on anemia has a number of advantages for both doctor and patient. Most fatigue is caused by plain old hard work, or by problems at home or at work, or, worst of all, it has no known cause. By blaming anemia, we avoid dealing with a difficult subject ("You think this is all in my head, don't you, doctor? Well, I know it isn't.") or avoid admitting that no cause can be found. ("It must be cancer. I need a doctor who knows what he's doing.") In either case, treatment may be difficult or impossible. But with anemia, treatment is not only possible but has a number of advantages. The two most frequent treatments, iron pills and vitamin B_{12} shots, are relatively safe. If the patient needs "proof" of a medical problem, then frequent visits to the doctor's office for B_{12} shots will do nicely. In addition, the shots are quite profitable for the doctor.

Because B_{12} shots are relatively safe, their use has been justified as a placebo treatment for fatigue due to psychosocial factors. (See Chapter 3 for a discussion of the placebo effect.) If the physician believes that the patient's neurosis is such that it cannot be treated with a more direct approach, this makes a good deal of sense. It is safe, less expensive than visits to a psychiatrist, and may allow the patient to function more adequately. Unfortunately, this argument is often used to justify B_{12} shots given in a haphazard manner and with little thought. The sad fact is that the major motive in many situations is profit. In general, the more B_{12} shots given, the less competent the physician. True vitamin B_{12} deficiency, termed pernicious anemia, is an uncommon disease. Competent physicians rarely give B_{12} shots even if they believe that it is proper to use them as a placebo treatment.

Anemia is also big business. As you can see by our table, women normally have lower hematocrits and hemoglobins than men. It seemed logical that menstrual bleeding might cause an iron deficiency in virtually all women and thus gave support to the notion that all women needed iron supplements. In reality, there is little evidence to indicate a need for iron in most women or even in women who complain of fatigue. It has been shown that the difference between the hematocrits of men and women persists even when women have hysterectomies and, therefore, are no longer losing the blood, or when women are given iron in abundance. Furthermore, when iron deficiency does occur in women, it is usually of such a mild degree that it almost never accounts for problems of fatigue. Nevertheless, the myth persists that most women are slightly anemic and could use some extra iron. Upon this myth rest the fortunes of numerous unneeded concoctions whose advertisements imply that the user will have high energy, a youthful appearance, and a handsome, considerate spouse. Even if you need iron, these products are poor choices. You pay up to 25 times more for each milligram of iron than if you had purchased the iron pill doctors most commonly recommend.

Similar notions persist concerning anemia in "all" infants and pregnant women. It is true that bottle-fed infants need iron if their formula does not contain it. Some pregnant women may become deficient in folic acid and a supplement of this vitamin makes sense. But few will develop severe anemias even if they do not receive extra amounts of this substance.

In addition to deficiencies of vitamin B_{12} and iron, anemia may also be caused by a lack of folic acid and pyridoxine. These deficiencies are rare in persons eating normal diets. A mild anemia often does accompany serious chronic diseases, but these anemias do not respond to vitamins or iron. Treatment should be directed toward the chronic disease itself. Chronic blood loss, usually through the gastrointestinal tract, may lead to an anemia. Sickle-cell disease (a severe anemia) and sickle-cell trait (a very mild anemia) are inherited disorders. They are limited almost entirely to blacks and are due to an abnormal hemoglobin. Beyond these problems there are a whole multitude of causes of anemia which are, fortunately, very infrequent.

Can We Prevent Anemia?

A balanced diet is effective preventive medicine for anemias due to deficiencies of vitamins or iron. Most breads and cereals are routinely fortified with iron by the manufacturer. Milk is not, so iron deficiency may be seen in infants whose diet consists mainly of milk. Folic acid should be added to the diets of pregnant women.

Can We Treat Anemia?

Deficiency anemias usually respond readily to the replacement of the deficient substances. Anemias associated with chronic diseases are resistant to therapy and tend to vary as the chronic disease itself varies. In the case of blood loss, if the source of the blood loss can be located and treated successfully, the anemia will be cured. Treatment of sickle-cell disease is disappointing whereas sickle-cell trait does not require treatment. Many of the relatively rare types of anemia may be improved by treatment, although few can be cured.

Can We Detect Anemia Before It Causes Symptoms?

Attempts to detect anemia before it causes symptoms have not been shown to be particularly beneficial. A very simple test for hematocrit can be done at very low cost by means of a "microhematocrit" procedure. In this procedure, the tip of the finger is pricked with a sterile stylet and a drop of blood is drawn up into a tiny tube. The tube is then sealed, spun in a centrifuge and the hematocrit determined. This test should cost only a dollar or so and might be useful to do occasionally. It is not to be confused with the "complete blood count," which includes a number of tests and should not be recommended routinely (it costs from six to 15 dollars). For adults, it is even difficult to justify the cost of the hematocrit, and it must be restated that, in general, screening for anemia has not been very helpful except in children who may not be receiving an adequate diet. Screening programs can detect sickle-cell trait, but there seems little point since it is not treated. Sickle-cell disease usually makes itself known in early childhood.

What Should You Do About Anemia?

Be reluctant to diagnose yourself as anemic. Remember that fatigue and dizziness may be due to anemia but this is an infrequent cause of these problems. For children, an occasional microhematocrit determination may be worthwhile. For adults, it is much less likely to be useful. Finally, know that the mysterious anemia slowly robbing you of your strength, vitality, and happiness is a fiction created by Madison Avenue for the benefit of itself and its clients. A balanced diet will give you all the vitamins and minerals you need.

28
Thyroid Problems

AS WITH ANEMIA, THE THYROID OWES MUCH OF ITS POPULARITY TO its connection with fatigue. Hypothyroidism ("low thyroid") is a cause of fatigue but an infrequent one. Of those persons referred to a university hospital for fatigue, less than six percent had hypothyroidism. If other symptoms of hypothyroidism are absent, the chance that fatigue is due to this problem is near zero.

On the other hand, the diagnosis of hypothyroidism has many advantages for both patient and physician. The common causes of fatigue—stress and strain, obesity, boredom, plain old hard work—are more difficult to deal with than a nice, clear-cut disease that can be treated with a pill. Giving thyroid pills for fatigue has some of the same advantage as giving iron pills for anemia. As long as only small amounts are given, it is quite safe. The body possesses a wonderful mechanism to regulate the amount of thyroid hormone. If you take extra thyroid in the form of a pill, the thyroid gland simply puts out less of its own thyroid hormone so that the total amount of hormone in the body is normal. This protection lasts only as long as the amount taken is small (less than four per day of the usual type of pill). If you take a whole bottle of iron pills, constipation is about the worst thing that can happen. But if you take a bottle of thyroid pills, you will be very sick and could even do yourself in.

In addition to fatigue, the thyroid has two other connections going for it. Since it is true that persons with hypothyroidism tend to be overweight, the temptation is great to think of thyroid pills as the answer to a fat problem. But people with hypothyroidism have other symptoms as well. Weight gain is usually one of the lesser problems. If your problem is obesity, the chances that your excess pounds are due to a little low thyroid are very slim.

Cholesterol is also related to thyroid hormone and persons who have hyperthyroidism (too much thyroid hormone) usually have low cholesterol. As noted in Chapter 18, the notion that the risk of heart attack depends on your total cholesterol has been oversold in this country. More importantly, the Coronary Drug Project revealed that the use of thyroid to lower cholesterol actually *increases* the chances of dying from a heart attack. So while it is true that if you take enough thyroid you will feel peppier, lose weight, and lower your cholesterol, you will have done so by giving yourself a new disease, hyperthyroidism. And you will have made your future a good deal bleaker in the process.

The amount of thyroid hormone controls the body's rate of metabolism. Too little and everything slows down: fatigue, weight gain, constipation, and slow reflexes result. Too much and you have the opposite problem: nervousness, weight loss, diarrhea, and a pounding heart. Metabolic rate is related to the body's temperature; people with hypothyroidism feel cold and dislike cold weather, whereas people with hyperthyroidism feel hot and dislike hot weather. A person with a thyroid problem often has several of these symptoms as well as a change in the appearance of hair, skin, or eyes. Without at least a hint of other symptoms, those persons with fatigue and obesity should *not* be tested for thyroid problems. The fact that they often are is one reason why we get very little benefit for all the dollars that we spend on laboratory tests.

The cause of either hyperthyroidism or hypothyroidism usually cannot be determined. Malignant tumors almost never are responsible for these conditions.

There is one important point to make about tumors of the thyroid, however. At one time it was common to give radiation treatments for acne, ringworm of the scalp, and to reduce the size of tonsils and adenoids. Persons who have had this type of treatment have an increased risk of developing tumors of the thyroid. Fortunately, these tumors are slow to spread. Still, it is very important for you to record a history of this type of treatment in your LifePlan as well as schedule the thyroid exams discussed below. Remember that most enlargements and lumps in the thyroid gland are *not* cancer, so don't jump to conclusions if you find a lump or if you have had radiation to the head and neck.

Can Thyroid Problems Be Prevented?

The only preventable cause of hypothyroidism is iodine deficiency. In certain areas of the country, iodine does not occur naturally in the drinking water. An area in the mid-West was once known as "the goiter belt" (goiter is an enlarged thyroid). The addition of iodine to salt (iodized salt) and other foods has eliminated this problem for all practical purposes.

Are Thyroid Problems Treatable?

Hypothroidism is treated simply by taking thyroid hormone in the form of pills. It is usually effective and has few, if any, side effects. Hyperthyroidism is more complicated and involves decreasing the activity of the gland through surgery, radiation, or with drugs. All of these are hazardous to some extent, and the choice depends on a number of variables including the patient's own feelings and wishes. Radiation and drugs are safer and easier at the beginning, but the long-term risks are difficult to project. Remember, it took 20 years to discover that radiation was causing tumors of the thyroid. Surgery has more risk initially, but its long-term side effects are usually small or nonexistent. Currently the vast majority of patients receive either radiation or drugs. In my view, surgery should be given careful consideration.

Can Thyroid Problems Be Detected Before They Cause Symptoms?

For hyperthyroidism and hypothyroidism, there is no evidence that programs to detect small elevations or deficiencies in thyroid hormone in adults would be of benefit. (As of now it appears that routine testing of newborn babies is worthwhile in order to find those with congenital hypothyroidism and prevent cretinism.) One problem is that there has always been a problem in interpreting thyroid blood tests. Beyond this, if the abnormality is so small that it causes no symptoms, treatment will not provide any benefit.

A malignant tumor is clearly a different matter. Most of these will not cause any symptoms before they spread. Fortunately, they seem to spread beyond the gland rather late in the game. This allows a good chance of detecting them before spread occurs. Most are discovered by the patient who notices a small lump just to the side of the Adam's apple. However, there is no evidence that a periodic thyroid examination is an effective screening procedure *unless* there is a history of radiation (x-ray) treatment to head or neck.

What Should You Do About Thyroid Problems?

If you have had radiation to the head or neck for acne, ringworm, enlarged tonsils or adenoids (this does *not* mean a routine diagnostic x-ray of the skull or spine), then you should have your thyroid examined by a physician once a year without fail. If you have not had this type of radiation treatment, ask your doctor to feel the thyroid when you are in the office for something else. If you like, ask that you be taught how to do the examination so that you can do this for yourself and your family. No data tell us exactly how often the thyroid should be examined, but once a year should be plenty.

29
Allergy and Asthma

ALLERGIES GET BLAMED FOR A LOT OF PROBLEMS THEY DON'T cause. This is most true where drugs are concerned. Less than one-third of reported allergies to medicines are really due to an allergic process. You are not allergic to a drug even though it causes nausea, diarrhea, fatigue, or dizziness, even if these occur with small doses. These problems are virtually always side effects of the drug and are caused by the drug itself, not a reaction to it. Clearly it is important to avoid taking a drug to which you are allergic, but it is also important not to deny yourself a drug that is needed. This may occur unnecessarily if you report that you are allergic to the drug when this is not really the case.

Allergy is an overreaction of the body's normal defense mechanism against invasion by foreign substances. This is the same mechanism that produces immunity to bacteria and viruses. Since the problem is one of degree rather than kind, physicians often speak of "hypersensitivity." This may contribute to the mistaken notion that persons who seem to be sensitive to the side effects of drugs even at low dosages are allergic to the drug. In fact, allergic reactions to drugs usually take only one of two forms: (1) skin rashes, especially hives, and (2) severe asthma-like attacks with difficulty in breathing and, sometimes, collapse of the circulation. Unless you have experienced one of these problems as a result of exposure to a drug, you should be reluctant to label yourself as allergic to that drug. If there is some question as to whether a symptom is due to allergy or not, then discuss this problem with the doctor or nurse by phone or on your next visit to the office for another reason.

Of the many types of allergic problems that have been described, five are important to you as part of your personal or family medical history: systemic reactions, local reactions, allergic rhinitis and conjunctivitis (better known as hay fever), eczema, and asthma. Systemic reactions consist of skin rashes or asthma-like attacks described above. This type of reaction may occur with bee stings, drugs, or foods to which the individual is allergic. Since these reactions can be very serious, it is most important that you be sure of any such allergy. Allergy to aspirin may occur in middle age (especially in women) and be associated with nasal polyps and sinusitis. Although not a common allergy, this is worthy of special note, since the systemic reactions are often severe.

Local reactions might be further divided into those in which the allergic process is well understood and those in which it is not. Contact dermatitis, of which poison ivy is the most common example, is an allergic reaction to a chemical applied to the skin. On the other hand, the local swelling, redness, itching, and pain some people experience with insect bites or stings may have an allergic component, but usually are due mostly to the chemicals injected by the insect. The most important thing for you to know is that these local reactions, whether or not they appear to have a significant allergic component, do not have the same implications for your health as do the systemic reactions. They do not indicate that you have the type of allergy that may be life threatening, or that requires the use of desensitization injections or the constant availability of adrenalin and other drugs to treat these reactions on an emergency basis. This is not to say that you will not avoid some discomfort by avoiding poison ivy or gnats, but it does mean that you needn't be in fear of your life at the possible exposure to these hazards.

Itchy eyes and runny noses are a familiar sight between August 15th and the first frost, since this is the time when ragweed releases its pollen into the air in merciless abundance. While the term "hay fever" was originally meant to apply to sensitivity to ragweed pollen only, it has come to be a handy label for all types of seasonal allergic rhinitis and conjunctivitis. The same type of problem may not be seasonal if the substance to which the person is allergic does not originate from plants. Common examples of nonseasonal problems are allergy to animal danders and house dust.

Eczema is not really an allergy to a particular substance or substances. It is a problem of easily damaged skin. Most of the damage is from the daily use of soap and water. Cleanliness is not next to godliness if you have eczema. Eczema is usually associated with a personal or family history of allergies. Such a history is an important criterion for making the diagnosis of eczema.

Asthma is commonly divided into two types. In about a third of patients, asthma seems to be the result of an allergy to identifiable substances like those responsible for allergic rhinitis and conjunctivitis. This is called allergic or extrinsic asthma, and it is more common in children. In another third of patients, there is no evidence of such an allergy. Attacks are often brought on by respiratory infections or emotional strain. This type is called nonallergic or intrinsic asthma and it usually starts after age 30. The remaining third of patients have asthma with some characteristics of each type. Air pollution and smoking may bring on an attack in any asthmatic.

What Causes Allergy and Asthma?
Allergy and asthma clearly tend to run in families, but in most cases the pattern of inheritance is not clear. Since these problems are overreactions of a normal body defense mechanism, it is likely that these families carry a trait of "hypersensitive defense." On the other hands, things that bring on attacks—pollens, dust, smoking, air pollution, emotional strain—also tend to be shared by families.

Can Allergy or Asthma Be Prevented?
There is no way to prevent the development of a hypersensitive defense mechanism. Hypersensitivity to a particular substance may be avoided by avoiding that substance. Attacks may be prevented by avoiding specific substances to which there is allergy and avoiding other factors that bring on attacks—soap and water in eczema, smoking in asthma, and so on. While there may be some quibbling about this, prevention of attacks is most properly thought of as treatment.

Can Allergy and Asthma Be Treated?
Symptoms may be controlled, but these problems cannot be cured. As mentioned above, avoidance of things that bring on attacks is most important. In addition, there is a wide variety of drugs that act to decrease the sensitivity of the defense mechanism (cortisone-like compounds, and such) or to reverse the effect of the defense mechanisms (decongestants, antihistamines, bronchodilators, and the like). In some individuals, desensitization injections (allergy shots) will decrease the need for drugs.

Can Allergy and Asthma Be Detected Before They Cause Symptoms?
Not really.

What Should You Do About Allergy and Asthma?

Accurate recording of your personal and family history of allergy in the PHR is most important. You do not want to deny yourself a drug you may need because you mistakenly thought yourself allergic. Obviously you do not want to be given a drug to which you are truly allergic.

If you have nasal polyps, sinusitis, and a family history of allergy to aspirin, consider yourself allergic to aspirin even if you have not had a reaction. Acetaminophen can be substituted for the aspirin. Use aspirin only with your doctor's approval.

30
Epilepsy

IN MEDICINE, THE TERM EPILEPSY IS USED MOST OFTEN AS A shortened form of "idiopathic epilepsy," a condition that may be defined as recurrent seizures or convulsions without a known cause. Despite advances in understanding the brain and its functions, we still are unable to say why most seizures occur and, therefore idiopathic epilepsy is still the most frequent type of seizure disorder.

There are many types of seizures. The most dramatic is a generalized convulsion (*grand mal* seizure) in which the person first loses consciousness, then the body stiffens and begins to jerk rhythmically. Control of bowels or bladder may be lost. Before the attack, there may be a peculiar feeling that warns of the attack, or aura, and afterward there is a lethargy or sleep called the postictal state. *Petit mal* seizures appear as "staring spells," or brief losses of consciousness without body movements or falling. They occur most often in children and young adults. *Psychomotor* seizures are highly variable, and are characterized by confusion, restlessness, and repetitive movements. These psychomotor seizures may be mistaken for emotionally disturbed behavior. *Focal* seizures involve convulsions or jerking, but only of one part of the body.

Single seizures do surprisingly little harm, injury coming only from falling or loss of control if the victim is operating machinery or driving an auto. The attack will end by itself and very little needs to be done for the person during the attack. Do *not* attempt to force anything between the teeth. The seriousness of biting the tongue has been vastly overrated and you could break the person's tooth or lose part of your finger. Anyone who has epilepsy should see a physician after any seizure. This is critical if the seizures are continuing, one right after the other— a condition called status epilepticus. While the cause of most seizures is unknown, there are many problems that can cause them. (By definition, these are not idiopathic epilepsy). Any injury to the brain may be responsible. Such injuries may be due to the infant receiving insufficient oxygen while in the womb or during birth, blows to the head, infections, brain tumors, or blood clots. Seizures may be associated with certain rare, inherited brain disorders. Seizures may be due to alcoholism and alcohol may trigger seizures in persons with idiopathic epilepsy. Problems with body metabolism, such as very low blood sugar in diabetics using insulin, may result in a seizure. High fever in young children may cause a seizure but this does *not* mean the child has epilepsy. However, a child who has such a seizure has an increased risk of developing epilepsy later.

It has been suggested that epilepsy is caused by a brain injury too slight to have been noticed. This is a logical supposition, but efforts to detect such injuries have failed. If heredity has any influence, it is slight, and epilepsy should not be regarded as an inherited disease.

Epilepsy itself has no effect on intelligence, although it may be associated with brain injuries of the type that also cause retardation. Epilepsy is not a direct cause of behavioral or psychiatric problems, but the reaction of society, friends, and family to the disease—as well as the disease itself—may expose the epileptic to intense emotional stress and strain. With treatment, most epileptics can lead normal lives if we will let them. Traditionally, epileptics have been discriminated against both by law and by custom. Although progress has been made, this discrimination is still imposing an enormous burden that the epileptic must bear in addition to that of the disease itself.

Can Epilepsy Be Prevented?

Idiopathic epilepsy cannot be prevented, but seizures due to alcohol, fever, and at least some due to injury during pregnancy and birth can be. Alcoholism is discussed in Chapter 11. Fevers are controlled through the use of aspirin, acetaminophen, and sponge baths. Avoiding injury to your child during pregnancy and birth is discussed in Chapter 6.

Can Epilepsy Be Treated?

Although there is no cure, seizures may be controlled with drugs in most cases. Unfortunately, the need for these drugs usually continues for years, perhaps even for a lifetime. Over such long periods, the toxic effects of these drugs may accumulate so that the drugs themselves do extensive damage. This makes continuing care by a thoughtful physician mandatory, so that the person with epilepsy has the best chance at controlling seizures while using the smallest amount of drugs possible.

Can Epilepsy Be Detected Before It Causes Symptoms?
There is no known method of predicting who will have epilepsy.

What Should You Do About Epilepsy?
Make sure that you and your family make every effort to avoid the known causes of seizures.

Do not participate in attaching a social stigma to epilepsy. Lord Byron, Julius Caesar, Handel, Alexander the Great, and William Pitt, among others, had epilepsy. You should do as well.

If you need more information on epilepsy, the Epilepsy Foundation of America will be glad to provide it. The address is:

Epilepsy Foundation of America
1828 L Street N.W.
Washington, D. C.

31

Genetic Disorders

IN THE PAST THERE WOULD HAVE BEEN LITTLE POINT IN PROVIDING information concerning genetic diseases. It was impossible to predict with any accuracy whether an unborn child would be affected. Since these diseases could not be treated, parents could only play a chilling game of chance with their fate and that of their child.

Things have changed. The advent of amniocentesis, a procedure by which the fluid surrounding the fetus may be sampled, now allows detection of the disease at a time when the pregnancy may be interrupted safely. When genetic disorders are possible, the decision to have a child now may be based on whether or not that child *is* affected, not a vague probability that it might be. A decision to interrupt a pregnancy can never be taken lightly, but may be the best that can be made. For example, Tay-Sachs disease is about 100 times more common in Ashkenazic Jews than in the rest of the population. It is characterized by mental retardation, blindness, and other severe neurological problems. The child may appear normal at birth and for a varying period thereafter. Untreatable, the disease relentlessly progresses, with death occurring at age two to five. Testing parents to determine whether they are carriers of this disease is often inconclusive. In contrast, amniocentesis can reliably determine whether the unborn child has the disease. It is no longer necessary to condemn parents to the torture of caring for a child during a slow and inevitable death.

It now appears that there is an exception to the rule that none of these diseases can be treated. Phenylketonuria (PKU) is due to an inherited enzyme deficiency that causes the breakdown products of certain foods to accumulate abnormally. This accumulation causes severe mental retardation. Although results are not absolutely conclusive, a special diet seems to be able to prevent this accumulation and the mental retardation that results from it.

A few definitions will help. Genetics is the branch of biology that deals with heredity. A gene is the smallest piece of genetic information. We now know that genes are carried by a substance called desoxyribonucleic acid (DNA). But the term "gene" was used long before this was discovered. A gene is now defined as a piece of DNA that controls the inheritance of a particular feature of the organism, such as hair color, eye color, an enzyme, and so on. Today it is still rare to determine what piece of DNA actually contains a gene. For the most part, genes are known to exist when some particular feature is inherited according to the laws of genetics. This is a somewhat circular definition, to be sure, but it has served this science well for centuries. However, keep in mind that as a rule genes cannot be seen under any kind of microscope, and their exact chemical composition is not known. No one knows exactly how many genes there are.

Chromosomes are strands of DNA that are visible under the microscope. They are the carriers of the genes. Every normal human cell has 23 pairs of chromosomes, each parent being responsible for one of each pair. Having two of each chromosome is the greatest insurance plan you will ever have. If one fails, there is a second there to do the job. It has been estimated that each of us has from four to eight defective genes, but few of us suffer any real problems because we have a backup gene ready to take over and do the job of the one that failed.

A genetic disease is one that is inherited. Since many diseases seem to be influenced by heredity (heart disease, gout, and the like), it would cover a vast number of diseases if used in its broadest sense. Most often it is used to indicate diseases in which the role of heredity is striking and relatively well-defined. Many of these diseases are quite rare, but taken altogether they have considerable impact on our society. Twenty-five to 30 percent of admissions to children's hospitals are for genetic disorders. The cost of caring for children with just one of these diseases, Down's syndrome, is estimated at more than 60 million dollars.

Most genetic disorders involve just one gene, so the defect in the DNA is not visible under the microscope and cannot be defined in chemical terms. On the other hand, chromosomal disorders involve many genes and can be seen under the microscope. There may be too many chromosomes (as in Down's syndrome or mongolism), not enough chromosomes, or damaged and broken chromosomes. Chromosomal disorders are usually regarded as genetic disorders. However, many of these abnormalities arise at the time of conception and are not present in either parent. They are of special interest because: (1) their appearance increases markedly as the age of the mother increases, and (2) they may account for a significant number of spontaneous abortions (miscarriages) and stillbirths. The accompanying table, from an Australian study, shows the effect of the mother's age on the risk of Down's syndrome.

Before the advent of amniocentesis, it was possible to give only a general probability for the risk of a genetic disease in an unborn child. Such probabilities were vague and imprecise by necessity—clearly not the sort of information you would like in making the decision whether to have a child. Amniocentesis makes it possible in many cases to tell whether the fetus is affected with one of the more than 100 diseases detectable by this method. (At the end of this chapter is a list of some of the most common of these diseases.) As with all medical procedures, amniocentesis carries with it some risk and is not 100 percent accurate (see below).

Can Genetic Disorders Be Prevented?

With the possible exception of chromosomal abnormalities, we do not have specific preventive measures for these diseases. We do know

The risk of Down's syndrome as a function of mother's age

Mother's age	Risk of Down's syndrome
Under 20	1/2325
20–24	1/1612
25–29	1/1201
30–34	1/869
35–39	1/285
40–44	1/100
45 and over	1/45

Source: E. A. Murphy and G. A. Chase, *Principles of Genetic Counseling.* Copyright © 1975 by Year Book Medical Publishers, Inc., Chicago. Used by permission.

that radiation can cause genetic damage, so that the less radiation exposure you have the better. Remember this the next time you are inclined to think you need an x-ray.

It is true that the risk of chromosomal abnormalities increases as the age of the mother increases. It makes sense to have your children earlier rather than later, but this advice seems a little too facile, given the complexity of the decision to have children.

Despite publicity about the *possibility* of manipulating genetic material, it is very unlikely that deleterious genes can be altered in the near future. In the meantime, prevention will have to be limited to preventing the birth of affected children.

Can Genetic Disorders Be Treated?

None of these diseases can be cured. It appears that mental retardation due to phenylketonuria can be prevented through a special diet. Otherwise, treatment consists of training at best. Often custodial care is all that can be offered.

Can Genetic Disorders Be Detected Before They Cause Symptoms?

Phenylketonuria can be detected by blood tests several days after birth. For over 100 other genetic diseases, including those listed at the end of this chapter, amniocentesis can make the diagnosis in about the fourteenth week of pregnancy. This requires that a needle be inserted into the uterus under local anesthesia to collect the fluid surrounding the fetus. Its main hazard is to the fetus. The best information indicates that the procedure causes the death of no more than one normal fetus in 100. There have been reports of injury to the fetus from the needle. Mothers may rarely experience infection or blood loss. In from 5 to 10 percent of cases, a repeat procedure is necessary because the first was unsuccessful in establishing a diagnosis. Errors in diagnosis appear to be rare, but it is difficult to be precise as to their frequency. In up to 2 percent of cases, the child will be born with some abnormality, but these will seldom be one of the detectable genetic disorders.

What Should You Do About Genetic Disorders?

If you are not pregnant or contemplating having a child, do nothing. If your abnormal genes are not causing you any trouble and you are not going to pass them on, why worry about them?

If you are interested in childbearing, there are three considerations:

■ If you know of a genetic disease in your family or that of your spouse, consult your physician. This does not mean that amniocentesis or some other procedure is necessary, but counseling is.

Down's Syndrome and Tay-Sachs are among the most common genetic diseases.

■ If you are over the age of 40, discuss with your physician the benefits and risks of amniocentesis.

■ Have your child tested for phenylketonuria within a few days after birth.

Remember that amniocentesis cannot be done until the fourteenth week of pregnancy, and the tests require about two weeks to run after the fluid is obtained. (Cells from the fluid must be grown in a cell culture in order to test for genetic problems.) Since interruption of pregnancy becomes more hazardous as the pregnancy progresses, you should have all discussions completed and a decision on amniocentesis made before the fourteenth week.

Genetic disorders that can be diagnosed by amniocentesis*

■ *Chromosomal disorders*
  Down's Syndrome (Trisomy 21, Mongolism)
  Klinefelter's Syndrome (XXY)
  Turner's Syndrome (XO)
  Cri-Du-Chat Syndrome (Deletion of Short Arm of Chromosome 5)
  Wolf's Syndrome (Deletion of Short Arm of Chromosome 4)
  Many other unnamed chromosomal abnormalities.

■ *Developmental abnormalities*
  Anencephaly
  Spina Bifida

■ *Lipidoses*
  Fabry's disease
  Gaucher's disease
  Generalized gangliosidosis (GM_1 gangliosidosis type 1)
  Juvenile GM_1 gangliosidosis (GM_1 gangliosidosis type 2)
  Tay-Sachs disease (GM_2 gangliosidosis type 1)
  Sandhoff's disease (GM_2 gangliosidosis type 2)
  Juvenile GM_2 gangliosidosis (GM_2 gangliosidosis type 3)

Source: Modified from Aubrey Milunsky, *Prevention of Genetic Disease and Mental Retardation.* © 1975 by the W. B. Saunders Company, Philadelphia. Used by permission.

GM$_3$ sphingolipidystrophy
Krabbe's disease (globoid cell leukodystrophy)
Metachromatic leukodystrophy
Niemann-Pick disease
Refsum's disease
Wolman's disease

■ *Mucopolysaccharidoses*
MPS I—Hurler
MPS I—Scheie
MPS—Hurler/Scheie
MPS II—Hunter
MPS III—Sanfilippo
MPS IV—Morquio's syndrome
MPS VI A—Maroteaux-Lamy syndrome
MPS VI B—Maroteaux-Lamy syndrome
MPS VII—b-glucuronidase deficiency

■ *Amino acid and related disorders*
Argininosuccinic aciduria
Citrullinemia
Cystinuria
Maple syrup urine disease: (Severe infantile form)
Methylmalonic aciduria

■ *Disorders of carbohydrate metabolism*
Galactosemia
Glycogen storage disease (type II)
Glycogen storage disease (type III)
Glycogen storage disease (type IV)

■ *Miscellaneous hereditary disorders*
Acatalasemia
Adenosine deaminase deficiency
Chediak-Higashi syndrome
Congenital erythropoietic porphyria
Congenital nephrosis
Cystinosis
Lesch Nyhan syndrome

V

YOUR HEALTH RECORDS

THIS SECTION IS IN TWO PARTS. THE PERSONAL HEALTH RECORD (PHR) is the plan for recording your personal health facts. The LifePlan Record portion of the PHR will help you keep track of your progress— or lack of it—in securing a healthy future. Your PHR also will help health professionals understand your health history and plans for the future.

The second part consists of forms that can help you achieve your goals with respect to exercise, diet and weight control, and smoking. The process of keeping such forms up to date has been demonstrated to be of aid in the tough job of changing habits.

32

Personal Health Record (PHR)

THE PERSONAL HEALTH RECORD (PHR) MUST SERVE A VARIETY OF functions. It records not only what has happened in the past but also what you have planned for the future. It should make this information easily available not only to you but to health professionals as well. Information from your LifeScore, LifePlan and the medical record kept by your doctor will also be in your PHR.

If you will have a Health Evaluation and Planning (HEP) session, it is most important that you complete the PHR before you attend the HEP. If you will not have the opportunity for a HEP session, discuss your PHR with your doctor. It will allow him or her to become familiar with your medical history quickly. It also makes it clear that you are willing and able to take responsibility for your health and would like help in meeting that responsibility.

I. Problem List

This is your health agenda. It is also the most important way of letting others understand your health history. Having completed your LifeScore and LifePlan, you should have an excellent idea of what threatens your health and what you can do about it. Lifestyle problems—smoking, obesity, excessive drinking, lack of exercise, and so on—should be at the top of your list. If you have a chronic disease such as diabetes or hypertension, list it as well. Be sure to include any allergies, especially to medications, but see Chapter 29, Allergy and

Asthma, to be sure that these really are allergies. If an immunization is out of date, it should be listed here until it is made current. If there is a continuing exposure—that is, if you still work with asbestos—include this. Finally, include any other part of your health history that you consider to be of particular importance even though it is not continuing at present. For example, it will help to indicate a history of tuberculosis or breast cancer even though there are no signs of the disease now. Most of what has happened in the past and is over (appendectomy, measles, etc.) should be recorded in the sections that follow rather than on the Problem List itself.

Problems that are resolved should be crossed out and the date they ceased to be a problem recorded in this manner: 1/78

II. Habits

You recorded what you are doing in LifeScore. Now just add how long you have been doing it. Under Diet, record your weight and how long that has been your weight. Also include any information with regard to an unbalanced diet—for example: "Vegetarian," or "I eat only hamburgers."

III. Stress

Record your scores and the date when the questionnaire was completed.

IV. Immunity

If you have been immunized against the disease listed, just give the dates of the immunizations. For an adult, the dates of all "baby shots" are not crucial as long as you know that you had them. But it is very important to know at least the date of your last tetanus booster, since you need a booster every 10 years.

If you have actually had the illness listed, put the date you were ill preceded by the letter "I"—for example: "I-1967."

The most common immunization to be listed under "Other" will be that for small pox (variola). This immunization is no longer required or recommended. Others may be typhoid, typhus, rabies, or one of the many vaccines available for use in special circumstances. There are over 50 different vaccines available.

V. Drugs

List any drugs you take regularly. Give the dosage and how you take the drug—for example: "Hydrochlorothiazide 50 mg. (milligrams) twice a day." If you do not know the dosage, it's time you found out.

VI. For Women Only

If you ever sneaked a peek at your medical record, you must have been puzzled by the "G__ P__ Ab__" notation. Gravida means pregnancy and para means delivery. In medical terms, "abortion" means any interrupted pregnancy, so it includes miscarriages as well as those intentionally interrupted. Thus a history of three pregnancies with two being successful and one miscarriage would be abbreviated by a doctor into $G_3 P_2 Ab_1$. The PHR uses the words rather than the letters; enter your history in the blanks provided.

Menarche means the onset of menses (menstrual periods) and menopause indicates the end of regular menses. Enter the *ages* at which these occurred.

Give your contraception method and how long you have used it.

VII. Hospitalizations

Listing the hospital and its address as well as date and problem will help in getting hospital records if they are ever needed.

VIII. Serious Illness or Injuries

Giving the name of the doctor and his or her address will help in obtaining records if they are ever needed.

IX. Family History

Record any positive responses from the corresponding section of LifeScore.

X. Exposures

A. List any exposures (tuberculosis, asbestos, and so forth) as you did in your LifeScore.

B. List your x-rays by date, type, and where they may be found.

XI. Review of Systems

Doctors have traditionally asked a long series of questions about possible symptoms as a part of a "complete history and physical." Since these questions are usually organized by body system, this has been termed the "Review of Systems (ROS)." The ROS is something of a fishing expedition and its value is controversial. This controversy is mainly due to the large number of "false positives"—"yes" answers that really should have been "no" answers—and the difficulty of demonstrating that what is detected is of much importance. Much of the problem may be the patient's difficulty in understanding what the symptoms are and what their significance is.

You can use *Take Care of Yourself* and *Taking Care of Your Child* to help with this problem. Below are some symptoms that *might* be of importance. If you have any of these, consult the books above for more information. On the PHR list only those which the books indicate need attention or about which you still have some questions. These can be discussed at the time of your HEP session or other visit to a health professional. If you do not have access to these books, you will have to make your best guess as to whether these symptoms are significant.

System	*Symptoms*
Skin	Rashes, sores, bumps and lumps
Bones, joints, and muscles	Swelling, pain, stiffness, weakness, cramps
Heart and blood vessels	Shortness of breath, chest pain, palpitations
Lungs and throat	Wheezing, shortness of breath, chronic cough, chronic hoarseness
Stomach and intestines	Abdominal pain, vomiting, diarrhea, very dark or bloody stools
Kidneys, bladder	Painful or frequent urination, blood in urine, very dark urine, incontinence
Female genitalia	Heavy or painful periods, vaginal discharge or sores
Male genitalia	Penile discharge or sore
Head, ears, eyes, nose	Headaches, fainting, seizure, decrease in vision or hearing, chronic runny nose
General	Depression, nervousness, marked weight gain or loss, allergies, chronically swollen glands

Personal Health Record (PHR)

I. PROBLEM LIST   1. _____   5. _____

2. _____   6. _____

3. _____   7. _____

4. _____   8. _____

II. HABITS

Smoking: _____ per day for _____ years.

Drinking: _____ per day for _____ years.

Exercise: _____ conditioning minutes per week for _____ years.

Diet: _____ pounds for _____ years.

Seat belts: Worn _____% of the time.

III. STRESS

Holmes Score: _____   Date _____

IV. IMMUNITY (dates)

Tetanus _____   Mumps _____

Diphtheria _____   Rubella _____

Pertussis _____   Polio _____

Measles _____

Other:

V. DRUGS

_____

_____

_____

VI. FOR WOMEN ONLY

Gravida _____   Para _____   Abortions _____

Menarche _____   Menopause _____

Contraceptive method _____

VII. HOSPITALIZATIONS

Date   Reason   Hospital

_____   _____   _____

_____   _____   _____

_____   _____   _____

_____   _____   _____

VIII. SERIOUS ILLNESSES OR INJURIES NOT REQUIRING HOSPITALIZATIONS

Date   Reason   Doctor

_____   _____   _____

_____   _____   _____

_____   _____   _____

_____   _____   _____

IX. FAMILY HISTORY

_____   _____

_____   _____

_____   _____

_____   _____

X. EXPOSURES

A. _____   _____

_____   _____

_____   _____

_____   _____

B. X-rays

Date   Type   Available from:

_____   _____   _____

_____   _____   _____

_____   _____   _____

_____   _____   _____

XI. REVIEW OF SYSTEMS _____

_____

_____

LIFEPLAN RECORD

This record is in three sections:

1. What You Need To Do For Yourself

   These are the things each of us should be doing. They are the major factors in your health.

2. What You Need From Your Doctor's Office

   These really are only a few preventative and screening procedures everyone needs. Cost and inconvenience are poor excuses for ignoring this small, select group.

3. What Your History Suggests You Need

   In addition to those things we should all be doing, your personal or family history may have indicated that certain other procedures would be worthwhile. For example, if you had x-ray treatments for large adenoids, you should have a yearly thyroid examination by your doctor.

Pick one day a year to review your records and to enter that year's information. New Year's Day would be appropriate. If the entry has a number value, such as blood pressure, enter the number. If the test is reported simply as negative or positive, record − or +. For Yes and No, you may want to use a check (√) and a zero (0). For habits, record them as you did in your LifeScore. For example, smoking would be cigarettes per day, and alcohol would be cocktails (or the equivalent) per day.

LIFEPLAN RECORD

Age   21 22 23 24 25 26 27 28 29 30 31 32

I. What You Need To Do For Yourself

Smoking
(cigarettes per day)

Exercise
(conditioning minutes
per week)

Drinking
(cocktails per day)

Seat belts
(% of time worn)

Weight

Holmes score

Monthly breast
self-examinations

Contraception

LifeScore pts. (p. 63)

II. What You Need From Your Doctor's Office

Immunizations
up to date

Blood pressure

Pap smear

Breast exam

VDRL

Tuberculosis
skin test

Tonometry

Test stool for
hidden blood

III. What Your History Suggests You Need

LIFEPLAN RECORD (cont.)

33 34 35 36 37 38 39 40 41 42 43 44 45 46 47 48 49 50

LIFEPLAN RECORD

Age   51 52 53 54 55 56 57 58 59 60 61 62

I. What You Need To Do For Yourself

Smoking
(cigarettes per day)   — — — — — — — — — — — —

Exercise
(conditioning minutes
per week)   — — — — — — — — — — — —

Drinking
(cocktails per day)   — — — — — — — — — — — —

Seat belts
(% of time worn)   — — — — — — — — — — — —

Weight   — — — — — — — — — — — —

Holmes score   — — — — — — — — — — — —

Monthly breast
self-examinations   — — — — — — — — — — — —

Contraception   — — — — — — — — — — — —

LifeScore pts. (p. 63)

II. What You Need From Your Doctor's Office

Immunizations
up to date   — — — — — — — — — — — —

Blood pressure   — — — — — — — — — — — —

Pap smear   — — — — — — — — — — — —

Breast exam   — — — — — — — — — — — —

VDRL   —   —

Tuberculosis
skin test   —

Tonometry   —   —   —

Test stool for
hidden blood   —   — — — — — — — — —

Proctosigmoidoscopy   —

III. What Your History Suggests You Need

——————————   — — — — — — — — — — — —

——————————   — — — — — — — — — — — —

——————————   — — — — — — — — — — — —

——————————   — — — — — — — — — — — —

LIFEPLAN RECORD (cont.)

63 64 65 66 67 68 69 70 71 72 73 74 75 76 77 78 79 80

33
Charts

EXERCISE CHART

Date	Resting Heart Rate	Minutes of Conditioning	Pulse Two Min. After Exercise	Week of	Total Min. of Conditioning for Week

DIET CHART

Date _____   Weight _____

Time	Food	Amount	Location	Reason	Place-setting Used

WEIGHT CHART

Week of	Mon.	Tue.	Wed.	Thur.	Fri.	Sat.	Sun.	Week's Average

SMOKING CHART

1. Pick the day to stop: _____

2. The two weeks before you stop:
   Keep a record of your *decreasing* use of tobacco:

Week 1

	How Much	*When*	*Where*
1.	_____	_____	_____
2.	_____	_____	_____
3.	_____	_____	_____
4.	_____	_____	_____
5.	_____	_____	_____
6.	_____	_____	_____
7.	_____	_____	_____

Week 2

	How Much	*When*	*Where*
8.	_____	_____	_____
9.	_____	_____	_____
10.	_____	_____	_____
11.	_____	_____	_____
12.	_____	_____	_____
13.	_____	_____	_____
14.	_____	_____	_____

3. The Big Day:
   Activities planned:

   Rewards planned:

   Substitutes planned:

4. What you will do when you feel down:

Appendix

TABLE OF VALUES FOR MANY COMMON FOODS

Group 1. The Milk Group

	Portion	Wt./Vol. (ounces)	Calories	Protein (grams)	Carboh. (grams)	Fat (grams)
Milk, cow's						
fresh, whole	1 glass	8	165	9	12	9
fresh, nonfat (skim)	1 glass	8	80	8	11	.2
buttermilk (from skim milk)	1 glass	8	80	8	11	.2
buttermilk (from whole milk)	1 glass	8	100	8	10	3
evaporated (undiluted)	1 cup	8	348	18	24	20
condensed, sweetened (undiluted)	1 cup	8	1005	25	170	25
powdered, whole	¼ cup	2	148	8	11	8
powdered, nonfat, dried	¼ cup	2	88	9	13	Trace

Source: Pharmaceutical Division, Pennwalt Corporation. Used by permission. (See closing paragraph for more information.)

Group 2. The Vegetable Group

	Portion	Wt./Vol. (ounces)	Calories	Protein (grams)	Carboh. (grams)	Fat (grams)
Asparagus						
fresh, cooked	12 spears	7	42	4	8	.3
canned	12 spears	8	40	4	7	.8
frozen	12 spears	7	48	7	8	.4
Beets						
fresh, cooked	1 cup	5	68	2	16	.2
canned, drained	1 cup	5	68	2	16	.2
Beet greens						
cooked	1 cup	7	54	4	11	.6
Broccoli						
fresh, cooked	1 cup	5	44	5	8	.3
frozen		3½	28	3	5	.2
Brussels sprouts						
fresh, cooked	1 cup	5	66	6	12	.8
frozen		3½	36	3	7	.2
Cabbage						
raw, shredded	1 cup	3	24	1	5	.2
fresh, cooked	1 cup	6	40	2	9	.4
Carrots						
raw, diced	1 cup	3	42	1	9	.3
fresh, cooked	1 cup	5	46	1	10	.4
canned, drained	1 cup	5	46	1	10	.4
Cauliflower						
fresh, cooked	1 cup	4	30	3	6	.2
frozen		3½	22	2	4	.2
Celery, raw, diced	1 cup	3	16	1	3	.2
Chard greens						
cooked	1 cup	6	48	5	5	.8
Chicory or Endive	20 small leaves	2	12	1	2	.1
Collard greens						
cooked	1 cup	7	80	8	14	1.2
Beans, lima, green						
fresh, cooked	1 cup	5	152	8	29	.6
canned	1 cup	8	162	9	31	.8
frozen		3½	121	8	23	.2
Cucumber, raw	1 medium	3	12	1	3	0
Dandelion greens	1 cup	7	85	5	18	1.4
Eggplant, raw	1 cup	7	48	2	11	.4

	Portion	Wt./Vol. (ounces)	Calories	Protein (grams)	Carboh. (grams)	Fat (grams)
Escarole	20 small leaves	2	12	1	2	Trace
Kale						
fresh, cooked	1 cup	3	40	4	7	.6
frozen		3½	31	3	5	.5
Lettuce, raw	20 small leaves	7	30	2	6	.4
Leeks, raw	4 stalks 5″ long	3	40	3	8	.4
Mixed vegetables						
canned	1 cup	7	60	2	12	.2
frozen		3½	65	3	14	.3
Mushrooms						
canned	1 cup	9	50	3	10	.6
sautéed	9 small	3	100	2	4	10
Mustard greens						
cooked	1 cup	7	44	5	8	.6
Okra, cooked	10 pods	3	30	2	6	.2
Onions						
raw	1 (2″ diam)	3	45	1	10	.2
cooked	1 cup	7	75 ·	2	17	.4
scallions (5″ long; ½″ diam.)	10	3	45	1	11	.2
Peas, green						
fresh, cooked	1 cup	5	112	8	19	.6
canned, drained	1 cup	5	145	7	28	1
frozen		3½	74	5	13	.3
Pepper, green, raw	3″ diam	2	15	1	4	.2
Pumpkin, canned	1 cup	8	75	2	18	1
Radishes, red, raw	3 (1″ diam)	1	6	.3	1	Trace
Rhubarb						
raw, diced	1 cup	3	15	.5	4	Trace
cooked, sweetened	1 cup	9	280	1	70	.2
frozen, sweetened	1 cup	8	184	1	46	.4
Rutabagas, cooked	1 cup	5	52	1	12	.2
Sauerkraut						
canned	1 cup	7	44	3	9	1
Spinach						
fresh, cooked	1 cup	6	46	6	7	1.2
canned, drained	1 cup	6	46	6	7	1.2
frozen		3½	25	3	4	.3

	Portion	Wt./Vol. (ounces)	Calories	Protein (grams)	Carboh. (grams)	Fat (grams)
String beans (green or yellow)						
fresh, cooked	1 cup	4	27	2	6	.2
canned, drained	1 cup	4	27	2	6	.2
frozen, French style	1 cup	4	31	3	7	.1
Squash, summer						
boiled	1 cup	7	32	1	8	.2
Squash, winter						
boiled	1 cup	7	75	3	18	1
frozen		3½	21	1	5	.1
Tomatoes						
raw	1 medium	5	30	2	6	.5
canned	1 cup	7	38	2	8	.4
Tomato juice	1 cup	8	50	2	10	.6
Tomato catsup	1 tbsp.	½	17	.3	4	Trace
Turnips, white						
cooked	1 cup	5	40	1	9	.3
Turnip greens						
cooked	1 cup	5	44	4	8	.6

Group 3. The Fruit Group

	Portion	Wt./Vol. (ounces)	Calories	Protein (grams)	Carboh. (grams)	Fat (grams)
Apple, fresh	1 (3″ diam)	8	100	.5	25	.2
Applesauce canned						
sweetened	1 cup	8	185	.6	50	.4
Apricots, fresh	1 medium	1	17	.3	3	Trace
canned with syrup	1 medium	2	40	.3	11	Trace
Bananas, sliced	1 cup	5	130	2	35	.3
Blackberries, fresh	1 cup	5	92	2	20	2
Blueberries, fresh	1 cup	5	98	1	24	1
Cantaloupe, fresh	½ (5″ diam)	6	37	1	8	.4
Cherries						
fresh, sweet	10 large	2	40	.4	10	.3
Cranberry sauce (jelly)	1 tbsp.	1	47	Trace	13	Trace
Cranberry juice	1 cup	8	26	.4	3	1.2
Dates, dried, pitted	1	¼	21	Trace	6	Trace
Figs, fresh	1 large	1½	40	.7	10	.2
dried	1 large	½	55	1	17	.3

	Portion	*Wt./Vol. (ounces)*	*Calories*	*Protein (grams)*	*Carboh. (grams)*	*Fat (grams)*
Grapefruit, fresh, white/pink sections,	½ (4″ diam)	6	72	1	18	.4
canned, in syrup	1 cup	8	160	1	43	.4
juice, canned	1 cup	8	110	1	30	.2
Grapes	24	3	70	1	15	1
Grape juice canned	1 cup	8	160	1	44	Trace
Honeydew melon fresh	½ (5″ diam)	7	64	1	17	0
Mango	1 small	3	66	1	17	.2
Orange, fresh	1 (3″ diam)	5	68	1	17	.3
Orange juice Florida, fresh	1 cup	8	100	1	23	Trace
frozen concentrate	1 cup (diluted)	8	110	2	27	Trace
Papaya, fresh	1 medium	10	115	2	30	.3
Peaches fresh	1 medium	3	46	1	12	.1
canned, in syrup	2 halves	4	90	1	24	.1
Pears fresh	1 (3″ diam)	6	100	1	25	.1
canned, in syrup	2 halves	4	80	.3	22	.1
Pineapple fresh	1 slice (3½″ diam ¾″ thick)	3	45	.3	12	.2
canned, in syrup	1 small slice	3	46	.3	13	Trace
Pineapple juice canned	1 cup	8	122	.8	32	.2
Plums, fresh	1 (2″ diam)	2	30	1	8	.1
Prunes dried, raw	1 medium	⅓	27	.2	8	Trace
cooked, no sugar	4 medium	2½	85	.7	23	.2
Prune juice canned	1 cup	8	170	1	46	Trace
Raisins dried, seedless	1 cup	5	380	3	100	1
Raspberries red, fresh	1 cup	4	70	2	18	.5

	Portion	Wt./Vol. (ounces)	Calories	Protein (grams)	Carboh. (grams)	Fat (grams)
Strawberries						
fresh	1 cup	5	55	1	13	.8
frozen, sliced	1 cup	8	280	1	71	.4
Tangerines, fresh	1 large	3	44	1	11	.3
Watermelon	1 slice (6″ diam 1½″ thick)	20	170	3	42	1

Group 4. The Bread Group

	Portion	Wt./Vol. (ounces)	Calories	Protein (grams)	Carboh. (grams)	Fat (grams)
Bread						
White, plain	1 slice	⅔	63	2	12	.7
White, enriched	1 slice	⅔	63	2	12	.7
White, toasted	1 slice	⅔	63	2	12	.7
Whole wheat	1 slice	⅔	55	2	11	.6
Rye, dark, oval	1 slice	1	70	2	16	.4
French or Vienna	1 slice	1	80	3	16	.8
Italian	1 piece	1	80	3	16	.3
Corn	1 piece (2″ sq.)	1½	140	3	22	4
Thomas Protein	1 slice	⅔	45	2	9	.2
Biscuit						
baking powder	1 (2″ diam)	1	110	2	15	4
Brownies	1 (2×2× ¾″)	1	140	2	17	8
Cake						
Angel food (8″ diam)	2″ sector		110	3	23	Trace
Chocolate, fudge icing (10″ diam)	2″ sector		426	5	70	14
Coffee, iced	1 piece (4¼″ diam)	2	200	4	32	6
Cup, without icing	2¾″ diam		115	3	23	3
Pound	2¾×3×⅝″		130	2	15	7
Sponge (8″ diam)	2″ sector		120	3	22	2
Cereal, cooked						
Oatmeal	1 cup	8	150	5	26	3
Wheatena	1 cup	1½	150	5	33	1
Cereal, dry						
Bran flakes	1 cup	1	130	4	30	1
Corn flakes	1 cup	1	95	2	21	Trace
Cheerios	1 cup	1	100	3	18	2
Rice Krispies	1 cup	1	110	2	25	Trace
Puffed Rice	1 cup	½	50	1	12	Trace
Special K	1 cup	½	60	3	13	Trace
Shreaded wheat	1 biscuit	1	85	2	18	.3

	Portion	Wt./Vol. (ounces)	Calories	Protein (grams)	Carboh. (grams)	Fat (grams)
Cookies						
Chocolate chip	1 cookie	⅓	51	.5	8	2
Fig newton	1 cake	1½	55	.5	11	1
Lemon snaps	1 cookie	⅛	16	.3	3	.4
Macaroon	1 cookie	¾	107	1	14	5
Oatmeal	1 cookie	¾	86	1	13	3
Vanilla wafers	1 wafer	⅛	15	.2	2	.5
Pretzels, three ring	1 pretzel	⅛	12	.3	2	Trace
Corn, sweet (white or yellow)						
fresh, cooked	1 ear (7–8″ long)	7	125	4	30	1
canned, cream style (white or yellow)	1 cup	8	185	5	45	1.4
canned, kernel, drained	1 cup	5	140	5	33	1.2
Crackers						
Graham	1 cracker	¼	30	1	5	.7
Oyster	10 crackers	¼	30	1	5	.7
Saltines	1 cracker	⅛	14	.3	2	.4
Soda	1 cracker	¼	30	1	5	.7
Triscuit	1 wafer	⅓	21	.4	3	.8
Round, thin	1 cracker	⅛	17	.4	3	.3
Ry-Krisp	1 cracker	¼	21	.8	5	Trace
Doughnut						
jelly center	1	2	225	3	30	9
Flour						
All purpose	1 cup	4	400	12	84	1
Corn	1 cup	4	410	9	85	3
Gluten	1 cup	5	500	58	66	3
French toast	1 slice	2	185	6	14	12
Ice Cream						
Chocolate	1 cup		300	5	33	16
Chocolate, covered bar	one		162	2	15	11
Vanilla	1 cup		290	6	30	16
Vanilla, dietary	1 cup		266	6	29	14
Sherbet	1 cup	8	244	3	58	Trace
Yoghurt (partially skimmed milk)	1 cup	8	120	8	13	4
Macaroni						
elbow, cooked	1 cup	5	210	7	42	1
Muffin, cornmeal	1	1½	130	3	19	4
Noodles						
egg, cooked	1 cup	5	110	4	21	1

	Portion	Wt./Vol. (ounces)	Calories	Protein (grams)	Carboh. (grams)	Fat (grams)
Pancake	1 (4″ diam)	1½	60	2	11	1
Pies (9″ diameter)						
Apple	4″ sector		338	3	53	13
Cherry	4″ sector		349	3	55	13
Custard	4″ sector		263	7	34	11
Lemon meringue	4″ sector		304	4	45	12
Mince	4″ sector		340	3	62	9
Pumpkin	4″ sector		264	5	34	12
Potatoes, white,						
baked	1 medium (2½″ diam)	3	98	2	23	.1
boiled	1 medium (2¼″ diam)	3	90	2	22	.1
canned	1 cup	8	145	4	33	0
french fried	10 pieces ½ × ½ × ½″	1½	200	3	26	10
hashed brown	1 cup	7	480	6	64	24
mashed (milk and butter)	1 cup	7	246	4	32	12
Potato chips	15 chips (2″ diam)	1	162	2	15	11
Potatoes, sweet,						
baked	1 medium (2×4)	4	185	3	41	1
candied	1 medium (2×4)	7	360	3	72	7
canned	1 cup	8	245	4	64	.2
Rice, white, cooked	1 cup	1	140	3	30	Trace
Roll						
White, hard	1	1	95	3	18	1
Parkerhouse	1	1	80	2	14	2
Spaghetti, cooked	1 cup	5	157	5	32	1
with tomato sauce	1 cup	5	213	6	36	5
with meat and cheese sauce	1 cup	5	282	13	35	10
Vegetables						
Lima beans, dry	1 cup	5	532	33	98	2
Navy beans, dry	1 cup	7	676	43	123	3
Baked beans, canned (with pork and tomato sauce)	1 cup	8	257	14	42	5
Lentils, dry	1 cup	7	680	50	120	2
Cooked	1 cup	6	200	15	36	.6
Waffle, plain	1 (5½″ diam)	2½	230	5	21	14

Group 5. The Meat, Poultry, Fish, Shellfish, Related Products Group

	Portion	Wt./Vol. (ounces)	Calories	Protein (grams)	Carboh. (grams)	Fat (grams)
Beef						
Pot roast or braised						
lean and fat						
(1 thick or						
2 thin slices,						
4 by 2½")		3	236	23	0	16
lean only		3	160	26	Trace	6
Hamburger						
regular ground						
beef		3	237	23	0	16
lean ground round		3	145	27	Trace	4
Rib roast,						
over-cooked, no						
liquid added						
lean and fat		3	390	16	0	36
lean only		3	200	23	0	12
Bottom round roast						
lean and fat		3	218	23	0	14
lean only		3	145	25	0	5
Sirloin steak,						
broiled						
lean and fat		3	185	23	0	10
lean only		3	145	25	0	5
Club steak						
lean and fat		3	260	23	0	18
lean only		3	160	24	0	7
Corned beef hash	½ cup	3	229	10	9	17
Dried or chipped						
beef		3	173	29	0	5.4
Beef and vegetable						
stew	1 cup	8	210	15	15	10
Beef potpie, baked:	1 pie,					
4¼ inch diam	before					
	baking		443	17	37	26
Meat loaf						
beef and pork	4×4×⅜	3	340	13.5	15	25
Fish						
Anchovies, canned	4 thin fillets	½	27	3	Trace	2
Bluefish						
baked or broiled		3	125	22	0	4

	Portion	Wt./Vol. (ounces)	Calories	Protein (grams)	Carboh. (grams)	Fat (grams)
Clams,						
raw, meat only	4 med. clams	3	65	11	3	1
canned, solids and liquid	3 med. clams and juice	3	45	7	2	1
Cod, fresh, raw	3×3×¾"	3	72	17	0	.4
fish cakes	1 large cake	4	200	22	10	8
Crabmeat,						
cooked or canned	1 cup	3	80	14	1	2
casserole		5	315	17	12	22
soft shell, fried		2	180	11	9	12
Fish sticks						
breaded, cooked, frozen	5 sticks (4×1×½")	4	200	19	8	10
Flounder or Sole, raw	3×3×⅜"	3	68	15	0	.5
Haddock, fried	4×2½×½"	3	210	24	8	9
Halibut, raw	3×2×1"	3	120	19	0	5
Lobster, boiled or broiled	¾ lb. 2 tbsp. butter	12	310	20	1	25
Mackerel, raw	4×3×½"	3	190	19	0	13
Oysters						
raw, meat only (selects)	½ cup (6-10 med.)	4	75	10	4	2
fried	6	4½	400	15	18	30
Salmon						
steak, baked		4	175	33	0	5
loaf		4½	210	22	11	9
smoked	2-3 small slices	2	105	13	0	6
Salmon, pink or red, canned	³/₅ cup	3	115	17	0	5
Sardines						
canned in oil	5-7 med.	3	175	22	1	9
Shad						
baked or broiled	3×3×¾"	3	250	24	3	16
roe, baked, 2 slices bacon	1 serving	3	370	25	.5	30

	Portion	Wt./Vol. (ounces)	Calories	Protein (grams)	Carboh. (grams)	Fat (grams)
Shrimp, canned, meat only	17 med.	3	100	23	0	1
Swordfish, broiled	3×3×¾"	3	140	24	0	5
Tuna, canned in oil, drained solids	²/₅ cup	3	165	25	0	7
Frankfurter, cooked	5½ × ¾" diam	2	124	7	1	10
Lamb *Roast, leg* lean and fat	1 slice 4×3×¼"	3	260	20	0	20
lean only		3	160	25	0	7
Loin chop, cooked lean and fat		3	170	26	0	7
Liver *Beef*, fried	1 slice 3×2¼×⅜"	1	86	9	5.6	3
Calf, cooked	1 slice 3×2¼×⅜"	1	74	8	2	4
Chicken, cooked	1 med.	1	74	9	1	4
Pork, fried	1 slice 3×2¼× ⅜"	1	85	9	4	4
Liverwurst	1 slice 3×¼"	1	79	5	1	6
Bologna	1 slice 4½×⅛"	1	66	4.4	1	5
Pork sausage, cooked	1 link 3×½"	⅔	94	3.5	0	9
Salami	1 slice 3¾×¼"	1	130	7	0	11
Scrapple	1 slice 3½×2¼× ¼"	2	209	5	26	9
Pork *Ham*, canned, boneless	1 slice 3½×3½"	3	145	16	0	9
Ham, cured, lean only	1 slice 2×4"	3	190	25	.2	10
Loin chop, cooked Lean and fat		3	357	29	0	26
lean only		3	228	32	0	11

	Portion	Wt./Vol. (ounces)	Calories	Protein (grams)	Carboh. (grams)	Fat (grams)
Spareribs, roasted	meat from 6 med. ribs	3	246	15.4	0	20
Poultry						
Chicken, broiler, fried	¼ bird no bone	3	232	22.4	3.1	13.6
	½ bird no bone	6	464	45.3	6.2	27.2
Creamed chicken	½ cup sm. serving	4	208	18	7	12
	1 cup lg. serving	8	416	35	13	24
Roast chicken	2 slices 3×3×¼"	3	160	23	0	7
Turkey, roasted	2 slices 3×3×¼"	3	160	25	0	6
	4–5 slices lg. serv.	5	300	47	0	12
Veal						
Cutlet, round, cooked						
lean and fat	¼ cutlet	3	235	28	0	13
lean only (trimmed)	¼ cutlet	3	185	24	0	10
Cheese						
Blue or roquefort		1	108	6	.6	9
Camembert		1	85	5	.5	7
Cheddar, American						
ungrated	1" cube	1	110	7	.5	9
grated	1 tbsp.		28	2	Trace	2
Cottage	1 round tbsp.	1	29	6	1	Trace
Swiss		1	105	8	.5	8
Spread		1	80	4	2	6
Egg, whole, medium (21 oz. per dozen)	1 whole		77	6	Trace	6
	white only		16	4	Trace	Trace
	yolk only		61	3	Trace	5
Eggs, cooked						
boiled, soft or hard	1 medium		77	6	Trace	6
scrambled, with milk and butter	1 medium		120	7	1	10
Peanut butter	1 cup	8½	1486	67	54	123
	1 tbsp.	½	86	4	3	7

Group 6. The Fat Group

	Portion	Wt./Vol. (ounces)	Calories	Protein (grams)	Carboh. (grams)	Fat (grams)
Avocado	1 large	7	370	4	12	36
Bacon, broiled or fried crisp	1 strip		50	2	Trace	5
Butter						
salted (16 pats), ¼ lb. stick	½ cup	4	825	.7	.9	91
	1 tbsp.	½	100	.1	.1	11.3
	1 pat	¼	50	Trace	Trace	5.6
unsalted (16 pats) ¼ lb. stick	½ cup	4	825	.7	.9	91
	1 tbsp.	½	100	.1	.1	11.3
	1 pat	¼	50	Trace	Trace	5.6
Cooking fat, vegetable	1 tbsp.	½	110	0	0	12
Cream						
light	1 cup	8	536	7	10	52
	1 tbsp.	½	31	Trace	1	3
medium	1 cup	8	758	6	8	78
	2 tbsp.	1	94	Trace	1	10
heavy	1 cup	8	885	5	7	93
	2 tbsp.	1	110	Trace	1	12
Half-and-Half (milk and cream)	1 cup	8	337	8	11	29
	2 tbsp.	1	42	1	1	4
cream cheese	2 tbsp.	1	97	2.4	.6	9.4
Mayonnaise	1 tbsp. ½	110	.2	.2	12	
Nuts						
Almonds, shelled	13–15 nuts	½	95	3	3	8
Brazil, shelled	4 nuts	½	105	2	2	10
Cashew, roasted	6–7 nuts	½	90	3	4	7
Coconut, fresh	1×1×⅜″	½	55	.5	2	5
dried, shredded	1 cup	2	360	2	33	24
Mixed nuts, shelled	8–12 nuts	½	105	3	3	9
Peanuts, roasted, shelled	1 cup	8	1370	61	54	100
Pecans, shelled	6 nuts	½	115	1.4	2	11
Walnuts, black,	4–5 nuts	½	105	3	3	9
English	4–7 nuts	½	100	2.3	2.3	10
Oils, cooking or salad						
Corn	1 tbsp.	½	124	0	0	14
Olive	1 tbsp.	½	124	0	0	14
Peanut	1 tbsp.	½	124	0	0	14
Vegetable shortening	1 tbsp.	½	125	.2	0	14

	Portion	Wt./Vol. (ounces)	Calories	Protein (grams)	Carboh. (grams)	Fat (grams)
Margarine						
(¼ pound stick)	½ cup	4	825	.6	1	91
	1 tbsp.	½	100	Trace	.1	11.3
Olives, canned						
Green	12 "extra large"		71	1	1	7
Ripe	12 "extra large"		93	1	2	9
Salad dressings						
Blue cheese	1 tbsp.	½	98	1	1	10
French	1 tbsp.	½	60	.1	2	6
Russian	1 tbsp.	½	58	.4	3	5
Thousand Island	1 tbsp.	½	76	.3	1	8

Group 7. Miscellaneous Group

	Portion	Wt./Vol. (ounces)	Calories	Protein (grams)	Carboh. (grams)	Fat (grams)
Sandwiches						
white bread (with average portions of fillings)						
Bacon, lettuce, tomato			290	7	29	16
Chicken salad			255	14	27	10
Chicken, sliced, lettuce			310	16	27	15
Club (chicken, bacon, tomato)			570	39	43	26
Cream cheese and jelly			370	7	50	16
Egg salad			285	11	31	13
Ham			285	11	24	16
Liverwurst			260	10	27	12
Peanut butter			350	12	30	20
Tunafish salad			275	11	26	14
Turkey			400	29	28	19
Soups						
Bean	1 cup	8	190	8	30	5
Beef	1 cup	8	105	6	11	4
Bouillon; broth; consomme	1 cup	8	10	2	0	Trace
Chicken	1 cup	8	75	4	10	2
Clam chowder	1 cup	8	85	5	12	2
Cream soup (asparagus, celery, mushroom)	1 cup	8	208	7	18	12
Noodle; rice; barley	1 cup	8	110	6	13	4
Pea	1 cup	8	145	6	25	2
Tomato	1 cup	8	100	2	18	2
Vegetable	1 cup	8	90	4	14	2

	Portion	Wt./Vol. (ounces)	Calories	Protein (grams)	Carboh. (grams)	Fat (grams)
Beverage (non-alcohol)						
Coca-Cola	1 glass	8	105			
Ginger ale	1 glass	8	80			
Pepsi-Cola	1 glass	8	105			
Chocolate milk	1 glass	8	280			
Sweet cider	1 glass	8	124			
Milk eggnog	1 glass	8	290			
Beverages (alcohol)						
Ale	1 glass	8	100			
Beer	1 glass	8	115			
Brandy	1 brandy glass	1	75			
Daiquiri	1 cock-tail	3	125			
Eggnog	1 punch cup	4	335			
Gin	1 jigger	1½	105			
Highball	1 glass	8	165			
Manhattan	1 cock-tail	3½	165			
Martini	1 cock-tail	3½	140			
Old fashioned	1 glass	4	180			
Rum	1 jigger	1½	105			
Tom Collins	1 glass	10	180			
Rye	1 jigger	1½	120			
Scotch	1 jigger	1½	105			
Table wines, (Chablis, Claret, Rhine Wine, Sauterne)	1 wine glass	3	75			
Dessert wines (Muscatel, Port, Sherry, Tokay)	1 wine glass	3	125			

Information on fats and cholesterol is based on material from the EXCHANGE LISTS FOR MEAL PLANNING prepared by committees of the American Diabetes Association, Inc. and The American Dietetic Association, in cooperation with The National Institute of Arthritis, Metabolism and Digestive Diseases, and the National Heart and Lung Institute, National Institutes of Health, Public Health Service, U.S. Department of Health, Education and Welfare.

INDEX

INDEX

Swine influenza, 165, 171
Syphilis, 237-239
  testing, 50
  testing, LifeScore and, 62
Systemic reactions, 252
Systems, review of, 269-270

Tabs, 227
Take Care of Yourself, 270
Taking Care of Your Child, 270
Tay-Sachs disease, 258, 262
Teenagers, rubella vaccination of,
    170
Tennis as conditioning, 108
Testes
  cancer of, LifePlan and, 77
  self-examination of, 212
Tes-Tope, 227
Tests
  false positives, defined, 28
  limits of, 27-30
  of medical and surgical
    procedures, 15-16
  predictive value of, 28, *48*
  sensitivity of, defined, 28
  specificity of, defined, 28
  value of, 10-11
  see also tests and diseases by name
Tetanus
  booster, 167-168, 172
  illness, nature of, 168
  immunization, nature of, 168
  immunization schedule, *167*
Tetanus immune globulin, 168
Texas, University of, experiments on
    exercise, 108
Thalidomide, 26, 65
Thiamine deficiency, 116
Thiazide diuretics, drug problems
    from, 38
Thirst, 227
Thyroid hormone pills, 247, 249
Thyroid problems, 247-250
  causes, 248
  early detection, 249
  examination for, 50, 212, 214
  LifePlan and, 74, 76

  nature of, 247-248
  personal implications, 250
  prevention, 249
  tests for, 11, 50
  treatment, 249
  tumors and cancer, 248
  x-rays and, 208, 210
Tine test, 9, 62, 229
Tonography, 242
Tonometry, 242
  effectiveness of, 50
  LifeScore and, 62
  New You Score and, 81
Tonsillectomy and adenoidectomy
    (T&A)
  effectiveness of, 15-16, 41-42
  risk, 32
  sore throats and, 31-32
Tonsils
  surgery; *see* Tonsillectomy and
    adenoidectomy
  x-ray therapy on, 46, 208, 248, 250
Tooth decay, 117-118
Tophi, 234
Toxemia, 68
Tranquilizers
  use of, 158-159, 175
  value of, 39
Transient ischemic attack (TIA), 216-
    217
  stroke and, 218-219
Transient situational disturbances,
    175
Treadmill tests; *see* Stress tests
Treatment before symptoms appear,
    48; *see also problem or disease by
    name*
Tricyclic antidepressants, brand-
    name and generic, 39
Triglycerides, 196-197
Trinity School of Medicine (Dublin)
    study on exercise, diet, and heart
    disease, 106-107
Tuberculosis (TB), 228-230
  causes, 229
  death rate, 19-20
  decreasing rate, 166